Getting The Best From Your

ICE CREAM
MACHINE

Getting The Best From Your

ICE CREAM
MACHINE

All you need to know about using
your ice cream maker, with more
than 150 recipes

Joanna Farrow
& Sara Lewis

SELECT
EDITIONS

Select Editions imprint specially produced for Selectabook Ltd

Produced by Anness Publishing Ltd
Hermes House, 88–89 Blackfriars Road, London SE1 8HA
tel. 020 7401 2077; fax 020 7633 9499
info@anness.com

A CIP catalogue record for this book is available from the British Library.

PUBLISHER: Joanna Lorenz
EDITORIAL DIRECTOR: Judith Simons
EXECUTIVE EDITOR: Linda Fraser
EDITORS: Lucy Doncaster and Margaret Malone
DESIGNERS: Bill Mason and Luise Roberts
PHOTOGRAPHY: Gus Filgate, William Lingwood
and Craig Robertson
FOOD FOR PHOTOGRAPHY: Joanna Farrow, Annabel Ford
and Lucy McKelvie
STYLING: Penny Markham and Helen Trent
COPY EDITORS: Jenni Fleetwood and Jan Cutler
PRODUCTION CONTROLLER: Pedro Nelson

10 9 8 7 6 5 4 3 2 1

NOTES

Bracketed terms are intended for American readers.

For all recipes, quantities are given in both metric and imperial measures
and, where appropriate, in standard cups and spoons. Follow one set,
but not a mixture, because they are not interchangeable.

Standard spoon and cup measures are level.
1 tsp = 5ml, 1 tbsp = 15ml, 1 cup = 250ml/8fl oz

Australian standard tablespoons are 20ml. Australian readers
should use 3 tsp in place of 1 tbsp for measuring small quantities
of gelatine, cornflour, salt etc.

American pints are 16fl oz/2 cups. American readers should use
20fl oz/2.5 cups in place of 1 pint when measuring liquids.

Medium (US large) eggs are used unless otherwise stated.

Main front cover image shows White Chocolate Castles – for recipe, see page 194.

contents

Introduction

An ice cream maker is an invitation to indulgence. With this simple appliance you can create all your favourite flavours in your own kitchen, stocking the freezer for future feasts, making elaborate dinner-party sweets or simply impressing children or grandchildren with the magic transformation of basic ingredients into cool treats.

No longer will you need to dash to the supermarket for tubs of comfort food, or be unable to find your favourite sorbet when shops run out of stock. An ice cream maker enables you to produce a wide range of delectable desserts, from the healthy refresher to the unashamedly sinful. What is more, because you decide which ingredients to use, you know precisely what the ice cream contains and can avoid additives or ingredients to which friends or family are intolerant.

Of course, making your own ice cream doesn't quite provide the instant gratification available to those who simply lever a lid off a tub, but the half hour or so it generally takes to produce the home-made product provides the ideal opportunity for musing on the pleasures ahead: the velvety texture, the sensuous way the ice cream slips off the spoon, the delicious coolness as it touches first your lips and then your throat, and finally the increasing intensity of the flavour as the ice cream warms to the heat of your body.

Ice cream is a winner with young and old alike. Statistically, the most enthusiastic consumers are those aged between two and twelve, and over the age of 45. Toddlers get the taste early, intrigued by what it is that gives older children such obvious satisfaction. The first scoop of ice cream usually ends up on the floor, but small children soon master the art of holding the cone steady while circumnavigating the icy globe, keeping the licks smooth and even so that not a drop is lost.

It is said that it takes about 50 licks to demolish a single scoop of ice cream, but this statistic presupposes a measured eater, neither a nibbler nor a greedy guzzler and certainly not one of those people who bite off the bottom of the cone and attack it at both ends.

BELOW: *Crisp wafers, bittersweet dark chocolate and crunchy nuts add flavour and texture to creamy scoops of home-made ice cream.*

ABOVE: *Elegant ice cream bombes and terrines make the perfect dinner-party dessert.*

For the older generation, ice cream evokes nostalgia for days when the sound of an ice cream van could spell refreshment on a warm summer afternoon: a neat rectangle of vanilla ice, perhaps sandwiched between two wafers, or a tub of Italian ice cream with its own little spoon.

Ice cream represents treat days and holidays, and today ice cream parlours are proliferating as never before. Home consumption of ice cream is also rocketing, and it has become a year-round treat. It is so convenient to open the freezer and reach for a lolly or a tub of ice cream or sorbet, and if you have made it yourself, you can indulge in a superior product that has probably cost you considerably less than the closest equivalent the supermarket can provide.

Ice creams, in all their guises, are the perfect conclusion to a meal, whether you are feeding the family or entertaining in a more formal fashion. Fruit sorbets and granitas are ideal for serving between courses to cleanse the palate during an elegant supper or a relaxed al fresco meal, while bombes and terrines – apparently elaborate but actually very easy to create – make an impressive finale to the most sophisticated dinner.

AN ICE CREAM LOVER'S GUIDE

You'll find recipes for everything from simple sorbets and granitas to luxurious terrines and hot desserts in this comprehensive guide. First, though, there's a detailed reference section. We explore the history of this fascinating food, take you on a cook's tour of specialities from around the world, and offer advice on the best ingredients to use for perfect results every time. For those of you who haven't already bought an ice cream maker, there is a guide to the various types of machine available, plus plenty of tips for their use. Having made your ice cream, you'll want to know the best way to store and serve it, and these aspects are also explored fully. Instructions are given for making ice bowls, rippling raspberry and vanilla ice cream and making marbled mixtures. Sauces and dessert cookies are described in detail, and you'll even get the low-down on lollies (popsicles).

A WORLD OF FLAVOURS

The recipe section includes ice creams and ices from the Mediterranean, Eastern Europe, India, the British Isles and the Americas. They range from a light and fresh Apple and Cider Water Ice to wickedly rich Mocha, Prune and Armagnac Terrine. Among the more contemporary offerings are Pomegranate and Orange Flower Water Creams and Date and Tofu Ice, while for those who fancy an alcoholic kick there is a Bloody Mary Sorbet. Laced with vodka, it makes for intriguing after-dinner conversation.

Every recipe is illustrated with detailed, easy-to-follow step-by-step photographs, so that even the most inexperienced cook will feel confident about attempting every dessert, however complicated it may seem, and is guaranteed delicious home made frozen desserts every time.

ABOVE: *Tangy Blackcurrant Sorbet is perfect after a rich meal.*

One of the obvious benefits of iced desserts is that they can be prepared in advance, so even those that require a bit of time and patience to put together can be made days or even weeks ahead. Iced Raspberry and Almond Trifle Ice Cream, for instance, is a bit fiddly, as it requires you to make a sponge cake and beat together mascarpone, icing (confectioners') sugar and sherry, but the reaction that it produces when it is served more than repays the effort. The same can be said for Spiced Sorbet Pears – plump fruit poached in a red wine syrup, then cooled, hollowed out and filled with a delectable sorbet made from the scooped-out flesh and poaching juices. When thawed and served, these look and taste spectacular.

The book includes a chapter on cream-free, low-fat and low-sugar ices, many of which taste so rich and creamy that you may have difficulty convincing guests of their innocence. Blueberry and Honey Ripple Ice Cream, Honeyed Goat's Milk Gelato and Raspberry Sherbet are just some examples.

Ices and sorbets can also be transformed into delicious drinks. At the end of a busy day in the kitchen, when, with the help of your ice cream maker, you have stocked the freezer with delectable desserts, treat yourself to a Tropical Fruit Soda or a Strawberry Daiquiri and drink a toast to your finest frozen assets.

BELOW: *Light, crisp meringues and seasonal fruit complement simple ice creams.*

BELOW: *Iced Tiramisu will be loved by children and adults alike.*

The history of ice cream

No one knows for certain who produced the world's first ice cream, although it is probable that it was the Chinese who first developed the art of making frozen desserts in around AD618–97. They chilled fruit juices and tea, which led to their making primitive fruit-flavoured ices some two-and-a-half thousand years ago.

EARLY ICES

During Roman times, emperors such as Nero Claudius Caesar conceived the idea of serving a chilled dessert for a special feast. He is said to have sent his slaves into the mountains to gather fresh snow, which was dressed with honey and fruits and served as an early form of ice cream.

When Marco Polo returned from the East in the 13th century, he told of a frozen drink that consisted of a sweetened flower extract, paste or powder, which was diluted with water, then chilled with ice or snow. The drink was called *chorbet* in Turkish and *charab* in Persian, and it eventually evolved to become sorbet, or sherbet.

True frozen desserts were only made possible by the discovery that when ice and certain chemicals are combined, they form a liquid that is colder than the ice alone. One of the chemicals that works in this way is sodium chloride, or common salt. So when a mixture of ice and salt is packed around a container of a suitable liquid, the liquid in the container turns to ice.

As efficient ways of freezing were developed, the technique of making ices rapidly evolved into an art form and ices became a status symbol for the very rich. Soon banquet tables were glittering with beautiful ice pyramids. When Marie de Medici married Henry IV of France in the late 16th century, she introduced the French court to *sorbetti*. Like sorbets enjoyed today, these were frequently eaten between main courses, but they differ from modern equivalents in that they were based on alcohol. Making these *sorbetti* was very skilled work, carried out by expert *liqueristes* such as Massialot, who featured recipes for chocolate ice and

ABOVE: *A coloured engraving showing fashionable ladies choosing ice cream, "An Embarrassment of Choices", from "Le Bon Genre", Paris 1827.*

MASSIALOT'S FROMAGE A L'ANGLOISE

"Take 16oz of sweet cream and the same of milk, ½ lb powdered [icing/confectioners'] sugar, stir in 3 egg yolks and boil it until it becomes a thin pap. Take it from the fire and pour it into your ice mould and put it on ice for 3 hours. When it is firm, withdraw the mould and warm it a little in order more easily to turn out your cheese, or else dip your mould for a moment in hot water, then serve in a compotier."

This recipe from Massialot's book The Court and Country Cook *was reprinted in Elizabeth David's book* Harvest of the Cold Months, *London, 1994.*

RIGHT: *A Sevres dessert service was only for the very wealthy. It includes a* plat de ménage, *dish, cup and saucer and large ice cream bowl. From the Blue Cameo Service, Sevres, 1778–9. Part of a collection belonging to the Hermitage, St. Petersburg, Russia.*

EARLY RECIPES

Mary Eales, Confectioner to Queen Anne, was one of the first people to publish recipes for ice cream. Her book, *Mrs Eales's Receipts* (receipt being an early word for recipe) was published in 1718, some years after she supplied ice creams to the royal court. Her recipes call for very large amounts of ice to freeze these simple ice creams – as much as 10kg/20lb of ice mixed with 450g/1lb salt.

Mrs Eales' ice creams were frozen without the use of a churn, so would have tasted quite different from our modern ice creams. In 1722, a few years after Mary Eales published her book, Mary Smith included ten iced desserts in her publication *The Complete House-Keeper and Professional Cook*. These included Brown Bread Ice Cream, which is often considered a modern invention. Also on the list were Italian Ice Cream, Raspberry Cream, Orange Cream, Peach Cream and Apricot Cream.

Neither Mrs Eales' recipes nor those devised by Mary Smith contained eggs. Their inclusion was a later French refinement, which made ice cream considerably richer.

IMPROVEMENTS IN TASTE AND TEXTURE

A major advance that occurred in the 18th century was the discovery that beating ice cream until it was semi-frozen, then spooning it into a mould for a second freezing produced a much creamier and smoother result.

Flavourings became more adventurous at this time, and varied from exotic fruits such as bananas and pineapples to fresh berry fruit, preserves, chestnuts, cinnamon and white coffee cream. One of the more bizarre concoctions was a blend of lightly poached cucumber, ginger, brandy, coffee and cream. By 1885 books on making ice cream began to appear on the shelves, and cookery schools offered courses in making iced desserts.

custard ice in his cookbook published in 1692. Massailot referred to his ices as "cheeses", possibly because they were usually made in the dairy.

Fruit flavours predominated in these early sorbets, but flower waters, such as jasmine, violet, tuberrose, orange blossom and jonquil, were also used, as were infusions of green fennel, burnet and chervil. Ices were served on exquisite china, often in epergnes or bowls made specifically for the purpose.

Britain was slow to follow this new European fashion. It was not until 1675 that we have the first recorded instance of ice cream being served, when King Charles II enjoyed strawberries and ice cream at a grand banquet. Interest in frozen desserts grew during the reign of William and Mary, and by the time Queen Anne ascended the throne in 1702, they were extremely popular in court circles.

In Regency Britain, elegance and extravagance were all-important, and London society was at the heart of the British Empire. During the reign of George III and later the Prince Regent, ice creams became even more fashionable. Frozen desserts were spectacular scented and shaped creations, set in complicated hinged moulds and served at grand balls, or brought to elaborate summer picnics in portable "ice caves" or cabinets.

Although these frozen desserts were very impressive to look at, they must have tasted rather gritty, as the ice crystals were not broken down by beating, nor was air introduced into the mixture.

THE ITALIAN CONNECTION

Italy had always been famous for its superior ice creams, but it was not until the late 19th century that Great Britain and the United States discovered the joy of Italian ice cream. This came about when political upheaval in Italy led to a huge exodus of young Italians, many of whom set up as ice cream makers in the countries that gave them refuge, often in makeshift premises on the dockside.

In the early days, ice cream street sellers were a cross between wandering musicians and street hawkers. Their organ music first attracted customers to their barrows, which ranged from quite simple, crude affairs to highly decorated and colourful carts. Some sellers even made early carts look like gondolas.

As ice cream grew in popularity, so the number of street sellers increased, and by the turn of the century, 900 ice cream barrows were registered in Clerkenwell, London, alone. Competition was fierce, and as more and more street traders arrived on the scene, fights between rivals became frequent as each vied for the best pitch or spot.

HYGIENE ISSUES

Much of the ice cream sold at the time was produced in slum conditions in domestic kitchens. Milk was boiled and left to stand overnight, then frozen with ice the next morning. The dishes in which the ice cream, known as penny licks, was served were reused, often without being washed. The inevitable outcome was that bacterial infections and diseases like tuberculosis spread rapidly. Following an attempt to ban the sale of ice cream, manufacturing moved to much more hygienic business premises, and barrows were licensed to sell ice cream only at designated points.

These actions helped to resolve the hygiene problem and restore peaceful trading. However, the event that did most to reinstate the reputation of ice cream sellers was the invention of the ice cream cone in the early 19th century. The ice cream could be scooped directly into the wafer cones, bowls became largely obsolete and food safety standards improved considerably.

Many more Italian immigrants came to Britain and America after the end of World War II in a bid to rebuild shattered lives and homes. Family-run cafes, ice cream parlours and ice cream factories were quickly set up by the immigrants, and Italian bakers lost no time in switching from cookie-making to producing ice cream cones and wafers to meet the demands dictated by the growing popularity of ice cream on the streets.

ABOVE LEFT: *As ice cream vendors prospered, some stalls became very elaborate, fixed structures.*

ABOVE AND LEFT: *Many early hand carts were replaced by horsedrawn carts, and these evolved into the ice cream vans used today.*

LARGE-SCALE PRODUCTION

The world's first ice cream plant was founded in the United States in 1851 by Jacob Fussell, a Baltimore milk dealer who wanted to find a new market for cream during the summer months, when the supply peaked. As a milk dealer, he had the advantage over his rivals and was able to undercut their prices. As a result, his ice cream became so successful that by 1864 he had opened factories in Washington, Boston and New York.

By the 1920s England was also producing ice cream on a grand scale. Two major market leaders soon emerged: Wall's and Lyons. Originally known for his meat pies, Thomas Wall embarked on ice cream manufacture as a way of boosting summer profits. At first, ice cream production was small, but Thomas's use of American production techniques paid off. As popularity and production grew, the company expanded from just one ice cream factory in the London suburb of Acton, with seven street sellers, in the 1920s, to 136 depots and 8,500 stop-me-and-buy-one tricycles by 1939. Also highly successful was the Lyons group, famous for its triple-flavoured Neapolitan ice cream and the Lyons Corner Houses in London.

REFRIGERATORS AND FREEZERS

Most bought ice cream at this time was consumed on the spot. Mechanical refrigerators had only been developed at the start of the 20th century, and early models were noisy and prohibitively expensive. However, as technology advanced, prices came down, although in Britain refrigerators remained a luxury item for the very rich until after World War II. It was not until the 1960s that refrigerators became commonplace, and it would take another decade before many households owned a domestic deep freezer, making it possible to store both bought and home-made ice cream.

CONES AND WAFERS

It was a young Italian immigrant to America, Italo Marchiony, who first came up with the idea of an edible container for ice cream. When he started selling his ice creams and sorbets on Wall Street in New York, he spooned them into glasses. These were cumbersome and wasteful, so he started making shaped cups from waffle batter. The cups proved very popular, and he patented them in 1902. Two years later, he patented an ice cream cone, although the credit for this innovation is often given to a Syrian, Ernest A. Hamwi. According to the story, Mr Hamwi was selling waffles at the World's Trade Fair in 1904 when a neighbouring ice cream

ABOVE: *An ice cream parlour, popular in the United States since Prohibition, when enterprising brewers converted their liquor bars to milk bars and served chilled ice cream sodas, thick creamy milk shakes and sundaes instead.*

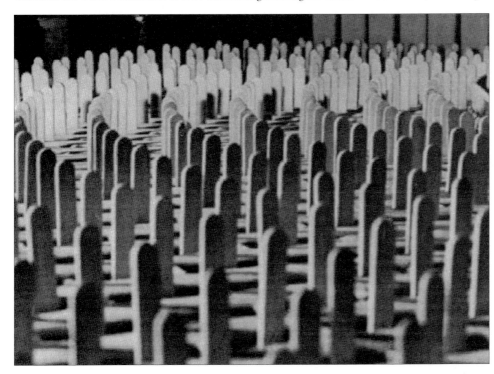

ABOVE: *The one-penny wafer of the 1930s, and later the larger American ice cream cones, quickly grew in popularity with the young and the "young at heart".*

LEFT: *Lolly (popsicle) sticks at a French factory, 1963.*

seller sold out of dishes. He persuaded Mr Hamwi to roll one of his waffles into a cone, let it cool and filled it with his ice cream. Made with a mixture of flour, milk and sugar, the ice cream cone quickly became a favourite. To help prevent spills, a ring of non-crushable biscuit (cookie) was moulded to the top.

Other traders of the 1920s were reluctant to sell these large imported cones, as they were quite expensive and required a considerable amount of ice cream to fill them. They preferred to sell ice cream briquettes sandwiched between the much cheaper rectangular wafers. In the 1930s a box of 1,200 wafers was very cheap to produce, making it possible to sell ice creams for one penny. However, by 1935, waffles for ice cream were introduced to supersede wafers, with the rather unusual advertising slogan of "Have a waffle in the cinema". Sales of wafers continued until the 1950s, until soft serve ice cream cornets (cones) appeared on the scene and the famous "99" was introduced, complete with its much-loved chocolate flake bar.

THE ICE CREAM SUNDAE

In late 19th-century America, chemists (drug stores) throughout the country sold drinks that were based on soda water (seltzer). Flavoured with fruit syrups and whipped cream, sodas were popular with both young and old alike. In 1874, Robert Green of Philadelphia ran out of cream when making sodas for the 50th anniversary of the Franklin Institute. With a long queue of customers waiting to be served, he substituted ice cream, much to the delight of the guests.

The ice cream soda soon became very popular, but you couldn't buy one on a Sunday. This was because many people believed that the sodas were alcoholic, even though they were nothing of the kind, and indulging was regarded as improper, especially on Sundays. An ingenious drugstore concessionaire got around the ban by serving the ice cream and syrup without the soda (selzer). He called it Ice Cream Sunday. The name was later changed to Sundae, which was judged more seemly.

ABOVE: *A welcome refresher from the heat, ice cream is sold at an ice cream parlour near Broken Hill in New South Wales, Australia.*

ABOVE: *Although ice cream making started off slowly in Italy, it soon developed, and Italian ice creams have enjoyed worldwide popularity ever since.*

ICE CREAM PARLOURS

The first ice cream parlour is reputed to have been opened in New York City in 1776, although it wasn't until the Prohibition years of the 1920s that business really started to boom. Bar owners had always served ice cream during the summer months, and when Prohibition came in 1920, the more enterprising among them had the foresight to realize that swapping ice cream for hard liquor was one way of staying in business. By 1930, ice cream parlours were very much a part of the American scene, and today there are ice cream parlours all over the world.

ICE CREAM MACHINES

Very early ice cream makers consisted of small earthenware or metal pots filled with milk or cream mixtures. These were then placed inside deep urns or cabinets lined with either wood or lead and surrounded with just ice, ice and straw, or ice and salt. The mixtures were then left to freeze. They must have been very hard and rather unpalatable by today's high standards, but such was their novelty value that they quickly became extremely popular with people of every age and social class.

ABOVE: *Despite the wintery weather, a young child enjoys ice cream near Winnipeg, Manitoba.*

George Washington, the first President of the United States, is said to have been so taken with ice cream when he was offered it in 1789 by Betsy Hamilton, wife of the Secretary to the Treasury, that he insisted that it be served regularly at official functions. Thomas Jefferson continued this presidential penchant for ice cream and even brought an ice cream maker back with him when he returned to the United States from a posting in France as Secretary of State.

By the middle of the 19th century, mechanized ice cream makers were introduced. These looked like wooden pails filled with an ice and salt mixture, and had a small metal canister inside for the ice cream.

HAND-CRANKED MACHINES

What really revolutionized the production of ice cream, however, was the hand-cranked ice cream machine. This kept the ice cream in continuous motion during freezing, preventing the formation of discernible ice crystals and introducing air. The most famous hand-cranked machine was invented in 1843 by Nancy Johnson, a naval officer's wife, in the United States. Later that century, in England, Agnes Marshall also developed a hand-cranked ice cream maker.

Traditional hand-cranked machines are handsome appliances. The outer casing is a tongue-and-groove wooden pail with a carrying handle. A stainless-steel ice cream container fits inside the tub, and the crank or turning handle powers the gear drive that turns the wooden dasher.

Operating the hand-cranked machine is simple, if tiring work. Having inserted the ice cream container into the pail, the dasher is fitted, and then chilled ice cream mixture is poured in. The lid is put on the container, the crank top is secured, and the space between the can and the pail is filled with a mixture of crushed ice and rock salt. After about five minutes, it is time to start churning.

With a manual machine, this means turning the crank continuously, slowly at first and then more rapidly, until the ice cream freezes and the crank becomes increasingly difficult to turn. At this point, water is drained from the machine, the top is lifted off and sufficient ice is cleared away to expose the top of the can. Ice cream on the dasher is scraped back into the can, and the dasher is removed. The ice cream can be eaten immediately, but purists prefer to repack it in the can, surrounding it with more ice, this time with a higher concentration of salt, and leave it to stand for 30 minutes to mature or 'ripen'.

The advantage of a hand-cranked ice cream machine is that very good ice cream can be made anywhere – on the porch, at a picnic – by anyone strong enough to turn the handle. Another plus is capacity. These machines make up to 6 litres/10 pints/6 quarts of ice cream in one sitting, which makes them ideal for entertaining. Perhaps these, plus their deliciously retro appearance, are among the reasons for their upsurge in popularity in America today. Electrically operated cranked machines are also available, mainly in the United States.

ABOVE: *With the introduction of mechanized ice churners, such as these wooden pails with metal canisters inside, ice cream could be produced and sold on a large scale by enterprising street sellers.*

FREEZER-AIDED MACHINES

As domestic refrigerators and freezers became more commonplace in people's homes, it was inevitable that someone would come up with the idea of an ice cream machine that could be operated inside the freezer. Several designs were pioneered in the early 1970s, including a simple rectangular stainless-steel box that was filled with a mixture of custard and cream and placed in the freezer cabinet of a refrigerator. The dashers or paddles were fitted on the underside of the lid. These turned constantly when the machine was connected to the electricity supply by means of a flattened flex, which enabled the door of the freezer to be closed while the ice cream maker was in operation. Some of these machines produced wonderfully smooth ice cream, but there were disadvantages. Most of them made only a small quantity and because the ice cream took a considerable amount of time to freeze, the motor was put under a lot of strain. The trailing flex was a hazard, and because the machine was out of sight during operation, the cook often failed to notice when the ice cream had frozen solid, causing paddles to snap and the motor to labour. Broken paddles and burnt-out motors contributed to the demise of this type of ice cream maker.

Making ice cream at home became a good deal simpler with the discovery that when a freezing solution was sealed within the walls of a container that was then frozen, the container became cold enough to freeze the ice cream mixture, even when operated at room temperature. The first machine to utilize this principle was invented in the 1980s. It resembled a traditional hand-cranked ice cream maker, but instead of a messy mixture of ice and salt, which needed to be replaced every time ice cream was made, the refrigerant was safely sealed inside the double-skinned bucket. The dasher that churned the ice cream had to be turned by hand every few minutes, but the machine didn't require the same amount of elbow grease as classic hand-cranked versions and was much more time- and energy-efficient.

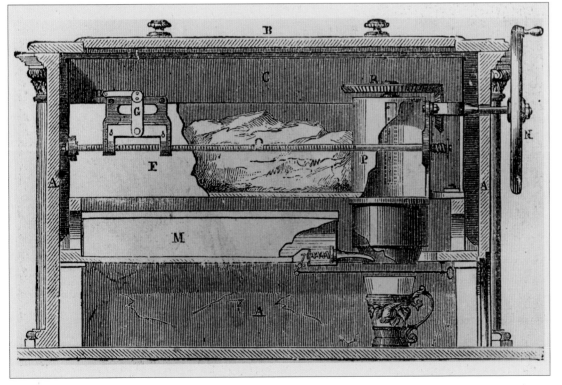

LEFT: *Illustration of an early ice cream machine using a hand-cranking device for churning the ice cream.*

ABOVE: *Commercial machines, like those used in this ice cream factory in Holstich, Germany in 1895, were the forerunners of modern ice cream makers.*

The next stage was to produce an ice cream maker that operated on the same principle, but in which the mixture could be churned automatically during freezing. The bucket was pre-frozen and then removed from the freezer. A lid that incorporated the dasher and motor was fitted on top, the machine was plugged in and switched on, and the ice cream mixture was poured in. The ice cream was frozen relatively quickly, and the dasher continued to turn until the thickening mixture caused it to become sluggish, which signalled that the ice cream was ready to be decanted and eaten.

Such machines remain the mainstay of the lower end of the market today. They come in various shapes and sizes, some with tall, bulbous ice cream tubs; others looking more like cake tins (pans). In some cases, the container that goes into the freezer is the base of the machine, merely requiring a dasher and motor to be fitted after freezing. In other models, the bucket is separate, and must be fitted into an outer casing once the refrigerant is frozen. The advantage of the former machine is that if you store it permanently in the freezer, as suggested by the manufacturer, then it is ready to be used at all times, and the only part that should be housed in a kitchen cupboard is the lid, with its motor and dasher. The type of machine that has a separate bucket is not ready for immediate use and takes up more storage space in the kitchen, but tends to be easier to assemble.

Freezer-aided machines take around 30–45 minutes to make ice cream. It is important that the dasher is rotating when the ice cream mixture is poured in (usually through an aperture in the lid) so that churning begins immediately and the dasher continues to move smoothly. If the cream or custard mixture is poured in before the dasher has been started, the mixture may freeze on contact with the sides or base of the bucket, preventing the dasher from turning easily, causing wear to the motor and preventing the production of perfect ice cream.

One of the latest machines to arrive on the UK market is the soft serve ice cream maker. Like the seaside treat that gave it its name, it includes a dispenser, so the ice cream comes out rather like toothpaste from a tube, and can be easily swirled into a dish or cone. Quite a lot of air is incorporated during the mixing and freezing process, so the ice cream is lighter and airier than the dense, rich ice cream produced by conventional machines.

MAKING ICE CREAM AT HOME

With the increased availability of affordable ingredients and improvements to ice cream makers, middle-class housewives sought the advice of highly skilled cooks, such as Mrs Agnes B. Marshall and Mrs Beeton. In 1885 Agnes Marshall published her first book, in which she included detailed advice on making a range of ice creams, such as "cheap", "ordinary" and "common" ice cream. Her "cheap ice cream" was made using 1 pint (600ml | 2½ cups) of cream, 8 egg yolks and ¼lb (115g | 4oz | ½ cup) of sugar. Next came her "ordinary ice cream", in which the cream was replaced with milk. Her "common ice cream" was made with the same quantity of milk and sugar, but only two whisked eggs, while the "ordinary ice cream" dispensed with eggs altogether, and thickened the sweetened milk with arrowroot (15g | ½ oz | 2 tbsp).

ABOVE: *An ice cream mould.*

RIGHT: *An early hand-cranked ice cream machine.*

RIGHT: *Illustration from* Süsse Speisen und Eisbomben, *published in Germany in 1907, showing a variety of iced confections.*

The soft serve machine is great fun for families with small children and could well become the main attraction at birthday parties. However, the machine is quite difficult to assemble and does have its limitations. It makes delicious ice cream, but it is not suitable for mixtures containing chunky ingredients, such as nuts, pieces of fruit or chocolate chips. It is recommended that only soft-serve recipes supplied with the machine be used, and these tend to be quite basic. Should hard ice cream be required, the soft-serve can be spooned into a tub and placed in the freezer until solid.

All of these machines are affordable and easy to operate, but because they depend on a period of pre-freezing of the tub, you can't make ice cream on impulse. If you have enough freezer space to keep the bucket or tub permanently frozen, as the manufacturers recommend, some spontaneity is possible, but you still won't be able to make successive batches of ice cream without a spare tub.

FREESTANDING MACHINES

If you really love ice cream – and make it often – it is worth investing in a top-of-the-range freestanding machine. These are worktop versions of the huge machines used in ice cream factories, and each has a built-in compressor. Pre-chilling is still necessary, but this only takes ten minutes at most, after which time the dasher is turned on and the ice cream mixture is poured in.

The three main advantages of this type of machine are convenience, speed and excellent texture. Use good quality ingredients, and the ice cream they produce will be virtually perfect, but you'll need to produce a lot of it to justify the price of the appliance. Another factor to consider is size. One of these, a food processor and a kettle and your working area will be severely restricted. Also these machines tend to be noisier than freezer-chilled types, so if you are trying to make a batch of Chunky Chocolate Ice Cream or Rocky Road Ice Cream without attracting the attention of the children, you may be rumbled.

Whatever type of machine you buy, making ice cream will be a great deal easier than the old-fashioned method of chilling in a shallow pan and beating it by hand at regular intervals during the freezing process. With the minimum of effort, you'll be able to transform top quality ingredients into a delectable iced dessert.

THE RISE OF THE ICE CREAM GIANTS

In the early 1930s a young man by the name of Reuben Mattus was often to be found on the streets of the Bronx in New York, selling his mother's home-made ice cream from a horse and buggy.

BELOW: *This traditional churn has been modified with the addition of an electric crank. These retro churns produce large amounts of ice cream and are very popular.*

ABOVE: *A traditional hand-cranked ice cream machine. The metal turning handle powers the gear drive and turns the wooden dasher.*

The family business prospered in the years that followed, and in 1961 Reuben launched a new product, a superior, richly flavoured ice cream containing butterfat, which did not incorporate very much air, producing a dense texture. He called it Häagen-Dazs. At first there were just three basic flavours – chocolate, vanilla and coffee – but the ice cream's fans soon demanded more, and the delis that stocked it found it difficult to keep up with demand.

In 1973 the first Häagen-Dazs shop was opened, and ten years later Mr Mattas sold out to the Pillsbury Company. Today Häagen-Dazs remains a world leader, with flavours such as blueberry cheesecake, chocolate cheesecake and macadamia brittle.

Five years before Mr Mattas sold his business, two young American college friends, Ben Cohen and Jerry Greenfield, began making ice cream in a renovated petrol (gas) station in Burlington, Vermont. They bought an old-fashioned hand-cranked machine, did an ice-cream-making course by correspondence and, after considerable experimentation, went into business. Sales soon rocketed and Ben & Jerry's ice cream is now sold all over the world.

ICE CREAM TODAY

Ice cream is one of the world's favourite foods, enjoyed in all countries and in all seasons. The countries with the highest rate of consumption include the United States, New Zealand and Australia. Sales in Japan are rising rapidly, and even in cooler countries such as Denmark and Finland, ice cream is extremely popular. Although more ice cream is sold in the summer than in the winter, it is bought, eaten and enjoyed all year round. In Russia, for instance, ice cream can be bought from street kiosks even when the ground is covered in deep snow.

It is now possible to buy luxury ice creams in a vast array of flavours from supermarkets, delis and ice cream parlours, but indulgence often comes at a price, and many individuals prefer to make their own ice cream, especially now that efficient and relatively inexpensive machines are readily available.

making
ice cream

Creating delicious ice cream at home is surprisingly simple, requires little equipment and is enormously satisfying. Covering every aspect of making ices in all of their variety, as well as sauces, cones, baskets and decorations, this chapter provides the skills and techniques necessary for even the most ambitious iced desserts.

Ice cream machines

Ice cream can be made by hand, but it is a time-consuming and laborious process. An ice cream maker produces excellent iced desserts, including low-fat ice cream and sorbets, with very little effort. There are a number of models on the market, priced to suit all pockets.

There are basically two types of ice cream maker on the market: freezer assisted machines, and machines that have their own compressors which do not need to go in the freezer.

FREEZER ASSISTED MACHINES

These machines are usually cheaper than machines with their own compressors, and there are many different models available, which perform in different ways.

Simple ice cream machines

The cheapest option is a simple machine that consists of a double-skinned bowl and a separate motor unit. Between the walls of the bowl is liquid refrigerant. When frozen solid – a process that can take up to 24 hours – the bowl becomes super-cooled, and when the dasher or beater and motor are fitted, the mixture to be

BELOW: *This simple freezer assisted machine is easy to use and relatively inexpensive.*

churned is rapidly transformed into ice cream or sorbet. The drawback with this type of machine is that it requires forward planning – unless you have enough room to keep the bowl permanently in the freezer – and the capacity is limited. Some of the machines are quite awkward to assemble, and because the aperture where the mixture is poured in is relatively small, spills are commonplace. You can't make successive batches of ice cream unless you have a spare frozen bowl, but that shouldn't prove a problem unless you are a serial ice cream eater! For the average family for whom ice cream is a regular but not daily dessert, this type of machine is ideal.

Quick ice cream machines

One type, which performs very well, only takes half an hour to make a batch of ice cream. The double-skinned bowl is lifted out of the casing and wrapped in a plastic bag before being frozen. When the refrigerant has cooled

ABOVE: *This compact freezer assisted model comes in both white and modern chrome finishes.*

sufficiently, the bowl is replaced and the lid, with the dasher, is fitted on top. The motor is turned on, and the mixture is poured in through the lid. The advantages of this machine are ease of assembly and operation, a quiet motor and a bowl with a large surface area for easy scooping. The drawback is that it requires quite a bit of storage space.

Quick churn ice cream machines

Other freezer assisted machines are available on the market with fewer parts, in which the ice-bucket-shaped bowl itself forms the base of the machine. Once it is fully frozen – which can take some time – all you need to do is fit the lid with the dasher and motor, switch it on and pour in the ice cream mixture to be churned. If you keep the bowl permanently in the freezer, it will be ready to use at all times and the remaining parts will take up little room in your kitchen cupboard. This type of model tends to come in two sizes, one delivering 650ml | 1 pint 2fl oz | 2⅔ cups of ice cream and the larger 900ml | 1½ pints | 3¾ cups. On the negative side, the motor is quite loud and fitting the lid can be difficult.

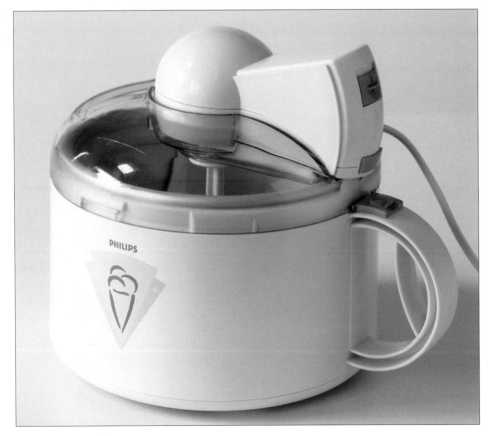

Soft serve ice cream machines

A third type of machine, and one that can be fun for the child in the family or even the child in you, is a soft serve maker. This type of machine dispenses soft serve ice cream in swirls and whirls, so you can make ices just like the ones sold at the seaside. It comes with four separate nozzles and is relatively easy to operate, although assembling the machine and cleaning it can be awkard. It is also very loud, so there's no question of making a sundae in secret, and it is not suitable for mixtures containing any chunks, such as nuts or chocolate chips or fruit.

BUILT-IN COMPRESSOR MACHINES

If you can afford it, and have plenty of space on your counter-top, consider buying an ice cream maker with a built in freezer unit or compressor. These machines are ready for use ten minutes after activating the compressor, and produce very good ice cream with ease. Most have both a fixed bowl, and a smaller bucket for quantities up to 600ml | 1 pint. To make successive batches of ice cream, you can use the bucket first, then lift it out and make a second lot of ice cream in the larger bowl.

ABOVE: *The soft serve ice cream maker is one of the latest types of machine available.*

The real advantage of a machine with its own freezing unit, or compressor, is that it needs only 5–10 minutes' pre-chilling before the dasher motor is switched on and the liquid is added. The major drawback is cleaning the machine, since the fixed bowl cannot be lifted out, nor should the machine be tilted. After scooping out the ice cream, the bowl must be washed thoroughly with a sponge filled with hot soapy water, then rinsed with cold water before being dried with kitchen paper. If you use the smaller bowl, you will avoid this chore, but will still need to wipe up the alcohol that must be used between the two bowls to conduct the cold.

Some models have the dasher motor inside the machine, so the operation is smooth and efficient. This type of machine is easy to use

ABOVE: *This handsome counter-top model has its own built-in compressor for creating luxury ice cream.*

but does take up a lot of space. It should not be tipped or tilted (the refrigerant must settle before use), so it is best kept permanently on the worktop.

THE FREEZER

An efficient freezer is essential for pre-chilling bowls or buckets for basic ice cream makers, and for storing the ice cream once you have made it. For making ice cream the temperature should be −18°C | −66°F. A freezer thermometer is a useful tool. The colder the freezer the more quickly the ice will freeze, resulting in smaller ice crystals and smoother ice cream.

BELOW: *This freestanding machine incorporates an internal dasher motor.*

TIPS TO CONSIDER WHEN BUYING

- Is the machine virtually ready to go or does it require lengthy pre-freezing?

- If the bowl needs to be pre-frozen, which shape will fit your freezer best?

- How much storage space does the machine require? Remember that a machine with its own compressor is best kept on the worktop.

- How noisy is the motor? (Ask to see – or hear – the machine in operation before you buy, if possible.)

- What is the maximum – and minimum – capacity of the machine?

- Is it possible to make successive batches of ice cream?

- How easy is it to assemble and take apart the machine for cleaning?

- Is there a decent-size aperture for pouring in the mixture to be churned?

- Can you buy extra bowls for pre-freezing?

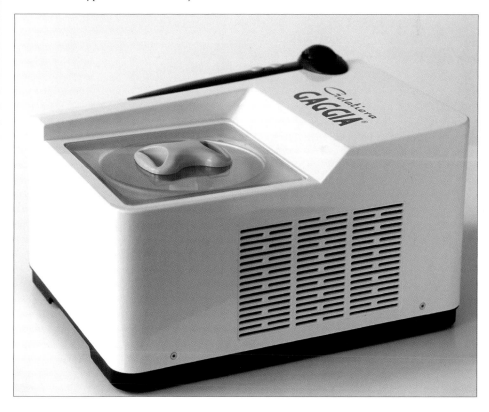

Basic equipment

You will probably already have most of the peripheral equipment required for making ice creams, or can adapt existing kitchen equipment. Spoons can double as scoops, bowls can be used as moulds, and plastic boxes with tight-fitting lids are ideal for storage. Some specialist items are useful, however.

SCOOPS, SPOONS AND SCRAPERS

There are plenty of ice cream scoops on the market. Choose from half-moon-shaped stainless-steel scoops with sleek steel handles, simple spoon-shaped scoops with metal handles or easy-grip moulded plastic handles, or brightly coloured plastic scoops with quick release levers. Among the most efficient scoops are those with antifreeze solution embedded in the handle. This is activated by the warmth of your hand, and enables the ice cream to slide effortlessly off the scoop.

When scooping ice cream out of a tub or box, do not dig deep: the trick is to draw the scoop smoothly across the surface of the ice cream so that a natural ball-shape is formed. Some people recommend dipping the scoop in water between uses, but this is not a good idea as the water will freeze on contact, spoiling the texture of the ice cream. For tiny balls of ice cream, use melon ballers. Arrange the scoops on a plate so that they resemble a bunch of grapes, or pile them up.

Use only plastic or rubber spoons and scrapers for removing ice cream from the buckets or bowls of ice cream makers, as scratching the containers will impair their efficiency and could trap germs.

MOULDS

Although you can buy bombe, dariole and ring moulds designed specifically for ice cream, such items can be costly and take up valuable space

ABOVE: *Specialized bombe, dariole and ring moulds will ensure a professional finish, but they can be expensive pieces of kitchen equipment.*

LEFT: *Individual metal steamed-pudding moulds can be used if lined with clear film.*

in the kitchen. Improvise by using mixing bowls, cake tins (pans) and individual steamed pudding moulds. Line them with several layers of clear film (plastic wrap) first, using a generous amount of wrapping so that there is enough overlap to cover the entire exposed surface of the ice cream to prevent it from drying out in the freezer.

EVERYDAY EQUIPMENT

To make rectangular ice cream bombes or terrines, you can use metal loaf tins (pans). Unless they have a non-stick finish, line them with clear film. Tins that have sloping sides can be adapted. Simply cut a piece of cardboard the length and height of the tin and use it to alter the shape of the tin. Line with clear film, pushing it carefully into the corners.

For bombes or cassatas you can use a plastic bowl with a lid. These make ideal ice cream moulds, as the thin plastic conducts the cold well in the freezer, and the dessert can be easily turned out by by running the basin under a hot tap and then flexing the plastic.

ABOVE: *Use melon ballers to make miniature scoops of ice cream and sorbet, and pile them up on a plate.*

ABOVE: *This wooden cone mould is a very simple but useful tool for making professional-looking cones.*

ABOVE: *Unmoulding kulfi is easy with a specially designed all-in-one kulfi mould.*

Instead of buying special moulds for kulfi, use conical lolly (popsicle) moulds or new disposable plastic cups, which work almost as well. For individual moulds, line old china cups, metal dariole moulds or individual metal steamed pudding moulds with several layers of clear film, which makes it easier to turn out the frozen dessert. If you can lay your hands on them, the tiny plastic pots with lids used for freezing baby food are ideal.

BELOW: *Ice cream scoops are available in many different shapes, materials and colours.*

STORAGE BOXES

For storage, you will need a selection of freezerproof containers in varying sizes, with tightly fitting lids to eliminate the transfer of strong smells and flavours and prevent the surface of the ice cream from drying out. Good quality bought ice cream tubs and air-tight sandwich boxes are ideal. Placing a piece of clear film on the surface of the ice cream is a sensible additional precaution, preventing frost build-up and preventing the surface from becoming dry. Try to keep the ice cream away from strongly flavoured products in the freezer.

TURNING OUT A FROZEN BOMBE

To unmould an iced dessert in a metal or plastic mould, dip it in hot, but not boiling, water, leave for a few seconds, then blot the excess water. If the mould is lined with clear film, carefully insert a knife between the film and the mould to loosen the ice cream. Invert the mould on a serving plate, lift off the mould and peel away the film.

If the mould is made of glass or china, do not dip it in hot water, or it may break. Instead, invert the basin on a serving plate, then warm the outside by covering it with a hot dish towel. Count to 20 and then lift the basin off.

When dipping moulds, use hot tap water rather than boiling water from the kettle, which would cause the outside of the ice cream to melt instantly and run over the plate when turned out. Boiling water would also be dangerous, as it could splash.

Basic ingredients

Nothing beats the cool, creamy smoothness of the ultimate indulgence, home-made ice cream. The choice of flavours and flavour combinations is limited only by your own imagination, so begin with our basic recipes and adapt or develop them to incorporate all the tastes you love. You will rapidly build a repertoire of wonderful iced desserts, all completely additive-free and made with only the ingredients that you choose to include.

Ice cream

Cream

You just couldn't make true ice cream without lashings of cream. Surprisingly, whipping cream, with its natural creamy taste, makes the best ice cream, especially when mixed with strong rich flavours such as coffee, toffee or chocolate. Double (heavy) cream is, however, a must for vanilla or Brown Bread Ice Cream. Clotted cream and crème fraîche, the thick, rich lightly soured French-style cream, make delicious additions to fruit, honey and spice ice creams. Do be careful when using double or clotted cream as their high butter-fat content can give the ice cream a buttery flavour and texture, especially if it is overchurned. Avoid UHT creams as the flavour is too strong.

Milk

There is a wide choice of milk in most supermarkets – from skimmed, semi-skimmed (low-fat), full-fat (whole) and breakfast milk, to the now more readily available goat's milk and soya milk. Skimmed milk is best avoided when making ice cream at home, due to its low fat content and "thin" taste, but it is difficult to distinguish between semi-skimmed or full-fat milk, especially when mixed with cream. Full-fat, semi-skimmed and goat's milk all make delicious ice cream.

Yogurt

The choice of yogurt is highly personal: it seems people either love ice cream that contains yogurt, or absolutely hate it! If you are not sure how your family will react, start with the mild bio-style natural (plain) yogurt, with its creamy smoothness, and, if that is successful, work up to the stronger, sharper sheep's and goat's milk yogurts.

ABOVE: *Freshly laid eggs and double or whipping cream gives home-made ice cream its luxury flavour.*

Cheese

Light, virtually fat-free fromage frais can be added to fruit or vanilla ice creams and is ideal for those who adore ice cream but have to watch their fat intake. Ricotta, an Italian whey cheese, has a white, creamy, soft texture. It is similar to a cross between cottage and cream cheese and can be used successfully in certain ice creams. For the richest results of all, try mascarpone, another Italian cheese. It has a deep buttery-yellow colour and a texture similar to that of cream cheese. For the best of both worlds, mix mascarpone with fromage frais for a rich-tasting, reduced-fat dessert.

Non-dairy products

Look out for soya milk, either unsweetened or sweetened, in long-life cartons, and canned coconut milk – both ideal for vegans or those on a milk-free diet. Coconut milk is also a great standby for a dinner-party ice cream when mixed with lime or lemon.

Eggs

Where possible use freshly laid, organic eggs for the best colour and flavour. They cost a little more than ordinary eggs but make a great difference to the finished result of home-made ice cream.

ABOVE: *Muscovado sugar can be a delicious sweetener.*

Sweeteners

Caster (superfine) sugar has been used in most of the recipes, as its fine crystals dissolve quickly in the custard, maintaining a smooth, silky texture. Granulated (white) sugar is used for making nut brittle (praline), a delicious ingredient in some of the speciality ices. Muscovado (molasses) and light muscovado (brown) sugar can also be used as a sweetener in some recipes, where the darker colour and stronger flavour is used to great effect. Honey and maple syrup also make delicious additions, either on their own or mixed with caster sugar. They are particularly good in ice cream flavoured with nuts.

Cornflour

Purists will throw up their hands in horror at the idea of cornflour (cornstarch) being used in the custard for an ice cream. They might well argue that it is far better to make the custard in a double boiler or a large heatproof bowl set over simmering water. It is certainly true that cornflour is not a standard ingredient in a classic custard, but it does help to stabilize the custard and reduces the risk of curdling. Custard that contains a little cornflour is easier to handle, so can be gently cooked in a heavy pan. It will thicken in 4–5 minutes, whereas it would take 15 minutes or more in a double boiler, thus greatly reducing the cooking time.

COOK'S TIP *Put leftover egg whites in a small plastic box. Cover with a tight-fitting lid and label the box clearly. Freeze up to 6 months and thaw at room temperature for 4 hours. Use to make pavlovas, sorbets, meringues and meringue-based ice creams.*

Water ices

Sugar syrup

A simple sugar syrup is made by heating a mixture of caster sugar and water in a medium pan, stirring until the sugar has dissolved. It is no longer thought essential to boil the syrup, just to heat it for long enough to dissolve the sugar. Caster sugar has been used for syrups in the recipe section of this book because it dissolves very rapidly, but granulated sugar can also be used, as can light muscovado sugar or honey. Once made and cooled, the syrup can be stored in the refrigerator for several days.

Flavouring

Choose from a wide range of fresh fruit purées such as strawberry, raspberry, peach or pineapple, or mix with some of the more exotic fruits such as passion fruit, mango and lime. Dried fruits can be steeped in apple or grape juice or in water and brandy or a liqueur mixture before being puréed and added to the custard mixture. Citrus rinds (orange, lemon or lime) can be infused in the hot syrup for extra flavour and then fresh juice added to heighten and strengthen the flavour. Spice infusions or mixtures of spices and fruits also work very well and create unusual ices that are particularly successful with people who prefer a light dessert that is not too sweet.

ABOVE: *Honey can be used on its own or with sugar.*

Egg white

The purpose of adding egg white to a semi-frozen sorbet is twofold. First, it helps to stabilize the mixture, which is important for those sorbets that melt quickly, and second, it can be used to lighten very dense or fibrous sorbets, such as those made from blackcurrants or blackberries. The egg white requires only the minimum of beating with a fork to loosen it and need not be whisked until frothy or standing in peaks as previously thought.

HOW TO SEPARATE AN EGG

Crack the egg on the side of a bowl. Gently ease the halves apart, keeping the yolk in one half and letting the white fall into the bowl below. Separate any remaining egg white from the yolk by swapping the yolk from one shell half to the other. Do this several times if necessary, until all the egg white has fallen into the bowl and what remains is the pure egg yolk. If you do drop any egg yolk into the bowl below, scoop it out with one of the eggshell halves; the jagged edges will trap the yolk and prevent it from sliding back into the bowl.

Flavourings

Visit a modern ice cream parlour and you'll be dazzled by the number of flavours available. Yet, there is no comparison to the endless possibilities you can create at home. Spices, herbs, fruits of every kind, flower waters, chocolate, coffee and nuts can all be used – singly or in combination. Experiment to find the tastes you and your family like best, remembering that freezing dulls some flavours, so you can often afford to be bold.

Herbs and flowers

Edible flowers

A sprinkling of just a few delicate, colourful petals or tiny flower heads from the garden can turn even a few simple scoops of home-made strawberry or vanilla ice cream into an elegant dinner-party dessert.

A few vibrant pansies or tiny violas mixed with primrose petals or even a few dainty violets would be perfect for a springtime party, while pastel-coloured rose petals, borage flowers or sprigs of lavender would make a fine decoration in summer, as would a misty haze of elderflowers or sweet cicely flowers.

For something bolder, use yellow or orange marigold petals (but not French marigolds) or nasturtiums. If selecting other flowers, please be aware that not all flowers are edible. Avoid plants that grow from a bulb or that would not be found in a herb garden, as these may at worst be poisonous or at best have an unpleasant flavour.

Flower waters

Orange flower or orange blossom water and rose water add a delicate fragrance to ground almond or summer berry ice creams and sorbets. Add a few drops and seal the bottle well to prevent evaporation.

Herbs

Rosemary, bay, mint and lavender make wonderful additions to creamy ice creams, sherbets or sorbets. For best results infuse a few sprigs of rosemary or lavender, two to three whole bay leaves or a small bunch of fresh mint in cream or sugar syrup that has just come to the boil. Leave in the liquid until cool, then strain. You can also add a little fresh chopped mint or other extra herbs to the finished ice cream or sorbet.

RIGHT: *Sprigs of flowers or flower water give a delicate flavour to ice creams and sorbets.*

Spices

Ginger

TYPES/FORMS: The rhizome of an elegant tropical plant, ginger appears in many guises. The root is widely available fresh and is also preserved in sugar syrup as stem ginger. Chopped candied ginger and crystallized ginger are other forms of this delicious spice.

USES: Ginger makes a wonderful ice cream ingredient just on its own, but it gives a glorious lift to fruit ices, especially with fruit such as rhubarb or pears, and it is a natural partner for tropical fruit. Preserved ginger, ginger syrup and ginger wine make delicious ice cream sauces.

PREPARATION: Peel root ginger, then slice or chop it thinly. Alternatively, grate it with the fine-toothed surface of a grater. Slice or chop preserved stem ginger; finely chop candied or crystallized ginger if pieces are large.

Using ginger

1 Peel away the skin on the ginger root, using a swivel-blade vegetable peeler or a small, sharp knife. Take care when peeling to remove only the thin outer skin.

2 Grate the ginger on the fine section of a regular grater or a nutmeg grater. This is easiest to do if the ginger is frozen. It will thaw instantly on being grated.

Vanilla

TYPES/FORMS: Seed pods of the climbing vanilla orchid plant are sold singly or in pairs. The spice is also finely ground, mixed with sugar and sold in sachets labelled vanilla sugar. It is best known, however, as vanilla essence (extract).

The pods are picked while still unripe. On drying, their yellow colour deepens to a dark brown and they acquire a natural coating of vanillin crystals, which are the source of the characteristic spicy aroma. The word "vanilla" comes from the Spanish *vainilla*, meaning "little sheath". Although always associated with sweet dishes, the vanilla pod is not itself sweet.

Beware of cheap vanilla flavourings as their harsh, almost bitter, flavour can be overpowering and could spoil the delicate flavour of some ice creams. The better quality vanilla essence is always labelled "natural vanilla essence".

USES: Vanilla is delicious in ice cream, whipped cream and custard and is used extensively when making patissiere cream and confectionery.

PREPARATION: Slit the whole vanilla pod, add it to cream or milk that has just come to the boil, then leave to cool and infuse. Lift up the pod, and holding it over the liquid, scrape the tiny black seeds with a small knife so that they fall into the liquid. The flavoured cream or milk makes excellent ice cream. Don't throw pods away after use. Rinse, pat dry with kitchen paper and store two or three in a jar of caster (superfine) sugar to make your own vanilla sugar. Vanilla essence is highly concentrated, and you only need 2.5–5ml | ½–1 tsp for ice cream.

Cinnamon

TYPES/FORMS: Cinnamon is obtained from the bark of the cinnamon tree, which is native to India. The bark is rolled into sticks or quills and dried. Cinnamon is also sold finely ground. The ground spice is seldom used in ice creams, except as a decoration, although it is widely used in baking. Cassia is a related spice. It resembles cinnamon in terms of aroma and flavour but is coarser and more pungent. Cassia is usually cheaper than cinnamon.

USES: Ice cream may not be the obvious use for cinnamon, a spice better known as an ingredient in cakes, biscuits and savoury dishes, but it adds a delicious flavour, especially with fruits such as peaches or nectarines.

PREPARATION: Infuse halved cinnamon sticks in milk or cream that has just come to the boil. Continue to simmer for 5–10 minutes until the cinnamon has imparted its flavour to the liquid, strain the milk or cream and use it to make custard as the basis for ice cream. Cinnamon sticks can also be used to flavour fruit purées or compotes by infusing in the liquid in the same way.

Using vanilla

Using a sharp knife, slit a whole vanilla pod. Add it to milk or cream that has just come to the boil. For maximum flavour, scrape out the tiny black seeds from the pod and let them fall into the milk or cream.

Nutmeg

TYPES/FORMS: Sold whole, nutmegs are the dried seeds of the fruit of the nutmeg tree, which is native to the tropics. Blades of mace, the pretty orange outer coating, are also sold separately, and both are sold ground.

USES: Nutmeg's wonderfully aromatic and slightly bitter flavour complements both sweet and savoury dishes. It is delicious in milk-based desserts such as ice cream.

PREPARATION: For the best flavour, grate a little off a whole nutmeg as and when you need it, using the fine-toothed surface of a grater or, better still, a small nutmeg grater. Ready-ground nutmeg rapidly loses its pungency when stored.

Cloves

TYPES/FORMS: The unopened flower buds of a tree related to the myrtle, cloves look like tiny nails. They are available whole and ground.

USES: Although cloves are most commonly used in savoury dishes, they are also widely used in desserts, particularly with apples and other fruits. Their pungent flavour means that they are a somewhat unlikely ingredient in ice cream, but if used sparingly, they add an intriguing flavour.

PREPARATION: Infuse whole cloves in milk or cream. This is especially appropriate when making a custard to form the basis of a fruit ice cream. Don't overdo this flavouring – the taste should be subtle and not strident.

Star anise

These pretty star-shaped pods are a favourite of Chinese cooks, but are becoming popular in the West. Use them whole for sauces and compotes, or infuse them in sugar syrups or custards for ices with a lovely aniseed flavour.

Using cardamom

If the recipe calls for cardamom seeds, crush the pods with the back of a cook's knife until they split. If necessary, use the tip of the knife to remove any remaining seeds from the pods. Use both the pod and the seeds for maximum flavour.

Cardamom

Traditionally used in Indian, Arabian and North African cooking, cardamom also adds a wonderful delicate aromatic fragrance to sorbets, ice creams and fruit compotes.

Lemon grass

Mainly known for the delicate lemon fragrance it contributes to Thai and Vietnamese cookery, lemon grass is now widely available. Most supermarkets stock the fresh stems, which are pale green and tipped with white; it is also available as dried whole stems or ground lemon grass and sold in jars. To extract the delicate flavour the dried stems must be soaked in warm water for at least two hours before use. Fresh lemon grass can be finely sliced or crushed and infused in the milk to be used for custard-based ice cream or infused in the sugar syrup for a granita or sorbet.

BELOW: *Star anise, vanilla pods, cinnamon sticks and ground ginger all add subtle flavours to ice creams.*

Chocolate

Choosing the best

A chocolate with a good, strong flavour is vital when making ice creams as the flavour of the chocolate is dulled when it is mixed with custard and cream. For the best and strongest flavour choose a good quality dark or bitter chocolate with a high proportion of cocoa solids. Confectioners and good food shops will have a selection of superior chocolates, but many of the larger supermarkets now stock several different types of good quality cooking chocolate. Choose one with "luxury" or "Belgian" on the label as it will almost certainly have at least 75 per cent cocoa solids, and good flavour and taste will be guaranteed.

Chocolate Menier can also be used. It has a stronger flavour and is less sweet than some other types of chocolate, but is well suited to ice cream making. Plain (semisweet) dessert chocolate contains between 30 and 60 per cent cocoa solids. Check the side of the pack for details – the higher the cocoa solids, the stronger the chocolate flavour will be, so avoid using any chocolate with less than 45 per cent cocoa solids if possible.

In general, chocolate cake coverings should be avoided, as these have a mild, less chocolatey taste. With their added vegetable fat, they are more suited to making chocolate curls or caraque. What you can do, however, is to mix equal amounts of cake covering and luxury dark (bittersweet) chocolate. This way, you get the easy melting and moulding qualities of the former, plus the superior taste of the latter.

How to melt chocolate

1 Pour water into a pan until it is about one third full. Bring to the boil, switch off the heat, then fit a heatproof bowl over the pan, making sure that the water does not touch the base of the bowl. Break the chocolate into equal-size small pieces and put it in the bowl.

Couverture

This pure chocolate contains no fats other than cocoa butter, and has a high sheen and a creamy texture. It is used mainly by professionals, and is only available from specialist suppliers. It generally requires "tempering" before use in order to distribute the cocoa fat evenly. This is quite a lengthy process that involves warming and working the chocolate until it reaches 32°C | 90°F. Couverture is usually used for moulding or decorating because of its glossy finish. It is available as white, milk and dark chocolate drops or as a block.

2 Leave the chocolate pieces for 4–5 minutes, without stirring, until the chocolate has melted – the chocolate pieces will hold their shape. Stir the chocolate briefly until it is smooth, before folding it into ice cream, or using it as the basis of a sauce.

White chocolate

As when buying dark chocolate, choose "luxury" white chocolate or "Swiss" white chocolate for the best flavour. White chocolate is made from cocoa butter extracted during the production of cocoa solids. Although it includes about 2 per cent cocoa solids, many purists would argue that this is not nearly enough to make it a true chocolate, especially as the cocoa butter is then mixed with milk solids, sugar and flavourings.

As a result of these additional ingredients, white chocolate does require extra care when being melted: it quickly hardens if overheated. Do check the pack before buying, and choose a brand with a minimum of 25 per cent cocoa butter, as any chocolate with less than this will be difficult to melt. The more cocoa butter there is, the creamier and softer the chocolate will be. Some brands may even include vegetable fat or oils, so always check the ingredients list.

Melting chocolate in a microwave

Break dark or milk chocolate into equal-sized small squares, and place them in a bowl that can be safely used in a microwave. Heat it on full power, allowing 2 minutes for 115g | 4oz chocolate and 3 minutes for 200g | 7oz. The chocolate will retain its shape until you stir it. Don't be tempted to heat it for longer as you may cause the chocolate to "seize", which spoils the chocolate and causes it to clump and harden. White chocolate melts easily and is best microwaved on medium power or in a bowl placed over a pan of just boiled water.

Cocoa

This rich, strong, dark powder is made by extracting some of the cocoa butter during chocolate production. What remains is a block containing around 20 per cent cocoa butter, but this varies with each manufacturer. The cocoa is then ground and mixed with sugar and starch. The addition of starch means that cocoa must be cooked briefly to remove the raw, floury taste. This can be done by mixing it to a paste with a little boiling water, which is the usual technique when flavouring ice cream. If the cocoa is to be used in a sauce, it will probably be mixed with hot milk.

The very best cocoa is produced in Holland. It is alkalized, a process that removes the acidity and produces a cocoa with a mellow, well-rounded flavour. The technique was devised by the manufacturer Van Houten, some 150 years ago, and this is still the very best cocoa available. Although it is more expensive than some other brands, it is definitely worth using for ice cream and chocolate sauces.

BELOW: *cocoa powder*

Milk chocolate

Mild and creamy, milk chocolate is made with up to 40 per cent milk or milk products and contains less cocoa solids than dark chocolate. Because it has a mild flavour, you will need to add more than when using dark chocolate, to obtain a strong flavour. You can use a combination of melted milk chocolate and chopped milk chocolate. As with white chocolate, the addition of milk products means that it requires more careful heating than dark chocolate.

Carob

Although not a true chocolate, carob is viewed by many as an acceptable alternative. It is the ground seedpod of the carob or locust tree and can be used as a chocolate substitute. It is usually available from health-food stores and is sold in bars or in a powdered form as a flour. Unlike chocolate, it does not contain any caffeine. If you are using a bar, be cautious as it is highly concentrated. The flour can be used in a similar way to cocoa.

STORING CHOCOLATE

Wrap opened packs of chocolate well or pack them in a plastic box. Store in a cool, dry place away from foods with very strong flavours, such as spices, which may taint the chocolate. Avoid very cold places, or the chocolate may develop a dull whitish bloom. Chocolate has a long shelf life, but check use-by dates before cooking.

Fruits

Soft berry fruits

TYPES/FORMS: Berry fruits make marvellous ice creams and sorbets. You can choose from standard raspberries, larger tayberries and loganberries, bright red strawberries and tiny alpine and Hautbois strawberries, blueberries and blackberries. Look out for golden raspberries, too. These tend to be grown in small quantities by keen gardeners and are often difficult to find in the shops, but they are well worth trying when available.

USES: Delicious in ice creams, sorbets and sherbets, berry fruits can easily be transformed into superb sauces. Melba sauce is an obvious example, but there are plenty more to choose from. A delectable iced summer pudding that teams sliced strawberries with strawberry ice cream and soft fruit sorbet makes perfect use of summer fruits. Blueberries and red berries look most attractive sprinkled over ice cream sundaes or crushed and added to just setting ice cream for added texture and colour. Expensive alpine and Hautbois strawberries can be used for decoration only.

PREPARATION: Purée ripe fruits, press them through a fine sieve to remove the seeds, then use the purée in ice creams, sherbets or sorbets. Berry fruit purées are also delicious spooned over ice cream or mixed with a sugar syrup and lemon juice for a refreshing ice cream sauce.

RIGHT: *redcurrants*

MAKING A PURÉE

Purée berry fruits in a food processor or blender until smooth, then press the purée through a sieve into a large bowl, using the back of a large spoon or ladle.

Cane fruits

TYPES/FORMS: This category includes black, red and white currants, green gooseberries and the more unusual red gooseberries. As their short midsummer season is soon over, enjoy them while they are available fresh and bursting with rich flavour.

USES: All cane fruits make good ice creams, sherbets and sorbets. They can also be used to make coulis and sauces. Currants look beautiful and are often used for decoration.

PREPARATION: Gently remove currants from their stems, using the tines (prongs) of a fork. As blackcurrants have such a sharp flavour, it is wise to poach them first with sugar and a little water until just tender. Red and white currants can be eaten raw or lightly poached. Gooseberries should be topped and tailed with scissors before being cooked. Purée and sieve currants or cooked gooseberries if adding to ice cream, sorbet or sherbet. Gooseberry and ice cream made with clotted cream is a wonderful summertime treat.

Orchard fruits

TYPES/FORMS: Choose from apples, pears, plums, damsons, cherries, apricots, peaches and nectarines.

USES: Orchard fruits, particularly peaches and nectarines, make irresistible ices. Use them in creamy ice creams, sorbets and similar desserts, with a little liqueur, if you like.

PREPARATION: Apples and pears should be peeled and cored; plums, peaches and apricots should be halved and stoned (pitted). The fruit should then be poached in a little water and sugar until tender before being processed to a smooth purée. Ripe peaches, nectarines and apricots can be puréed raw, then sieved to remove the skins. Damsons are small and difficult to prepare, so poach, then scoop out the stones (pits). Alternatively, press the cooked fruit through a sieve to remove the stones. Use stoned cherries whole or roughly chopped. Larger fruits can be used for decoration, provided they are ripe. Slice or chop them, and toss apples and pears in a little lemon juice to prevent discoloration.

How to stone and string cherries

1 Remove cherry stones easily with this handy gadget, which pushes the stones out of the fruit. Usually available from good cookshops.

2 Cherries threaded on a skewer or cocktail stick (toothpick) make an attractive decoration, especially for an iced drink.

Citrus fruits

TYPES/FORMS: Choose from lemons, limes, oranges, tangerines, clementines, kumquats and grapefruit.

USES: All citrus fruits can be used to make sorbets, granitas and sherbets. In addition to these uses, oranges make a very good ice cream. Citrus fruit can also be used to make tangy sauces, and the rind is frequently used as a decoration, either as it is or when it has been crystallized.

PREPARATION: Grate the rind or pare it thinly, taking care to remove only the coloured skin, leaving the bitter white pith behind. Cut the fruit in half and squeeze it, then pour the juice through a sieve to remove any pips (seeds). Mix it with cream and custard for ice cream or with sugar syrup for sorbets, sherbets and granitas. Kumquats can be poached whole or in slices and used to make a refreshing accompaniment to iced desserts.

RIGHT: *halved lemons and limes*

Rhubarb

TYPES/FORMS: Strictly speaking, these pretty pink stems are not a fruit at all, but are actually a member of the vegetable family. For making iced desserts, choose the young, slender, baby-pink stems of early forced rhubarb, as it has a much more delicate flavour. Maincrop rhubarb has thicker, darker stems and a coarser texture.

USES: Puréed cooked rhubarb makes an excellent sorbet and granita, or flavour it with ginger for an old-fashioned ice cream. Lightly poached rhubarb can be served as an accompaniment to vanilla, cinnamon or goat's milk ice cream.

PREPARATION: Both early forced and maincrop rhubarb should be cooked with sugar and just a tablespoon or two of water. Put the rhubarb, sugar and water in a heavy-bottomed pan and cook gently for about 30 minutes, or until the rhubarb has softened.

Melons

TYPES/FORMS: Choose from canteloupe, Charantais, Galia and Ogen melons. Test them for ripeness by pressing the stalk area of the skin. The melon should yield under your thumb and smell quite perfumed.

USES: With their delicate perfume, melons make the most wonderfully refreshing sorbets and granitas. The shells make excellent and attractive containers for serving melon ices.

PREPARATION: Cut the melon in half, scoop out the seeds, then purée the flesh before use. Watermelons can also be used, but as the seeds are speckled throughout the flesh it is often easier to leave them in when processing the fruit. Sieving the purée will remove them. As watermelons have rather a bland flavour, mix the purée with grated lime rind and juice.

How to segment an orange or a grapefruit

1 Using a sharp knife, start by cutting a slice off the top and bottom of the orange or grapefruit so that you just can see the flesh inside.

2 Using a small serrated knife, slice off the skin and pith cleanly. Work your way from the top down to the base of the fruit.

3 Holding the fruit over a bowl to catch the juices, carefully cut between the membranes to remove the whole fruit segments.

Tropical fruits

TYPES/FORMS: Choose from bananas, pineapples, mangoes, passion fruit, grapes and kiwi fruit. These fruits are now available year-round and are a welcome alternative to seasonal fruits.

USES: Mash or purée peeled bananas with a little grated or pared lemon or lime rind – to prevent discoloration – and make them into smooth ice creams by combining with honey, ginger, chocolate or cinnamon. Puréed or chopped pineapple flesh makes wonderful ice cream, especially when chunky pieces of crushed meringue or a few tablespoons of rum are added. Pineapple can also be puréed and made into tangy sorbets. Look out for the extra sweet varieties, with their bright yellow, juicy flesh. Mix puréed mango with ginger, lime or coconut for a sorbet with a Caribbean flavour. Grapes and kiwi fruit are best served as a colourful accompaniment to iced desserts, although both can be made into sorbet.

PREPARATION: Sliced or diced tropical fruits can be used as a decoration or sautéed in a little butter and sugar and then flamed in a little brandy, rum or orange liqueur for an easy ice cream accompaniment. To prepare pineapples, slice the top off the pineapple, then cut it into slices of the desired width. Cut away the rind with a small sharp knife. Cut away any remaining eyes from the edges of the pineapple slices. Remove the central core of each slice with an apple corer, pastry cutter or knife.

PREPARING PASSION FRUITS

Passion fruits are easy to prepare. Just slice them in half and scoop out the fragrant seeds with a teaspoon. If necessary, press the pulp through a sieve.

Preparing a mango

1 Place the mango, narrow side down, on a board. Cut a thick, lengthways slice off the sides, keeping the knife blade as close to the central stone as possible. Turn the mango around and repeat on the other side.

Dried fruits

TYPES/FORMS: Sultanas (golden raisins), raisins, prunes, apricots, peaches, dates and figs are all suitable for use in ice creams, as are dried apples and pears, although these are seldom used for making ice creams and sorbets. Several types of dried fruit – such as apricots, figs and dates – are sold in vacuum packs labelled "ready to eat" and these do not need soaking before use, although they are sometimes macerated in wine or liqueur for extra flavour. More unusual dried fruit includes mango, cranberries and blueberries, all of which can provide an unusual twist to simple family favourites.

USES: Using dried fruits in ice creams is nothing new – rum and raisin is a classic combination. Drying seasonal fruits such as peaches and apricots intensifies their flavour, so they make excellent purées once they have been soaked in fruit juice or alcohol. These can then either be incorporated in ice creams or sorbets, or used as sauces for any ice cream dessert.

PREPARATION: Use the smaller varieties of dried fruit whole or chopped, and steep them in fruit juice, wine, spirits or liqueur if you like. For the best results, ensure that the fruit is totally submerged in the liquid and leave to soak overnight. The smaller varieties do not need to then be puréed before being used. Larger fruits such as apricots and peaches must be soaked overnight and then puréed before being added to ice cream or used as a topping, although chopped fruit can be added when the ice cream is partially frozen to give extra texture and colour.

Preparing a mango (continued)

2 Make criss-cross cuts in the mango flesh, cutting down only as far as the skin, then turn the large slices of mango inside out so that the diced flesh stands proud. Scoop it into a bowl.

3 Cut all the remaining fruit away from the stone (pit), remove the skin and dice the flesh.

Glacé fruits and candied peel

These vibrant, jewel-like fruits make a pretty addition to partially frozen ice cream, and are the traditional flavouring in classic Italian Tutti Frutti Ice Cream. They can also be used to decorate elaborate ice cream sundaes. Most fruits can be glacéd (candied), and a wide selection is available in supermarkets and cookshops. Choose from glacé cherries of various colours, glacé or candied pineapple and candied fruit peels. Large whole or sliced glacé fruits tend to be expensive, but are great for special occasion desserts. Sugar is a natural preservative, and glacé fruits will keep well in an airtight container, but they are best used as soon as possible and purchased fresh as needed.

Using glacé fruits

Use a small, sharp knife to finely chop the glacé (candied) fruits, then fold into just setting vanilla ice cream for a classic Tutti Frutti.

Nuts

TYPES/FORMS: Choose from a wide range of whole shelled nuts such as almonds, hazelnuts, pistachios, walnuts and pecans, plus the less widely used macadamias, Brazil nuts, chestnuts and unsalted peanuts (groundnuts).

USES: Nuts are most popular in cream-based ice creams and are seldom added to water ices. Add chunky toasted nuts or nut brittle (praline) for extra crunch in ice creams, or sprinkle them over elaborate ice cream sundaes. Roughly chopped sugared almonds with pastel-coloured coatings look good and make an easy decoration when scattered on top of scoops of home-made ice cream. Ground nuts infused in milk or cream give a delicate flavour to ice creams that are inspired by recipes from the Middle East.

PREPARATION: Toast the nuts, chop them roughly and fold them into partially frozen ice cream. Alternatively, use them to make nut brittle, which can be broken up and folded into ice cream that is on the verge of setting. Finely ground almonds or cashews can be added to just boiled milk or cream, then left to cool. The flavoured milk can then be strained or used as it is to make a custard-based ice cream.

BELOW: *Pistachio nuts are an attractive addition to ice cream.*

Blanching nuts

1 Put nuts such as pistachios, hazelnuts or almonds into a bowl and pour over just enough boiling water to cover. Leave them to stand for a minute or two until the skins expand and soften.

COOK'S TIP *Canned coconut milk combines full flavour and convenience for an ice cream that tastes good and is very easy to make. Reduced-fat varieties provide a healthy alternative, and coconut milk powder can also be used.*

2 Drain the nuts. To pop nuts such as almonds out of their skins, simply pinch them. Skin hazelnuts or pistachios by tipping them into a clean, dry dish towel and rubbing them together vigorously.

Toasting nuts

For maximum flavour, toast whole or roughly chopped nuts in a dry frying pan on the hob, in a shallow cake pan (tin) under a hot grill (broiler) or on a baking sheet in a medium oven for just a few minutes, until golden and lightly roasted. You don't need to add oil, as they have such a high natural oil content that extra oil is uneccesary. You can then grind or chop the toasted whole nuts. Desiccated (dry unsweetened shredded) coconut can also be toasted in this way, but because it is so finely processed you will need to keep a very close eye on it. It browns in a matter of seconds.

Spread out whole, thinly sliced or roughly chopped nuts on a baking tin or sheet. Grill (broil) for 3–4 minutes, shaking the tin or sheet frequently so that the nuts brown evenly all over and don't burn. Leave to cool before either mixing into partially frozen ice cream or scattering on top once the ice cream has been scooped into dishes or cones.

Making nut brittle (praline)

1 Put granulated sugar, whole nuts and a little water into a heavy frying pan. Heat gently, without stirring. Do not use caster (superfine) sugar and do not stir as this would cause the sugar to crystallize, making it solidify and become opaque. Continue to heat the sugar, but don't be tempted to stir the mixture with a spoon. Tilt the pan gently if necessary, to mix any sugar that has not dissolved completely.

2 Keep a watchful eye over the nuts as the sugar and nuts begin to turn golden. Remember to keep the heat low.

3 Quickly pour a thin layer of the hot nut brittle (praline) mixture on to a cool, oiled baking sheet. Leave to cool and harden before removing as a single large layer.

4 Cover the cooled nut brittle with clear film (plastic wrap) or put it in a strong plastic bag. Break it into rough pieces with a wooden rolling pin.

5 If finely ground nut brittle is needed, you can either crush it further using a rolling pin or grind it up finely in a food processor or coffee grinder.

Other flavourings

Coffee

Iced desserts can be made successfully with freshly-made filter coffee or good instant coffee. Strong filter or espresso coffee is preferable for coffee granita, while coffee ice cream can be made with cracked coffee beans. Bring milk or cream to the boil, add the beans and infuse them, then strain the mixture and use the flavoured milk as the basis for the custard in the ice cream. Another way to make coffee ice cream is by blending cold, strong filter coffee or instant coffee dissolved in a very small amount of water with thick custard and cream. While cracked coffee beans give perhaps the best flavour and a pretty speckled finish (after straining), it can be difficult to judge quantities, so this method is more demanding. If too many beans are used or the custard is overcooked, the finished ice cream can be bitter.

Spirits and liqueurs

The addition of a favourite spirit such as brandy, Calvados or whisky to ice cream, gin or vodka to sorbet, or an orange-flavoured liqueur to a fruity granita can lift a simple iced dessert into the realms of gourmet dining. While it is important to add sufficient alcohol to flavour the mixture (bearing in mind that freezing will dull the flavour), it is also vital to note that too much alcohol can prevent the ice cream or sorbet from freezing hard.

Purists or professional ice cream makers test the density and balance of an ice cream before freezing, using a saccharometer, but a beer-making hydrometer may also be used. This enables the level of sugar to liquid to be checked, ensuring satisfactory freezing. The home cook is unlikely to go to these lengths, and the best guide when adapting or making up recipes is to taste the mixture before freezing. If it is bland, don't add extra spirit, but pour a little over the ice cream just before serving.

ABOVE: *Spirits and liqueurs can be used in small quantities to add flavour to ice creams.*

Honey

To make enough honey to fill a single standard-size pot, bees have to visit more than two million flowers. The type of flowers and the time of harvest determine the flavour, colour and texture of the finished honey. You can choose from clover, lavender or heather honey, and cheaper blends are also available that include honey from more than one country. Clear heather honey has the best flavour for making ice cream and tastes especially delicious mixed with goat's milk.

ABOVE: *Alcohol is an excellent flavouring for all iced desserts.*

Basic techniques

Making ice creams and sorbets is child's play if you use an ice cream maker. The basic techniques are outlined here, but in the first instance, it is vital that you read the handbook supplied with your own machine. Parfaits and granitas are made by hand; follow the instructions in individual recipes.

FREEZER ASSISTED ICE CREAM MAKERS
Before using the machine, ensure that the bowl or bucket is completely clean and sterile, otherwise bacteria could be transferred to the ice cream. If you are unsure about how clean it is, then wash the inside with hot soapy water using a sponge, rinse with cold water and then wipe dry using kitchen paper. The bowl or bucket must then be placed in the freezer for the time stipulated in your handbook (usually up to 24 hours).

Manufacturers often recommend that you store the bowl or bucket in the freezer so that is ready for immediate use at all times and so that it doesn't take up too much cupboard space. With some machines it is recommended that you wrap the container in a plastic bag first.

1 Make the ice cream, frozen yogurt or sorbet mixture, ensuring that the quantity is suitable for the capacity of your machine. Pour it into a jug (pitcher) and cool it in the refrigerator or freezer until the machine has been set up.

2 Remove the bowl or bucket from the freezer and shake it gently to ensure that the refrigerant is frozen solid. If it is designed to fit inside a casing, lower it into position. Fit the dasher and motor and switch it on.

3 With the dasher rotating, pour the chilled ice cream mixture through the aperture in the lid of the machine in a steady stream, using a rubber or plastic spatula to make sure that all of the mixture is added.

4 During freezing, check the mixture often. Depending on the ingredients used, the temperature at which they were added and the ambient air temperature, the ice cream will be ready in 25–40 minutes. Sorbet freezes more quickly than a rich custard ice cream. Add extra ingredients, like chopped ginger, chocolate or crushed cookies just before the ice cream is ready.

5 As soon as the mixture is thick and creamy, ladle out the ice cream into dishes or an airtight plastic container. You should try to use a plastic spoon so as not to scratch the container. The ice cream can be served immediately, but it will be quite soft. It will firm up a little more if you leave it in the ice cream maker or put it in the freezer for up to 10 minutes.

6 For ice cream that is firm enough for scooping, scrape the mixture into a tub and chill in the freezer for 2–3 hours. It will keep in the freezer for up to two months, but for the best flavour you should aim to use it within two weeks. Ensure that you label the tub with the type of ice cream and the date on which it was made.

FREE STANDING ICE CREAM MACHINES

With this type of machine, which has its own built-in compressor, there is no need for lengthy pre-freezing, but before you use it for the first time, it is important to leave the machine to stand on a level surface for 24 hours, to allow the refrigerant to settle. If you wanted to, you could prepare the ice cream mixture and chill it in the refrigerator so that it is ready for immediate use after the 24 hour period.

Most free-standing machines have additional removable buckets for making smaller amounts of mixture (up to 600ml | 1 pint | 2½ cups). For making larger quantities of ice cream (not more than 900ml | 1½ pints/3¾ cups), use the fixed bowl.

TIP *One word of warning – when you first start to use a machine of this type, it is all too easy to turn off the compressor instead of turning on the dasher motor. If you do this inadvertently – or if there is a power cut – it is vital to wait at least 10 minutes before starting it again. This is because the compressor has a safety device to prevent any damage to the motor unit. If you switch the machine on immediately, the compressor will appear to be working but it will not freeze.*

1 Switch on the freezer unit (compressor) 10 minutes before adding the ice cream mixture. If you are using the removable bucket, pour the recommended quantity of alcohol into the fixed bowl. This will act as a conductor, speeding up the freezing process.

2 If you are using the bucket rather than the bowl, fit it in place inside the machine casing. Insert the appropriate dasher (there will probably be separate dashers of different sizes for the bucket or bowl).

4 With the dasher rotating, pour the chilled mixture in a steady trickle through the aperture in the lid so that it flows into the bucket or bowl. Once you have poured all of the mixture in, the ice cream, frozen yogurt or sorbet will be ready in 20–40 minutes. When the iced mixture has reached the correct consistency, switch off the dasher motor and lift off the lid and dasher.

3 Close the lid, lowering it gently over the lid and motor unit so that it connects with the dasher spindle. Switch on the dasher motor, being careful not to accidentally turn off the compressor motor.

5 For slightly firmer ice cream, the motor operating the compressor or freezing unit can be left on for 5–10 minutes more, but do not leave it on for longer than this or the ice cream will become too solid to remove from the container. Scoop out the ice cream with a plastic spoon. Serve at once or transfer to a tub and place in the freezer.

TIPS FOR USING AN ICE CREAM MAKER

- Try to always use good-quality ingredients whenever possible.
- Always pre-chill the machine or the double-skinned bowl for the time recommended. If possible, keep the bowl or machine in the freezer all of the time.
- To get the best results make sure that you chill the mixture thoroughly before churning in the ice cream maker.
- Use only the quantities stipulated in your handbook. Air will be incorporated during churning so there must be plenty of room for expansion.
- Add extra ingredients only when the ice cream is already starting to thicken. Check that your machine can cope before adding large chunks.
- Clean your ice cream machine very carefully before putting it away, and wash before using if it has been in storage for a while. Good kitchen practice is particularly important when dealing with dairy products.

STORING

- For maximum flavour, don't store your ice cream at all. Eat it right away. If it is too soft for your liking, leave it in the ice cream machine for 10 minutes or so to firm up.
- If you do want or need to store your ice cream, use a clean freezerproof container with a tight-fitting lid, and which is the correct size for the volume of ice cream you wish to store. When filling, leave a little headspace at the top of the mixture to allow for expansion during freezing. Label the container with the type of ice cream and the date on which it was made.
- If the container is only part-filled, either because you do not have a container of a suitable size, or because you've already removed some of the ice cream, cover the surface of the ice cream with clear film (plastic wrap) to prevent the formation of ice crystals.
- Home-made ice cream contains no preservatives or stabilizers, so will not keep for as long as the commercial product. For the best flavour, it is preferable to use home-made ice cream within two weeks. Do not store for longer than two months.

Basic recipes

Many classic ice creams are based on a custard made from eggs and milk. It is not difficult to make, but as it is used so frequently, it is worth perfecting by following these very simple guidelines.

Classic custard base

Making the custard base for ice cream

INGREDIENTS

FLAVOURING to INFUSE (optional)

300ml | ½ pint | 1¼ cups
SEMI-SKIMMED (LOW-FAT) MILK

4 medium EGG YOLKS

75g | 3oz | 6 tbsp CASTER (SUPERFINE) SUGAR

5ml | 1 tsp CORNFLOUR (CORNSTARCH)

BATCH COOKING

If you are planning to make ice cream for a party, make double quantities of custard to save time. It is not advisable, however, to increase the quantities any more than this, or it would be difficult to heat the custard evenly. It is quicker and easier to make up two double-quantity batches in separate pans and a lot safer than running the risk of curdling one pan of custard made with a dozen eggs!

1 Prepare any flavourings. Split vanilla pods (beans) with a sharp knife; crack coffee beans with a mallet. Cinnamon sticks, whole cloves, fresh rosemary and lavender sprigs or bay leaves can be used as they are.

2 Pour the milk into a pan. Bring it to the boil, then remove the pan from the heat, add the chosen flavouring and leave to infuse for 30 minutes or until cool.

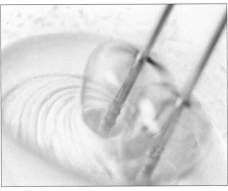

3 If you have used a vanilla pod, lift it out of the pan, and scrape the seeds back into the milk to enrich the flavour. Whisk the egg yolks, caster sugar and cornflour in a bowl until thick and foamy. Bring the plain or infused milk to the boil, then gradually whisk it into the yolk mixture. Carefully pour the combined mixture back into the pan.

4 Cook the mixture over a low heat, stirring it continuously until it approaches boiling point and thickens to the point where the custard will coat the back of a wooden spoon. Do not let the custard overheat or it may curdle. Take the pan off the heat and continue stirring, making sure to take the spoon right around the bottom edges of the pan.

5 Pour the custard into a bowl and cover the surface with clear film (plastic wrap) with a light sprinkling of caster sugar to prevent the formation of a skin. Leave to cool, then chill until required. When making the ice cream in a machine, chill the custard for 1–2 hours in the refrigerator or 20 minutes in the freezer.

6 Follow the preliminary instructions for your specific ice cream maker, pre-cooling the machine or chilling the bowl in the freezer. Stir whipping cream, whipped double (heavy) cream or any soft cream cheeses into the chilled plain or flavoured custard, and then churn until firm.

COOK'S TIP *Reduce the temperature of custard by pouring it into a cool bowl. Stand this in a larger bowl of cold or iced water and change the water as it warms.*

Parfait

Making a basic parfait

Made correctly, a parfait is a light, cream-based confection with a softer, smoother texture than ice cream. Unlike ice cream, it does not need beating during freezing.

Parfaits are traditionally set in moulds, tall glasses, china dishes or, more recently, in edible chocolate cups. The secret of a good parfait lies in the sugar syrup. Dissolve the sugar gently without stirring so that it does not crystallize, then boil it rapidly until it registers 115°C | 239°F on a sugar thermometer, or when a small amount of the syrup, dropped into a cup of cold water, solidifies and can be moulded into a ball.

Quickly whisk the syrup into the whisked eggs. Cook over hot water until very thick. Cool, then mix with flavourings, alcohol and whipped cream. Freeze until solid and serve straight from the freezer.

SERVES FOUR

INGREDIENTS

115g | 4oz | generous ½ cup CASTER (SUPERFINE) SUGAR

120ml | 4fl oz | ½ cup WATER

4 medium EGG YOLKS

FLAVOURINGS

300ml | ½ pint | 1¼ cups DOUBLE (HEAVY) CREAM

1 Mix the sugar and water in a pan. Heat the pan gently, without stirring, until the sugar has dissolved completely. Meanwhile, half fill a medium pan with water and bring it to simmering point.

2 Bring the sugar syrup to the boil and boil it rapidly for 4–5 minutes until it starts to thicken. It will be ready to use when it registers 115°C | 239°F on a sugar thermometer, or will form a soft ball when dropped into water.

FLAVOURINGS

Traditionally flavoured with coffee or chocolate and a dash of brandy or whisky, parfaits are also delicious made with ground spices such as cinnamon with apple or ginger with banana. Double (heavy) cream adds just the right degree of richness and a velvety texture, although crème fraîche or whipping cream can also be used with very good results. Another traditional combination is a fruit purée mixed with a liqueur such as kirsch, Cointreau or Grand Marnier; these make a sophisticated iced dessert at a dinner party.

3 Put the eggs in a heatproof bowl and whisk until light and frothy. Place the bowl over the simmering water and gradually whisk in the hot sugar syrup. Whisk steadily until creamy. Take off the heat and continue whisking until cool, when the whisk leaves a trail across the surface when lifted.

4 Fold in the chosen flavourings, such as melted chocolate and brandy, ground cinnamon and coffee, whisky and chopped ginger, kirsch and raspberry purée or kir and strawberry purée. In a separate bowl, whip the cream lightly until it just holds its shape. Fold it into the mixture with a metal spoon, being careful not to knock out too much air.

5 Pour the parfait mixture into prepared moulds, dishes or chocolate-lined cases. Place in the freezer and leave for at least 4 hours or until firm. Decorate, if liked, with whipped cream, spoonfuls of crème fraîche, caramel shapes or chocolate-dipped fruits. Serve immediately.

COOK'S TIP *Double (heavy) cream adds just the right degree of richness to parfaits, although crème fraîche or whipping cream can also be used as a lighter or lower-fat alternative.*

Making water ices

Sorbets are made with a light sugar syrup flavoured with fruit juice, fruit purée, wine, liqueur, tea or herbs.
They should not contain milk or cream (ingredients found in sherbets), and are best made in an ice cream
maker, as the constant churning ensures that the ice crystals are as tiny as possible.

Sorbet

Making a basic sorbet

SERVES SIX

INGREDIENTS

150–200g | 5–7oz | ¾–1cup CASTER
(SUPERFINE) SUGAR

200–300ml | 7–10fl oz | ¾–1¼ cups WATER

FLAVOURING

1 EGG WHITE

FRUIT PURÉES

As an approximate guide, 500g | 1¼lb | 5 cups
of berry fruits will produce about 450ml | ¾
pint | scant 2 cups purée. Mix this with
115g–150g | 4–5oz | generous ½–¾ cup caster
(superfine) sugar (depending on the natural
acidity of the fruit), which has been dissolved
in 300ml | ½ pint | 1¼ cups boiling water and
then made up to 1 litre | 1¾ pints | 4 cups with
extra cold water, lemon or lime juice.

1 Put the sugar and water in a medium pan and
heat the mixture, stirring, until the sugar has
just dissolved.

2 Add pared citrus rinds, herbs or spices,
depending on your chosen flavouring. Leave to
infuse. Strain and cool, then chill well in the
refrigerator. Add extra flavourings such as fruit
juices, sieved puréed fruits, herbs or tea.

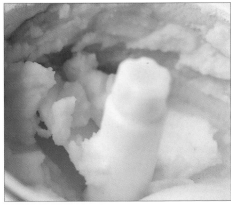

3 Having prepared your ice cream maker, pour
the syrup mixture into the machine with the
dasher rotating and churn until it is thick but
still too soft to scoop.

4 Lightly beat the egg white with a fork and
pour it into the ice cream maker, either adding
it through the top vent or removing the lid and
stirring it in, depending on the method
recommended by the manufacturer of your
machine. Continue churning the sorbet until it
is firm enough to scoop with a spoon.

5 BY HAND: Pour the mixture into a plastic tub
or similar freezerproof container. It should not
be more than 4cm | 1½in deep. Cover and freeze
in the coldest part of the freezer for 4 hours or
until it has partially frozen and ice crystals have
begun to form. Beat until smooth with a fork, or
hand-held electric whisk. Alternatively, process
in a food processor until smooth.

6 BY HAND: Lightly beat the egg white and stir
it into the sorbet. Freeze for a further 4 hours or
until firm enough to scoop.

COOK'S TIP *If making by hand, ensure that the*
freezer temperature is as low as possible to speed up the
freezing process, and beat at regular intervals.

Granita

Making a citrus granita

This wonderfully refreshing, simple Italian-style water ice has the fine texture of snow and is most often served piled into pretty glass dishes. You don't need fancy or expensive equipment, just a medium pan, a sieve or blender for puréeing the fruit, a fork and room in the freezer for a large plastic container.

INGREDIENTS

There are no hard-and-fast rules when it comes to the proportions of sugar to water, nor is there a standard amount of flavouring which must be added. Unlike sorbets, granitas consist largely of water, with just enough sugar to sweeten them and prevent them from freezing too hard. A total of 1 litre | 1¾ pints | 4 cups of flavoured sugar syrup will provide six generous portions of granita.

1 Squeeze the juice from six lemons, oranges or four ruby grapefruits. Add 115–200g | 4–7oz | generous ½–1 cup caster (superfine) sugar, depending on the natural acidity of the fruit. Dissolve the sugar in 300ml | ½ pint | 1¼ cups boiling water, then mix it with the citrus juice and rind. Top up to 1 litre | 1¾ pints | 4 cups with extra water or water and alcohol. Add enough alcohol to taste but don't be over generous or the granita will not freeze.

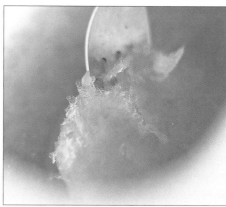

2 Pour the chilled mixture into a large plastic tub or similar freezerproof container. It should not be more than 2–2.5cm | ¾–1in deep. Freeze it in the coldest part of the freezer for 2 hours until it is mushy around the edges.

Take the container out of the freezer and beat the granita well with a fork to break up the ice crystals. Return the granita to the freezer. Beat it at 30 minute intervals for the next 2 hours until it has the texture of snow.

Making a hot infusion

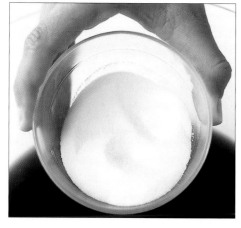

Some of the most delicious granitas are based on hot mixtures. Coffee is just one example. Pour hot, strong filtered coffee into a bowl or pan and stir in sugar to taste. For a ginger granita, infuse finely chopped root ginger in boiling water, then sweeten it. Chocolate granita is made by mixing unsweetened cocoa powder to a smooth paste with a little boiling water and sweetening to taste. All hot infusions must be left to cool, then chilled before being frozen.

Making a fruit-flavoured granita

To make a fruit-flavoured granita, purée berry fruits such as raspberries or strawberries, then sieve the purée to remove the seeds. Alternatively, purée ripe peaches, then sieve to remove the skins. To make a melon granita, scoop the seeds out of orange- or green-fleshed melons, then purée the flesh. Peeled and seeded watermelon can be puréed in the same way, or the flesh can be puréed along with the seeds and then sieved afterwards.

SERVING AND STORING GRANITAS

Coffee granita is classically served in a tumbler with a spoonful of whipped cream on top. Other types of granita look pretty spooned into tall glasses and decorated with fresh fruits or herb leaves and flowers. Because of its soft, snow-like texture, a granita is best served as soon as it is made. If this is not possible, you can leave it for a couple of hours in the freezer, beating it once or twice more if convenient. If you must freeze a granita overnight or for even longer, let it thaw slightly and beat it really well with a fork before serving. The ice crystals will become smaller but the taste will be the same. As a granita does not contain dairy products there are fewer concerns about food contamination or deterioration.

COOK'S TIP *Before you make the granita, make sure that the container you choose will fit in your freezer. A new stainless-steel roasting pan can be used to freeze the granita mixture. As this metal is such a good conductor, the granita will freeze very much faster than it would in a plastic container. Do not use aluminium, as the metal could react with the fruit acids to give a metallic taste to the finished granita.*

Layering and rippling

For a professional look and a dramatic effect, create different layers of harmonizing ice creams in large or small, rectangular or round moulds. There are plenty of possibilities – just let your imagination take over.

How to layer ices

Simple three-tier ice cream

1 When the first flavour has thickened and is semi-frozen, pour it into a 25 x 7.5 x 7.5cm | 10 x 3 x 3in terrine or loaf tin (pan) that has been lined with clear film (plastic wrap). Spread it in an even layer and freeze it in the coldest part of the freezer for 1 hour or until firm.

2 Pour in the second layer of semi-frozen ice cream and spread it out evenly. Freeze until firm, then add the final ice cream layer and freeze for 4–5 hours until hard. When ready to serve, turn out the ice cream from the mould, peel off the clear film and cut the terrine into slices, using a warm knife.

Chequerboard

1 Make a two-tier terrine, using two of your favourite ice creams layered in a terrine or straight-sided 900g | 2lb loaf pan. Invert the two-tier terrine on a board and cut it in half lengthways, using a hot knife.

2 Turn one of the halves over to reverse the colour sequence and wrap tightly in clear film to stick them together. Refreeze to harden. To serve, peel away the clear film and slice with a hot knife.

Iced roulade

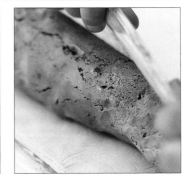

1 Prepare two quantities of semi-frozen ice cream with flavours that complement each other well. Line a 30 x 23cm | 12 x 9in baking sheet with clear film (plastic wrap) or waxed paper. Spread one quantity of thick, semi-frozen, flavoured ice cream. Freeze for 20 minutes.

2 Spoon the second batch of semi-frozen ice cream over a second piece of clear film or waxed paper to make a rectangle a little smaller than the first. Freeze for 20 minutes. Carefully place this sheet of ice cream over the first layer, then peel off the clear film or waxed paper.

3 Roll the layered ice cream, as if making a Swiss roll, starting from the longest edge and using the clear film or paper to roll it. Pat the ice cream into a neat cylinder, then wrap it in more clear film. Freeze for several hours, overnight if time permits, until the roll is hard.

4 Peel off the clear film (plastic wrap) or paper and put the roll on a board. Cut it into thick slices, using a warmed knife.

Classic cassata

This classic Italian iced dessert is traditionally made in a rounded metal mould with a lid. If you don't have a metal mould, a plastic or thick glass bowl can be used instead. Do not confuse this ice cream dessert with the Sicilian cake of the same name.

THE HISTORY OF CASSATA

Some think that cassata is modelled on the dome of the Brunelleschi cathedral in Florence; others believe that the famous dessert was the result of a culinary accident when cream and wine were accidentally spilled into a soldier's metal helmet that was being stored in a chilly cave. Whatever its true origins, cassata is traditionally served in Italy at weddings and Easter celebrations and comprises two or three layers of ice cream, depending on the size of the mould in which it is made.

1 Line a 1.2 litre | 2 pint | 5 cup pudding basin (mold) with clear film (plastic wrap). Line it with a 2cm | ¾in thick layer of semi-frozen strawberry ice cream, using the back of a metal spoon to press the ice cream down against the sides and bottom of the basin. Cover and freeze for 1–2 hours or until the ice cream lining is firm.

2 Again using the back of a metal spoon, press some chocolate ice cream on to the strawberry ice cream in the mould to make a second 2cm | ¾in thick layer of chocolate ice cream against the frozen strawberry layer. Leave a space in the centre. Cover and freeze for a further 1–2 hours or until the chocolate ice cream layer is firm.

3 Pack the centre with tutti frutti ice cream and smooth the top. Cover and freeze overnight until firm. Dip the mould in hot water for 10 seconds, insert a knife between the clear film and the basin, then invert it on to a serving plate. Lift off the basin and peel away the clear film and decorate with glacé (candied) fruits or chocolate caraque. Serve in wedges.

Individual bombes

1 Line four individual metal moulds with clear film, then press a 1cm | ½in layer of dark chocolate ice cream over the bottom and sides of each mould, smoothing the ice cream with the back of a teaspoon. Cover and freeze for 30 minutes or until the ice cream is firm.

2 Add a scoop of vanilla ice cream to the centre of each lined mould and insert a brandy-soaked prune or cherry into the middle. Smooth the surface, cover and freeze for 4 hours until firm.

3 Dip the filled moulds into a roasting pan filled with hot water for 2 seconds. Invert the moulds on to serving plates and quickly lift off the metal moulds.

4 Remove the clear film, then decorate the top and sides of each individual bombe with long sweeping lines of piped white chocolate. Serve immediately.

How to ripple ices

This dramatic and eye-catching effect is surprisingly easy to achieve, using ice creams and sauces in contrasting colours, which are lightly swirled together while the ice cream is semi-frozen.

Flavoured ice cream
Choose softly set ice cream that is too soft to scoop but thick enough to hold its shape. The colours should be markedly different for the most dramatic effect.

Sauces
Marble a chocolate, toffee or fruit sauce through ice cream that is on the verge of setting. Be careful with toffee sauces, as they can dissolve into the ice cream, so losing the effect.

Raspberry ripple ice cream

Fruit purée
Puréed and sieved fruit purées can be used unsweetened but can taste rather icy. It is better to mix them with a thick sugar syrup before swirling them with semi-frozen ice cream.

Jam
For the easiest rippled ice cream of all, use softly set extra fruit jam straight from the jar. You can use firmer jams, but they will need to be mixed with a little boiling water to soften before being used. Make sure the jam is cold when you use it, or it will melt the ice cream. Any fruit jam can be used but the contrast of berry fruits looks the most attractive.

RIGHT: *Use softly set jam for ice creams.*

1 Make the vanilla ice cream by hand or churn it in an ice cream maker until it is thick but too soft to scoop.

2 Mix 75g | 3oz | 6 tbsp caster (superfine) sugar with 60ml | 4 tbsp water in a pan. Heat until the sugar has dissolved, then boil for 3 minutes until syrupy, but not coloured. Cool slightly. Purée 250g | 9oz | 1½ cups fresh raspberries in a food processor or blender then press through a sieve over a bowl. Stir in the syrup and chill well.

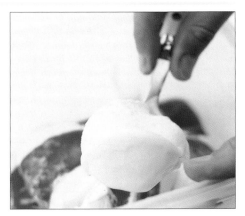

3 Add alternate spoonfuls of the soft, partially frozen vanilla ice cream and the chilled raspberry syrup to a 1 litre | 1¾ pint | 4 cup plastic tub or similar freezerproof container. Don't be alarmed if the contrasting layers look a little messy to begin with.

4 Stir through the syrup and ice cream two or three times to create a rippled effect. Freeze.

CLASSIC COMBINATIONS

Ripple one of the basic recipes in this book with one of your own favourite flavours. Use the same basic technique as for raspberry ripple.

Mixed berry swirl – strawberry ice cream with raspberry syrup.

Coffee toffee swirl – dark classic coffee ice cream swirled with a rich toffee sauce.

Double chocolate – smooth dark chocolate ice cream rippled with smooth white chocolate ice cream.

Apricot and orange ripple – orange and yogurt ice rippled with apricot sauce.

Creamy toffee ripple – rich toffee sauce rippled through creamy vanilla ice cream.

Raspberry ripple – try the home-made version made with the very best of ingredients for a truly timeless classic.

Marbling ice cream

Although very similar to the technique used when making a rippled ice cream, marbling creates softer, less defined swirls. The same combinations of ice cream and syrup, sauce or purée can be used as for making rippled ice creams, but the softer effect is achieved by mixing together more thoroughly.

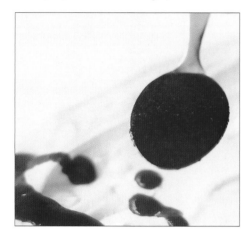

1 To achieve this effect, spoon alternate layers of partially frozen ice cream into a plastic tub or similar freezerproof container. Drizzle coloured liquid flavouring or syrup over each layer, using a spoon.

2 Pass the handle of a wooden spoon through the ice cream and liquid flavouring five or six times to produce a lightly marbled effect. Freeze the ice cream for 4–5 hours or overnight, until firm.

COOK'S TIP *Soft marbled ice cream need only be lightly swirled with the end of a spoon to create the required effect. Choose a coloured liquid flavouring that complements the base ice cream in colour and taste.*

ABOVE: *a single scoop of marbled ice cream*

SECRETS OF SUCCESS

- Line the mould with clear film (plastic wrap) so that it is easy to remove the frozen dessert.

- Choose flavours that contrast or complement each other, such as dark chocolate with pistachio, or vanilla and strawberry.

- Freeze ice cream after each layer has been added so that soft mixtures do not merge together. That way, the finished dessert will have well-defined layers.

- Make sure that the colours of the ice cream are in harmony, but are strong enough to be visible.

- Freeze the mould thoroughly after layering, preferably overnight, so that the layers will not separate when the ice cream is sliced.

- Dip the mould in hot water for 10–15 seconds so that the dessert will turn out easily. Peel off the clear film and use a knife dipped into warm water for slicing.

Ice cream lollies

Everyone loves an easy freezy ice lolly or popsicle, especially children, and these are particularly delicious.

Making your own is also a good idea because you know exactly what ingredients they contain.

SINGLE FLAVOURS

Milk maid

The simplest lolly (popsicle) of all. Made with full-fat (whole) milk poured into moulds and frozen until firm. Ideal for small children.

Orange refresher

Another very easy lolly, made by simply filling moulds with freshly squeezed orange juice or juice from a carton. The flavours can be varied. Try tropical fruit juices, apple, cranberry juice or mixed juices.

Strawberry yogurt

Mix a 150ml | ¼ pint | ⅔ cup carton of strawberry yogurt with the same quantity of full-fat (whole) milk. Stir in 10ml | 2 tsp strawberry milkshake powder, pour into lolly moulds and top up with extra milk if needed.

Banana custard

Mash two small ripe bananas with 5ml | 1 tsp lemon juice, then stir into a small carton of ready-made custard. Add enough full-fat (whole) milk to fill the moulds.

ABOVE: *Lolly moulds have handles to hold the ice lollies.*

MULTICOLOURED LOLLIES

Traffic-light lollies

Fill each lolly mould one-third full with sieved strawberry purée, then freeze until hard. Add a second layer, the same width as the first, of orange juice. Freeze that until hard, then top up with orange juice tinted with a little blue food colouring so that it goes green. Freeze until hard.

Rainbow lollies

Experiment with colour combinations. Fruit purées, sieved and sweetened with a little sugar if very sharp, work very well. Try mango, kiwi fruit, strawberry and blackberry, for example. Alternatively, create layers of different colours by tinting orange juice with drops of edible food colouring. A few drops of green will turn orange juice blue; a little blue will change it to green; red will intensify the orange colour. A combination of fruit purées and tinted juice also works well, and for creamy-tasting lollies you can use different flavours of sorbet or ice cream. Let your imagination run wild, but always use sorbet or ice cream that is partially frozen and be sure to freeze each coloured layer until it is hard before adding the next layer, or the colours will bleed into each other.

TWO-TONE AND DOUBLE-DECKER LOLLIES

Summer sunset

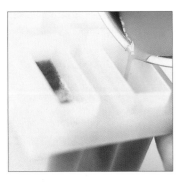

Pour a layer of sieved strawberry or raspberry purée into lolly moulds, and freeze. Top up with orange juice and freeze until solid. Add a little vodka or tequila for an adult version.

In the pink

Slide a strawberry slice down the side of each mould then half-fill with partially frozen home-made strawberry ice cream. Freeze until firm, then top with home-made strawberry sorbet, and freeze.

SWIRLED AND RIPPLED LOLLIES

Night and day

Add alternate spoonfuls of semi-frozen white and dark chocolate ice cream to lolly moulds. Lightly mix them together with a fine metal skewer for a swirled effect and freeze until solid.

Banana and raspberry ripple

Fill the lolly moulds with alternate spoonfuls of semi-frozen banana ice cream and raspberry syrup. Lightly stir them with a fine metal skewer and freeze until solid.

COATED AND DIPPED LOLLIES

Double choc

Fill moulds with partially frozen home-made chocolate ice cream, freeze until hard then remove from the moulds and coat the top half of each lolly with finely grated dark chocolate.

Strawberry sprinkle

Fill moulds with partially frozen home-made strawberry ice cream, freeze until hard, then remove from the moulds. Drizzle melted white chocolate over the top portion of each lolly, then sprinkle this with pastel-coloured sugar strands. For a simpler version, press the strands straight on to ice cream.

FREEZING LOLLIES

Lolly moulds come in various shapes and sizes. Some enable you to make six small lollies; others have space for four large ones. Many feature a drip catcher and straw as part of the handle. Pour the mixture into the moulds until it comes almost to the top, then press in the lolly handles. Freeze for at least 6 hours or overnight, until hard.

COOK'S TIP *If you don't have any lolly moulds or want to make lots of lollies for a children's party, use small disposable plastic cups or a deep ice cube tray. Empty mini pots that originally contained fromage frais can also be used, provided they are thoroughly washed. Lolly sticks can be saved and recycled.*

Turning lollies out

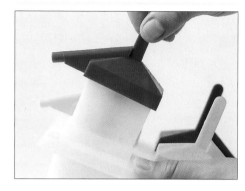

Hold the rounded ends of the moulds under running hot water or stand the moulds in a bowl of hot water. This should not be so deep that the water comes up to the handles – two-thirds of the way up is ideal. Count to 15, then flex the handles and lift out the lollies.

Ice cream petits fours

1 Place a toasted almond, hazelnut or brandy-soaked cherry in each of the sections of an ice cube tray. Cover each nut or cherry with a dollop of thick ice cream that is partially frozen. Level the top of each cube with a palette knife or spatula, put the tray back in the freezer and leave to freeze for a couple of hours until the ice cream cubes are solid.

2 Wearing oven gloves, pour just-boiled water from the kettle over the upturned ice cube tray over the sink. Allow the hot water to run off, then flex the tray to release the ice cream cubes. Arrange the cubes so that they are close together on a small fine-meshed cooling rack set over a plate or baking sheet to avoid ice cream dripping on the surface.

3 Spoon melted chocolate over the cubes, covering the tops and sides, and let it set. Turn each cube over and coat the underside and any gaps. Return to the freezer for a minute or two, then arrange on the inverted lid of a plastic container. Decorate with any remaining chocolate. Fit the upturned container and freeze until required. Allow to soften for a few minutes before serving.

Ice cream kebabs

1 Pour a little of your favourite fruit ice cream into each section of an ice cube tray, freeze until solid, then turn out and thread on to hot metal skewers, leaving a little space between the ice cream cubes. Quickly put the kebabs in the freezer so that the ice cream stays hard.

2 When you are ready to serve, arrange two skewers on each serving plate. Decorate each ice cream cube with a slice of strawberry or kiwi fruit and serve with Melba sauce.

COOK'S TIP *Vanilla or chocolate ice creams are perhaps the best choice for these dainty petits fours, but cashew and orange, pistachio, coconut or orange and yogurt are also delicious. Cover the ice cream cubes in batches of five or seven and work quickly so they don't melt before they are completely covered with chocolate. Using an upturned plastic box for storage in the freezer protects them from any knocks, and makes it easy to transfer them to plates for serving.*

Warm the skewers by dipping them in water that has recently boiled, or by holding them in an oven glove and warming them over the flame on a gas hob so that they pierce the hard ice cream easily. Kebabs can also be made from a solid block of ice cream that has been cut into cubes.

Serving ice creams and sorbets

Impress your friends at your next supper or dinner party by trying one of the following serving suggestions. They are not difficult to achieve, but look stunningly professional.

Oval shapes

These quenelle shapes are very easy to make and look attractive, especially when three different flavours of ice cream or sorbet are used. Arrange them on a plate flooded with chocolate sauce or Melba sauce and complete the picture with a sprig of redcurrants, a few whole fruits, a mint leaf or a few pieces of chocolate caraque.

1 You need two deep dessertspoons. Take a scoop of ice cream with one spoon. Slide the second spoon underneath the ice cream, transferring the oval, then repeat the process.

2 Gently ease the ice cream oval on to a plate, then draw the edge of the spoon along the top of the ice cream to create a decorative line.

Shavings

Pare off long shavings of ice cream or sorbet by pressing a dessertspoon into the surface and dragging it at an angle of 45°. Mixtures that are soft-set, can be scooped straight from the freezer, but in most cases ice cream or sorbet should be allowed to soften slightly before being scooped.

Using a melon baller

1 Press a medium or large melon baller into the frozen sorbet, rotate it, then put the ball in a dessert glass or serving dish.

2 Add more balls in the same way, piling them up attractively. Decorate with wafer biscuits or mint leaves dusted with icing (confectioners') sugar.

3 Another very effective presentation is to arrange balls of grape juice or apple sorbet on a flat plate to look like a bunch of grapes, adding a grape, strawberry or mint leaf to the top.

4 Balls of raspberry sorbet arranged in a circle on a plate flooded with apricot sauce look wonderful, especially when the centre is filled with fresh raspberries.

Using an ice cream scoop

Press the scoop into the ice cream and run the scoop along the surface, pressing it against the side of the ice cream container until a well rounded scoop has been formed. Put this on a serving dish. Make more scoops in the same way.

Piping shapes

Whirls of sorbet can be piped straight on to serving plates or into fruit cases or chocolate moulds from a large piping bag fitted with a cream nozzle. The ice cream or sorbet must be soft enough to pipe, so choose a variety that will not melt too quickly. If you are using sorbet, you may need to set it slightly with a little gelatine before piping and freezing it.

Creating a bed of ice

On very hot summer days, keep ice cream and sorbets cold by scooping them into dishes set over a plate or shallow dish filled with crushed ice. To crush the ice, wrap ice cubes in a clean dish towel and break them up by hitting them with a rolling pin. Keep the chunks of ice fairly large so that they will not melt too quickly.

Using citrus shells

1 Colourful fruit shells look very pretty filled with sorbet. Cut the top off a lemon, lime or orange, loosen the edges of the flesh with a small, sharp knife then scoop out all the flesh with a teaspoon, taking care to keep the shell intact. Having prepared more shells in the same way, rinse them all with cold water and drain them well. Use the flesh in another dessert.

COOK'S TIP *Do not be tempted to repeatedly thaw ice cream until it is soft enough to scoop and then refreeze the leftovers. The rich dairy content and fluctuating temperature will make this the perfect breeding ground for bacteria.*

2 Pipe or spoon the prepared sorbet into the hollowed fruit shells, wrap them in clear film (plastic wrap) and freeze them until they are needed. Serve garnished with fresh mint. Freeze with the "lids" replaced, if you like.

3 If you have a cannelle knife (zester), you can cut decorative grooves in the skin of the fruit before cutting a slice off the top, hollowing out the centres and filling them with sorbet.

SERVING TEMPERATURE

We have all been faced at some time with a tub of ice cream that is just too hard to serve. The majority of home-made ice creams will freeze very hard, so it is worth taking the ice cream out of the freezer and putting it in the refrigerator for 20 minutes or so before serving, or while you eat your main course. This allows the ice cream to soften slightly and also to "ripen", so that the full flavour of the iced dessert can be enjoyed. Alternatively, it can be thawed slightly in a microwave for 2–3 minutes on the defrost setting or for 1 minute on full power and then left at room temperature for 10 minutes. If you forget, serve the ice cream by dipping the scoop into a jug (pitcher) of hot water each time you form a ball of ice cream.

Baskets, biscuits and cones

Not only beautiful to look at, these sensational edible containers are surprisingly easy to make and are bound to impress your guests. They are the ultimate stylish and professional presentation and taste delicious too.

How to make baskets

Spun sugar baskets

These impressive baskets look stunning filled with ice cream, or upturned and placed over a single scoop of ice cream to form a cage, and arranged in the centre of a large white dinner

MAKES SIX

INGREDIENTS

3 ORANGES, to serve as moulds

a little OIL for greasing

250g | 9oz | generous 1 cup SUGAR

75ml | 5 tbsp WATER

VANILLA ICE CREAM and
FRESH SUMMER FRUITS, to serve

plate. Use an oiled soup ladle instead of oranges for slightly flatter baskets, and loosen with the tip of a small knife before removing. Add rich colour by decorating the plate with tiny clusters

of blueberries, a few raspberries and a sprig or two of redcurrants or any combination of summer fruits. Dust lightly with icing (confectioners') sugar for the final effect.

1 Smooth squares of foil over three oranges and brush lightly with oil. Put the granulated sugar and water in a thick-bottomed pan and heat gently, without stirring, until the sugar has completely dissolved. Increase the heat and boil the syrup until it turns golden and starts to caramelize.

2 Take the pan off the heat and plunge the bottom of it into a bowl of cold water to prevent the caramel from continuing to cook and overbrowning. Allow the caramel to cool for 15–30 seconds, stirring it gently until it starts to thicken, then lift the pan out of the water.

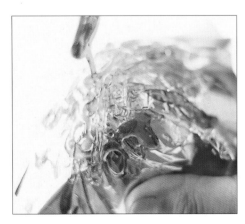

3 Hold a foil-wrapped orange over the pan and quickly drizzle caramel from a dessertspoon over half the orange, making squiggly lines and gradually building up layers to make the basket shape. Leave the caramel to set and make a second and third basket in the same way. Warm the caramel when it gets too stiff to drizzle.

4 Ease the foil off the first orange. Carefully peel the foil away and put the finished sugar basket on a lightly oiled baking sheet. Repeat with the remaining baskets, then make three more in the same way, reheating the caramel as needed and adding a little boiling water if it gets too thick to drizzle.

5 Use the baskets on the day you make them, filling them with vanilla ice cream and summer fruits and adding a dusting of sifted icing sugar. The baskets are extremely fragile, so scoop the ice cream on to a plate or baking sheet first and lower it carefully into each basket with the aid of two forks.

Chocolate tulips

These easy-to-make tulip baskets take only minutes to prepare and can then be set aside to harden. Fill with one large scoop of ice cream and decorate with blueberries and halved strawberries, or fill with tiny scoops of ice cream shaped with a melon baller and decorate with tiny chocolate shapes.

VARIATIONS *Any of the chocolate basket ideas suggested here are a perfect way of setting off your favourite chocolate, coffee or vanilla ice cream. You do not have to use dark (bittersweet) chocolate to make the baskets – Belgian white or milk chocolate work just as well.*

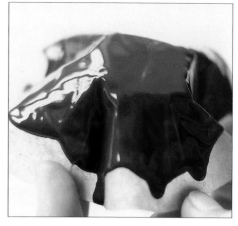

1 Using the back of a teaspoon, spread 175g | 6oz melted dark (bittersweet) chocolate over six 13cm | 5in circles of baking parchment, taking it almost, but not completely, to the edge, and giving it a swirly, wave-like edge.

2 Drape each paper circle, chocolate-side outwards, over an upturned glass tumbler set on a baking sheet. Ease the paper into soft pleats and leave the baskets in a cool place to set. When ready to serve, lift the baskets off the glasses and carefully peel away the paper.

A large chocolate bowl

3 Chill well until set, then carefully peel away the foil and place the bowl on a plate. Store in the refrigerator until ready to fill.

COOK'S TIP *This bowl can be made in any size. Small ones are perfect for individual portions, while larger bowls can serve up to four. Make it thicker than the other bowls and don't fill it too full, or the weight of the ice cream might cause the chocolate to crack.*

1 Smooth a double thickness of foil into a suitably sized mixing bowl or basin, so that it takes on the shape of the container. Carefully lift the foil out of the bowl.

2 Spoon melted chocolate into the bottom of the foil bowl. Spread it to an even, fairly thick layer, taking it over the base and sides with the back of a spoon or a pastry brush.

Individual chocolate cups

3 Fill each of the set chocolate cups with parfait. Chill again in the freezer, then carefully peel away the paper from each cup. Use a palette knife or spatula to transfer each filled cup to a plate, then decorate them with a light dusting of sifted (unsweetened) cocoa and serve immediately.

COOK'S TIP *When melting chocolate, it is important that the chocolate isn't overheated or allowed to come into contact with steam or small amounts of moisture, as these will cause it to stiffen or "seize". Make sure that the base of the bowl doesn't touch the water and don't allow the water to boil.*

1 Cut six 30 x 15cm | 12 x 6in strips of baking parchment. Fold each strip in half lengthways, roll into a circle and fit it inside a 7.5cm | 3in plain biscuit (cookie) cutter to make a collar. Secure with tape. Ease the cutter away and make five more collars, leaving the last collar inside the cutter. Place on a baking sheet.

2 Melt 250g | 9oz dark (bittersweet) chocolate in a heatproof bowl over a pan of hot water. Brush chocolate evenly over the base and sides of the paper collar, supported by the biscuit cutter, and make the top edge jagged. Carefully lift off the biscuit cutter and slide over the next paper collar. Make six cups and leave to set.

How to make biscuits

Tuiles

These classic French biscuits (cookies) are named after the similarly shaped roof tiles found on many old French homes.

SERVES SIX

INGREDIENTS

little OIL, for greasing

50g | 2oz | ¼ cup UNSALTED (SWEET) BUTTER

75g | 3oz | ¾ cup FLAKED (SLICED) ALMONDS

2 MEDIUM EGG WHITES

75g | 3oz | 6 tbsp CASTER (SUPERFINE) SUGAR

50g | 2oz | ½ cup PLAIN (ALL-PURPOSE) FLOUR, sifted

RIND of ½ ORANGE, finely grated plus 10ml | 2 tsp JUICE

SIFTED ICING (CONFECTIONERS') SUGAR, to decorate

1 Preheat the oven to 200°C | 400°F | Gas 6. Lightly brush a wooden rolling pin with oil, and line two large baking sheets with baking parchment. Melt the butter in a pan and set it aside. Preheat the grill (broiler). Spread out the almonds on a baking sheet and lightly brown under the grill. Leave to cool, then finely grind half; crush the remainder roughly with your fingertips.

2 Put the egg whites and sugar in a bowl and lightly fork them together. Sift in the flour, stir gently to mix, then fold in the melted butter, then the orange rind and juice. Fold in the finely ground nuts.

3 Drop six teaspoons of the mixture on to one of the lined baking sheets, spacing them well apart. Spread the mixture into thin circles and sprinkle lightly with the crushed nuts. Bake in the oven for 5 minutes until lightly browned around the edges.

COOK'S TIP *It is important to transfer the tuiles to t he rolling pin as quickly as possible. As the biscuits (cookies) cool they will set and become crisp and it will not be possible to shape them.*

4 Loosen one of the biscuits with a slim spatula and drape it over the rolling pin. Shape the remaining biscuits in the same way. Leave for 5 minutes to set while baking a second batch of biscuits. Continue baking and shaping biscuits until all the mixture has been used. Dust with icing sugar and serve with ice cream.

Cigarettes russes

These biscuits (cookies) are smaller and are rolled more tightly than tuiles, but they can be made using the same recipe. Omit the nuts, orange rind and juice. Add 5ml | 1 tsp vanilla essence (extract). Make 2–3 biscuits at a time, each time using 10ml | 2 tsp of the mixture spread into a thin circle. The mixture makes 15 cigarettes russes. Bake the biscuits until they are golden around the edges, then turn them over and wrap them around lightly oiled wooden spoon handles. Leave for 5 minutes to set.

Brandy snaps

Traditionally rolled into fat cigar shapes, these crisp, lacy biscuits (cookies) can also be made into tiny petits fours or even bowls.

MAKES 32

INGREDIENTS

a little OIL, for greasing

115g | 4oz | ½ cup UNSALTED (SWEET) BUTTER

115g | 4oz | generous ½ cup CASTER (SUPERFINE) SUGAR

115g | 4oz | ⅓ cup GOLDEN SYRUP or LIGHT CORN SYRUP

115g | 4oz | 1 cup PLAIN FLOUR

5ml | 1 tsp GROUND GINGER

15ml | 1 tbsp LEMON JUICE

15ml | 1 tbsp BRANDY

COOK'S TIP *Brandy snaps can be made the day before being served. Store them covered with greaseproof (waxed) paper in a cool, dry place. They can also be frozen. Pack in layers in a rigid plastic box, interleaved with greaseproof paper.*

1 Preheat the oven to 190°C | 375°F | Gas 5. Lightly oil the handles of two or three wooden spoons (or more if you have them). Line two baking sheets with baking parchment. Put the butter, sugar and syrup into a medium pan and heat gently, stirring occasionally until the butter has melted.

2 Once all of the sugar has dissolved and the butter has melted take the pan off the heat and sift in the flour and the ground ginger. Mix together well with a wooden spoon until the mixture is smooth, then stir in the lemon juice and the brandy. Mix well to combine, ensuring that there are no lumps.

3 Drop four teaspoons of the mixture on to the lined baking sheets, spacing them well apart. Cook for 5–6 minutes, until they are pale brown, bubbling and the edges are just darkening. Take the tray of biscuits out of the oven, leave them to stand for 15–30 seconds to set slightly, then loosen with a slim spatula.

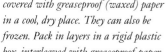

4 Quickly roll each brandy snap around the handle of an oiled wooden spoon and put join-side downwards on a wire rack to cool. Leave to set for 1 minute, then remove the spoon from the first biscuit and shape the others on the tray in the same way, by which time the second batch of biscuits will probably be ready.

CHOCOLATE SNAPS

For chocolate brandy snaps substitute 15g | ½oz | 2 tbsp of sifted (unsweetened) cocoa powder for 15g | ½oz | 2 tbsp of the flour. Do not use drinking-chocolate powder as this has added sugar and dried milk powder.

Mini brandy snap biscuits for petits fours

1 Spoon half teaspoons of the basic brandy snap mixture on to lined baking sheets and spread thinly to form circles. Bake until golden brown, then shape around oiled wooden satay sticks or metal kebab skewers. Work quickly, as the small biscuits (cookies) will cool rapidly. Leave to set for 5 minutes.

2 For mini cornets, shape the biscuits by wrapping them around oiled cream horn moulds or large piping tubes. Leave for 5 minutes to set. Remove the moulds or piping tubes once the biscuits are cool and dip the ends of the biscuits into melted white or dark chocolate, if liked.

Brandy snap bowls

1 Drop 15ml | 1 tbsp of the basic brandy snap mixture on to a lined baking sheet, spread it to a circle and cook for 6–7 minutes. Cool for a few seconds until firm enough to remove. Quickly lift the biscuit and drape it, textured side outwards, over an orange that has been lightly brushed with oil.

2 Flute the edges by easing the biscuit into folds with your fingertips. Leave to cool. As soon as it has set, lift it off the orange.

COOK'S TIP *These bowls are best made one at a time. They cook quickly and are shaped in a couple of minutes.*

How to make cones

Chocolate cones

1 Line the inside of as many cream horn moulds as you need with baking parchment so that it sticks out of the ends of the moulds slightly and the ends overlap inside.

2 Brush the inside of each paper cone with melted chocolate, chill for 15 minutes, then brush over a second layer of chocolate. Chill well, then fill with softly set ice cream. Stand the filled cream horn moulds in mugs to keep them upright or wedge them in a plastic tub, using crumpled kitchen paper or foil to keep them upright. Freeze until firm.

3 Carefully pull the chocolate cones out of the moulds, holding them by the paper, then gently peel the paper away. Lay the filled cones on individual plates and decorate with chocolate curls. Dust each plate lightly with sifted (unsweetened) cocoa.

Tuile ice cream cones

1 Use the basic recipe for tuiles, to make ten lacy ice cream cones on wooden moulds. They are extremely fragile so fill with care. These cones are best eaten on the day they are made. Make two cones at a time, using 15ml | 1 tbsp of mixture per cone. Spread thinly into 10cm | 4in circles, sprinkle with chopped nuts and bake at 180°C | 350°F | Gas 4 for 5 minutes, until golden around the edges.

2 Have ready an oiled, wooden ice cream cone mould. Loosen a biscuit (cookie), using a spatula, turn it over and put it on a clean, folded dish towel supported on the palm of your left hand. Lay the cone mould on top and wrap the biscuit around it to form the cone shape. Repeat with the second biscuit, then repeat with the remaining mixture.

Mini cones

1 Using about 10ml | 2 tsp of biscuit (cookie) mixture each time, make two well-spaced mounds on a lined baking sheet. Don't bother to spread them flat. Bake for 4 minutes until the biscuits are starting to brown around the edges.

2 Let the biscuits cool slightly, then loosen them with a slim spatula, turn them over and carefully roll them around cream horn moulds (see Cook's Tip).

COOK'S TIP *If you like, you can make cream horn moulds bigger by stuffing them with crumpled foil until they are about one third longer. Brush them lightly with oil before using them as moulds. Wooden ice cream cone moulds are available from specialist cook shops or by mail order.*

Transforming bought cones

1 Liven up ready-made cones by dipping the tops in a little melted dark (bittersweet), white or milk chocolate and then sprinkling with chopped toasted hazelnuts, toasted flaked almonds or roughly chopped pistachios.

2 Once the cones have cooled completely, coat the rims in melted white chocolate and sprinkle generously with grated dark chocolate or chocolate curls.

3 For children's parties, stud cooled cones with jewel-like arrangements of sugar diamonds or sugar flowers, sticking them on with dots of melted white chocolate. Alternatively, you could dip the rim of each cone into melted white chocolate, then into pastel-coloured sugar sprinkles.

Making ice bowls

These impressive ice bowls make a wonderful dinner party centrepiece. They are incredibly easy to make and need no specialist equipment – but make sure you have enough room in your freezer!

A decorated ice bowl

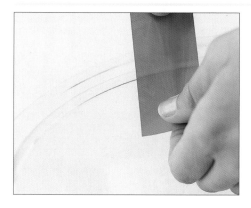

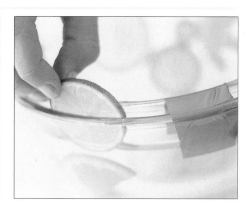

1 You will need two pyrex or plastic bowls that will fit one inside the other, leaving a gap of about 2–2.5cm | ¾–1in. Tape the bowls together using parcel (packing) tape. Make sure that the gap between them is constant all the way round.

2 Put the double bowl on a plate to catch any drips. Carefully fill the gap between the bowls with cooled boiled water. It should come almost to the top. For a more frosted look, use cold water straight from the tap.

3 Slide slices of citrus fruits, small flowers, herbs or spices into the water between the bowls, using a skewer to tease them into place if necessary. Freeze the bowl overnight until the water has frozen hard.

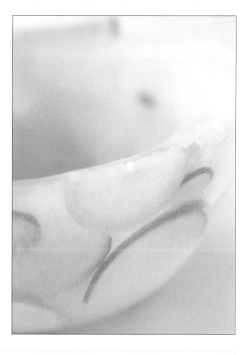

4 To unmould the ice bowl, remove from the freezer and peel off the tape. Place the bowls in a washing-up (dish-washing) bowl half filled with hot water and pour a little hot water into the smaller bowl. Count to 30 then lift the bowls out of the water, pour the water out of the smaller bowl and loosen the ice bowl with a thin, round-bladed knife.

5 Lift out the inner bowl, turn out the ice bowl and put it on a large plate. Decorate the plate with a few extra flowers or leaves and fill the bowl with ice cream. If you are serving it as part of a buffet you could unmould it ahead of time, fill it with ice cream and return it to the freezer until ready to serve. Decorate the serving plate just before taking it to the table.

BEAUTIFUL BOWLS

• In summer there are many edible garden flowers and herbs that can be used to decorate ice bowls. Try pansies and chives with rosemary and sweet cicely, or strawberry fruit, flowers and leaves for a very pretty effect. Fill the bowl with berry sorbet, or vanilla and strawberry ice cream.

• For a fresh citrus look, use orange, lemon and lime slices to make the ice bowl, adding a few sliced kumquats, if available. Decorate the serving plate with nasturtiums or calendula marigold flowers and fill with scoops of ice cream or sorbet in complementary colours.

• Celebrate the festive season with an ice bowl decorated with an arrangement of bay leaves and cranberries made to look like sprigs of holly. Add cinnamon sticks, whole star anise and a few orange slices too. Fill with a rich dairy ice cream, rum and raisin or a tutti-frutti ice cream.

Classic ice cream sauces

No ice cream sundae would be complete without one of these popular sauces. For convenience, they can all be made in advance and stored in the refrigerator until needed, and can be served hot or cold, as preferred.

Chocolate sauce

Rich, dark and irresistible. Pour the warm or cold sauce over vanilla or milk chocolate ice cream or serve with an ice cream sundae made with your favourite flavours.

MAKES 400ml | 14fl oz | 1⅔ cups

INGREDIENTS

25g | 1oz | 2 tbsp BUTTER

25g | 1oz | 2 tbsp CASTER (SUPERFINE) SUGAR

30ml | 2 tbsp GOLDEN SYRUP or
LIGHT CORN SYRUP

200g | 7oz LUXURY PLAIN (SEMISWEET)
COOKING CHOCOLATE

150ml | ¼ pint | ⅔ cup SEMI-SKIMMED
(LOW-FAT) MILK

45ml | 3 tbsp DOUBLE (HEAVY) CREAM

1 Mix the butter, sugar and syrup in a pan. Break the plain chocolate into pieces and add it to the mixture. Heat very gently, stirring occasionally, until the chocolate has melted.

2 Gradually stir in the milk and cream and bring just to the boil, stirring constantly until smooth. Serve hot or cool, refrigerate and reheat when required.

Butterscotch sauce

Smooth and glossy, this creamy toffee sauce is extremely rich. It is delicious with vanilla, coffee or yogurt ice creams. Once made, it can be stored in the refrigerator for up to 4 days.

MAKES 475ml | 16fl oz | 2 cups

INGREDIENTS

200g | 7oz | 1 cup CASTER (SUPERFINE) SUGAR

45ml | 3 tbsp each
COLD WATER and
BOILING WATER

75g | 3oz | 6 tbsp BUTTER

150ml | ¼ pint | ⅔ cup DOUBLE (HEAVY) CREAM

1 Put the sugar and 45ml | 3 tbsp cold water into a pan and heat very gently, without stirring, until all the sugar has dissolved.

COOK'S TIP *Don't be tempted to stir the sugar syrup when it is boiling or you may find that the sugar will crystallize and solidify. If this happens, the mixture cannot be retrieved. You will have to throw it away and begin again.*

2 Bring the mixture to the boil. Boil until the sugar starts to turn golden, then quickly take the pan off the heat and immediately plunge the bottom of the pan into cold water, to prevent the sugar from overbrowning.

3 Standing as far back as possible, and protecting your hand with an oven glove, add the 45ml | 3 tbsp boiling water to the caramel mixture, which will splutter and spit. Add the butter and tilt the pan to mix the ingredients together. Leave to cool for 5 minutes.

4 Gradually stir in the cream and mix well until thoroughly combined. Pour into a jug (pitcher) and serve warm or cool.

Melba sauce

Of all the classic ice cream sauces, this is perhaps the best known. It is very easy, requires no cooking and is delicious served with scoops of vanilla ice cream and sliced ripe peaches. Some versions of this sauce are cooked and thickened with cornflour (cornstarch), but this simple version is by far the best.

MAKES 200ml | 7fl oz | scant 1 cup

INGREDIENTS

250g | 9oz | 1⅓ cups fresh or thawed FROZEN RASPBERRIES

30ml | 2 tbsp ICING (CONFECTIONERS') SUGAR

1 Purée the raspberries in a food processor or blender until smooth.

2 Pour the purée into a sieve set over a bowl. Press the fruit through the sieve and discard the seeds that remain behind in the sieve. Sift in the icing sugar, stir the mixture until smooth and chill until required.

USING RIPE FRUIT

This is a wonderful way of using up very soft ripe raspberries. If they are particularly soft, don't purée them first; check them over, then simply press through a sieve with the aid of a wooden spoon.

Apricot Sauce

Delicious with vanilla ice cream, this fruity sauce is a good way of persuading children to eat fruit without realizing they are doing so.

MAKES 350ml | 12fl oz | 1½ cups

INGREDIENTS

200g | 7oz | scant 1 cup READY-TO-EAT DRIED APRICOTS

450ml | ¾ pint | scant 2 cups WATER

25g | 1oz | 2 tbsp CASTER (SUPERFINE) SUGAR

VARIATION *The apricots can also be poached in apple juice or a mixture of half apple juice and half water.*

1 Put the dried apricots in a pan and add the water and sugar. Cover and leave to simmer for 10 minutes until the apricots are tender and plump. Leave to cool.

2 Tip the mixture into a blender or food processor and process to a smooth purée. Scrape into a bowl and chill until ready to serve.

Combining sauces

Spoon a little Melba sauce over half a serving plate, then spoon apricot sauce over the other half. Tilt the plate very gently, first in one direction, then the other, to swirl the edges of the sauce together. Add the ice cream and decorate with sprigs of mint.

INSTANT DESSERTS

Serving plain ice cream with a combination of sauces is a very quick and easy way to produce an exciting dessert. Sauces that contrast in colour or texture are very attractive when used together, but avoid using flavours that are not complementary.

COOK'S TIP *Sauces that contrast with each other can be rippled or swirled in exactly the same way as rippling ice cream. Ice cream is then placed on the top.*

Decorations

Complete the simplest dish of beautifully scooped ice cream or a party-style sundae with one of these professional looking decorations and you will be sure to impress your dinner guests.

How to make decorations

Plain chocolate caraque

1 Using a slim spatula or the back of a spoon spread melted dark (bittersweet) chocolate over a marble slab or cheese board, to a depth of about 5mm | ¼in. Leave in a cool place to cool and harden.

2 Draw a long, fine-bladed cook's knife across the chocolate at a 45° angle, using a see-saw action to pare away long curls. If the chocolate is too soft, put it in the refrigerator for 5 minutes or in a cold place for 15 minutes.

Two-tone caraque

1 Spoon alternate lines of melted white and dark (bittersweet) chocolate over a marble slab or cheese board, and spread lightly so that all the chocolate is the same height. Leave to cool and harden.

2 Pare away long, thin curls of chocolate with a fine-bladed cook's knife in the same way that you do when making plain (semisweet) chocolate caraque.

Simple chocolate curls

Holding a bar of dark (bittersweet), white or milk chocolate over a plate, pare curls away from the edge, using a swivel-blade vegetable peeler. Lift the pared curls carefully with a flat blade or a slim spatula and arrange as desired.

Piped chocolate shapes

Spoon some melted dark (bittersweet) chocolate into a paper piping (pastry) bag and snip off the tip. Pipe squiggly shapes, hearts, butterflies, or even initials on to a lined baking sheet. Peel off when cool and chill until required.

Chocolate rose leaves

Brush melted dark (bittersweet) chocolate, as evenly as possible, over the underside of clean, dry rose leaves. Avoid brushing over the edges. Put the leaves on to a baking parchment-lined baking sheet and leave in a cool place to set. Carefully peel each leaf away and chill until they are required.

COOK'S TIP *If the chocolate used for decoration is not at the right temperature the curls will either be too brittle or won't hold their shape. Set the chocolate aside at room temperature for 20 minutes before working with it.*

How to make dipped fruits

Fruit looks and tastes fabulous when half dipped in melted dark (bittersweet) or white chocolate. Choose from tiny strawberries (still with their green hulls attached), tiny clusters of green or red grapes, physalis or cherries, with their stalks. It can also look very effective if you dip half the fruits in dark chocolate and the remainder in white chocolate. Leave the fruits to set on a large baking sheet lined with baking parchment.

Caramel-dipped fruits

For a more unusual fruit decoration for ice cream dishes, half-dip peeled physalis, whole strawberries or cherries (with the stalks intact) into warm caramel, then leave to cool and harden on an oiled baking sheet.

COOK'S TIP *Always carefully select fruit used for decoration and check that the fruit is perfect and free of any bruising as this will quickly spoil the decoration. Wipe them over with a damp cloth to remove any dust. A more even effect can be achieved if the stalks are still firmly attached to the fruit.*

Caramel shapes

The caramel used for making baskets is also suitable for making fancy shapes to decorate ice cream sundaes. Instead of drizzling the caramel on to foil-covered oranges, drizzle shapes such as treble clefs, graduated zigzags, spirals, curly scribbles, initials, stars or hearts on to a lightly oiled baking sheet. Vary the sizes, from small decorations about 5cm|2in long to larger 10cm|4in long shapes.

Using coloured chocolate

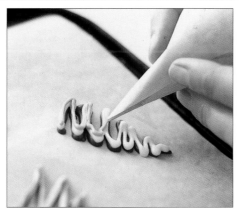

1 Pipe random lines of melted dark (bittersweet) chocolate over a piece of baking parchment. Overpipe with piped white chocolate. Using pink liquid food colouring, tint a little of the melted white chocolate.

2 Pipe a third layer of chocolate squiggles, this time in pink, over the dark and white layers. Chill in the refrigerator until set.

3 Break the coloured shapes into jagged fragments of varying sizes and stick them into ice cream to decorate. They look particularly good on top of ice cream sundaes.

Frosted flowers

1 Lightly beat an egg white, then brush a very thin layer over edible flowers such as pansies, violas, nasturtiums, tiny rose buds or petals. Herb flowers can also be used, as can strawberries, seedless grapes or cherries.

2 Sprinkle the flower or fruit liberally with caster (superfine) sugar and leave to dry on a large plate or wire cooling rack. Use on the day of making and handle with care as the flowers will be brittle and delicate.

Meringue dainties

1 Make a meringue mixture using 2 eggs and 115g|4oz|generous ½ cup caster (superfine) sugar. Spoon it into a large piping bag fitted with a small plain 5mm|¼ in or a 9mm|⅜in nozzle.

Citrus curls

1 Using a zester, pare the rind of an orange, lemon or lime, removing just the coloured rind of the skin and leaving the bitter white pith on the fruit.

2 Dust the citrus curls with a little caster (superfine) sugar and use them to sprinkle over citrus-based ices such as lemon sorbet. Use on the day or making or store in an airtight container until needed.

2 Pipe heart shapes, zigzags, shooting stars or geometric shapes on to baking sheets lined with baking parchment.

Corkscrews

1 Use a canelle knife (zester) to pare long strips of orange, lemon or lime rind. The strips should be as long as possible and very narrow.

2 Twist the strips of rind tightly around cocktail sticks (toothpicks) so that they curl into corkscrews. Carefully slide the sticks out of the corkscrews and hang the curls over the edge of ice cream dishes.

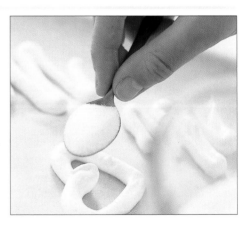

3 Sprinkle the shapes lightly with caster sugar and bake at low heat until they are firm enough to be lifted off the paper easily. Cool, then store in a cake tin (pan) for up to 1 week or until required.

Decorative effects with sauces

Spooning sauces over ice cream is a quick and simple method of decorating iced desserts, and this informal technique can look particularly pretty over ice cream sundaes. For a more elegant finish, sauces can also be piped in decorative shapes and patterns on scoops of ice cream, or used to create elaborate or dramatic backdrops on the surface of the dishes on which the ice cream is going to be served. These simple techniques are surprisingly quick and easy to use, and provide the perfect setting for home-made iced desserts.

Creating teardrops

1 Spoon a little Melba sauce over the base of a plate, tilt to cover, then pipe or spoon small dots of unwhipped double (heavy) cream around the edge of the plate.

2 Draw a skewer or cocktail stick (toothpick) through the dots to form teardrops. Scoop the ice cream into the centre of the plate.

Feathering

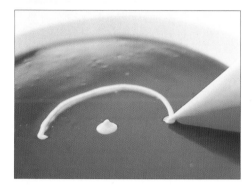

1 Spoon a little chocolate or butterscotch sauce over the base of a plate, then pipe a central dot and one or more circles of melted white chocolate or double (heavy) cream on the sauce, starting at the centre and working outwards.

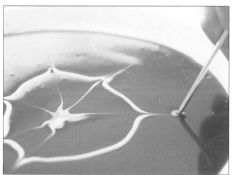

2 Draw a skewer or cocktail stick (toothpick) in lines radiating out from the centre of the plate to the rim, like the spokes of a wheel. Alternatively, you could mark lines in alternate directions for a spider's web effect.

Piping zigzag lines

Arrange scoops of ice cream on a plate. Spoon cooled chocolate sauce into a greaseproof (waxed) paper piping (pastry) bag, snip off the tip, and pipe zigzags over the plate and ice cream. For added effect, dust with sifted cocoa.

Piped border

1 Pipe a swirly border of sieved strawberry or apricot jam around the edge of a plate. Alternatively, use melted white or dark (bittersweet) chocolate and leave to set.

2 Using the jam or chocolate as a border, flood the centre of the design with fruit, chocolate or butterscotch sauce, or cream. Arrange the ice cream on top, keeping it within the border.

Decorative squiggles

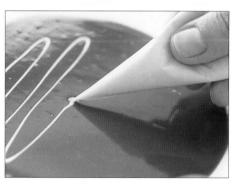

Spoon a little butterscotch or chocolate sauce over the base of a flat plate and tilt the plate to completely coat. Spoon melted white chocolate into a paper piping (pastry) bag, snip off the tip and pipe squiggly lines over the sauce. Leave to set, then arrange the ice cream.

the recipes

This section contains over 150 recipes for the exquisite desserts your ice cream machine was made for. Beautifully presented with easy-to-follow steps, recipes range from the classic flavours in ice creams and sorbets to imaginative low-fat, elegant and even hot ice cream desserts. With many different new and exciting flavours and combinations, every recipe will bring certain success.

classic sorbets& water ices

After a rich main course, nothing refreshes the palate better than a clean-tasting sorbet or water ice. Stock up the freezer when fruits are plentiful to make effortless desserts throughout the year. Flavours range from fruity favourites to more unusual twists using coffee, tea or alcohol.

Lemon Sorbet

This is probably the most classic sorbet of all. Refreshingly tangy and yet deliciously smooth, it quite literally melts in the mouth and is even more delicious topped with fresh summer berries.

SERVES SIX

INGREDIENTS

200g | 7oz | 1 cup CASTER (SUPERFINE) SUGAR

300ml | ½ pint | 1¼ cups WATER

4 LEMONS, well scrubbed

1 EGG WHITE

SUGARED LEMON RIND, to decorate

1 Put the sugar and water into a pan and bring to the boil, stirring occasionally until the sugar has just dissolved.

2 Using a swivel-blade vegetable peeler pare the rind thinly from two of the lemons so that it falls straight into the pan.

3 Simmer for 2 minutes without stirring, then take the pan off the heat. Leave to cool, then chill.

4 Squeeze the juice from all the lemons and add it to the syrup. Strain into a jug (pitcher) and chill before churning in an ice cream maker until thick.

5 Add the egg white to the mixture and continue to churn for 10–15 minutes until firm enough to scoop.

6 Scoop into bowls or glasses and decorate with sugared lemon rind.

COOK'S TIP *Cut one third off the top of a lemon and retain as a lid. Squeeze the juice out of the larger portion. Remove any membrane and use the shell as a ready-made container. Scoop or pipe sorbet into the shell, top with lid and add lemon leaves or small bay leaves. Serve on a bed of crushed ice allowing one lemon per person.*

VARIATION *Sorbet can be made from any citrus fruit. As a guide you will need 300ml | ½ pint | 1¼ cups fresh fruit juice and the pared rind of half the squeezed fruits. Use 4 oranges or 2 oranges and 2 lemons, or, for a grapefruit sorbet, use the rind of one ruby grapefruit and the juice of two. For lime sorbet, combine the rind of three limes with the juice of six.*

Pear and Sauternes Sorbet

Based on a traditional sorbet that would have been served between savoury courses in France, this fruity ice is delicately flavoured with the honied bouquet of Sauternes wine and is spiked with brandy for an extra kick.

SERVES SIX

INGREDIENTS

675g | 1½lb RIPE PEARS

50g | 2oz | ¼ cup CASTER
(SUPERFINE) SUGAR

250ml | 8fl oz | 1 cup WATER
plus 60ML | 4 tbsp extra

250ml | 8fl oz | 1 cup SAUTERNES
WINE, plus extra to serve

30ml | 2 tbsp BRANDY

juice of ½ LEMON

1 EGG WHITE

FRESH MINT SPRIGS,
dusted with icing (confectioners') sugar,
to decorate

1 Quarter the pears, peel them and cut out the cores. Slice them into a pan and add the sugar and 60ml | 4 tbsp of the measured water. Cover and simmer for 10 minutes, or until the pears are just tender.

2 Tip the pear mixture into a food processor or blender and process until smooth, then scrape into a bowl. Leave to cool, then chill.

3 Stir the wine, brandy and lemon juice into the chilled pear purée with the remaining water. Churn the mixture in an ice cream maker until thick.

4 Lightly whisk the egg white with a fork until just frothy. Add to the sorbet in the ice cream maker and churn for 10 minutes more.

5 Serve the sorbet in small dessert glasses, with a little extra Sauternes poured over each portion. Decorate with the sugared mint sprigs.

COOK'S TIP *Sorbets that contain alcohol tend to take a long time to freeze, especially when made in an ice cream maker. To save time, transfer it to a tub as soon as it thickens and finish freezing it in the freezer. If you make the sorbet by hand, freeze the mixture in a stainless-steel roasting pan to begin with. Transfer the sorbet to a plastic tub only after the egg white has been added.*

Red Berry Sorbet

This vibrant red sorbet seems to capture the true flavour of summer. Pick your own berries, if you can, and use them as soon as possible.

SERVES SIX

INGREDIENTS

150g | 5oz | ¾ cup CASTER (SUPERFINE) SUGAR

200ml | 7fl oz | scant 1 cup WATER

500g | 1¼lb | 5 cups MIXED RIPE BERRIES, hulled, including two or more of the following: STRAWBERRIES, RASPBERRIES, TAYBERRIES or LOGANBERRIES

JUICE OF ½ LEMON

1 EGG WHITE

small whole and halved STRAWBERRIES and STRAWBERRY LEAVES AND FLOWERS, to decorate

1 Put the sugar and water into a pan and bring to the boil, stirring until the sugar has dissolved. Pour the syrup into a bowl, leave to cool, then chill.

2 Purée the fruits in a food processor or blender, then press through a sieve into a large bowl. Stir in the syrup and lemon juice.

3 Churn in an ice cream maker until thick, then add the whisked egg white. Continue to churn until firm enough to scoop.

4 Scoop on to plates or bowls, and decorate with fresh strawberries, leaves and flowers.

VARIATION *For a fruity sorbet with a hidden kick, add 45ml | 3 tbsp vodka or cassis to the fruit purée. Don't be too generous with the spirits or the sorbet will not freeze firmly.*

Blackcurrant Sorbet

Wonderfully sharp and bursting with flavour, this is a very popular sorbet. If you find it a bit tart, add a little more sugar before freezing.

SERVES SIX

INGREDIENTS

500g | 1¼lb | 5 cups BLACKCURRANTS, trimmed

350ml | 12fl oz | 1½ cups WATER

150g | 5oz | ¾ cup CASTER (SUPERFINE) SUGAR

1 EGG WHITE

SPRIGS OF BLACKCURRANTS, to decorate

1 Put the blackcurrants in a pan and add 150ml | ¼ pint | ⅔ cup of the measured water.

2 Cover the pan and simmer for 5 minutes or until the fruit is soft. Cool slightly, then purée in a food processor or blender.

3 Set a large sieve over a bowl, pour the purée into the sieve then press it through the mesh with the back of a wooden spoon into the bowl below.

4 Pour the remaining measured water into the clean pan. Add the sugar and bring to the boil, stirring until the sugar has dissolved. Pour the syrup into a bowl. Cool, then chill. Mix the blackcurrant purée and sugar syrup together.

5 Churn in an ice cream maker until thick. Add the egg white and continue churning until it is firm enough to scoop.

6 Serve decorated with the blackcurrant sprigs.

Raspberry Sorbet

Sweet and silky smooth, sorbet is a good way of bringing out the flavour of slightly tart raspberries.

It's delicious served on its own or mixed with other sorbet flavours.

SERVES SIX

INGREDIENTS

150g | 5oz | ¾ cup CASTER
(SUPERFINE) SUGAR

200ml | 7fl oz | scant 1 cup WATER

500g | 1¼lb | 3 cups RASPBERRIES

juice of ½ LEMON

1 EGG WHITE

FRESH RASPBERRIES, to decorate

1 Put the sugar and water in a pan and bring to the boil, stirring until the sugar has dissolved. Pour into a bowl, leave to cool, then chill.

2 Purée the raspberries in a food processor or blender until smooth. Press through a sieve into a large bowl. Stir in the syrup and lemon juice.

3 Pour the mixture into the ice cream maker and churn until thick. Lightly whisk the egg white and add to the machine. Continue to churn until firm enough to scoop.

4 Scoop into bowls and decorate with fresh raspberries or turn into a freezer container and freeze until required.

Candied Clementine Sorbet

Clementines can usually be relied on at any time of the year for making a sweet, tangy juice that's full of flavour. Use them in this refreshing sorbet that's specked with pieces of candied fruit.

SERVES SIX

INGREDIENTS

800g | 1¾ lb CLEMENTINES

600ml | 1 pint | 2½ cups WATER

200g | 7oz | 1 cup CASTER (SUPERFINE) SUGAR

1 EGG WHITE

1 Cut half the clementines into quarters, discarding the stalk ends. Squeeze the juice from the remainder. Bring half the water to the boil in a heavy-based pan.

2 Add the quartered clementines, cover and cook gently for 15 minutes to soften the skins. Stir in the sugar and heat gently until the sugar has dissolved.

3 Simmer very gently, uncovered, for about 45 minutes until the clementines are very tender and the liquid has reduced to a thick syrup.

4 Lift out the clementines with a fork and stir the remaining water into the syrup left in the pan.

COOK'S TIP *The candied strips can be wrapped in clear film (plastic wrap) and stored in the refrigerator for up to a week.*

5 When the clementines are cool, scrape the pulp away from six of the wedges and finely shred the skin. Reserve for decoration.

6 Chop the remaining wedges into small pieces in a food processor or blender using the pulse setting.

7 Pour the syrup from the pan, plus the squeezed juice into the ice cream maker and churn until thick. Whisk the egg white with a fork until broken up and add it to the ice cream maker with the chopped clementines. Churn for 2–3 minutes until thoroughly mixed.

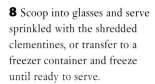

8 Scoop into glasses and serve sprinkled with the shredded clementines, or transfer to a freezer container and freeze until ready to serve.

Strawberry and Lavender Sorbet

Delicately perfumed with just a hint of lavender, this delightful pastel pink sorbet is perfect

for a special-occasion dinner.

SERVES SIX

INGREDIENTS

150g | 5oz | ¼ cup CASTER (SUPERFINE) SUGAR

300ml | ½ pint | 1¼ cups WATER

6 FRESH LAVENDER FLOWERS, plus extra to decorate

500g | 1¼lb | 5 cups STRAWBERRIES, HULLED

1 EGG WHITE

1 Bring the sugar and water to the boil in a pan, stirring until the sugar has dissolved.

2 Take the pan off the heat, add the lavender flowers and leave to infuse for 1 hour. Chill the syrup before using.

3 Purée the strawberries in a food processor or in batches in a blender, then press the purée through a large sieve into a bowl.

4 Pour the strawberry purée into the bowl and strain in the lavender syrup. Churn until thick. Add the whisked egg white to the ice cream maker and continue to churn until the sorbet is firm enough to scoop.

5 Serve in scoops, piled into tall glasses, and decorate with sprigs of lavender flowers.

COOK'S TIP *The size of the lavender flowers can vary; if they are very small you may need to use eight. To double check, taste a little of the cooled lavender syrup. If you think the flavour is a little mild, add 2–3 more flowers, reheat and cool again before using.*

Minted Earl Grey Sorbet

Originally favoured by the Georgians at grand summer balls, this refreshing, slightly tart sorbet is perfect for a lazy afternoon in the garden.

SERVES SIX

INGREDIENTS

200g | 7oz | 1 cup CASTER (SUPERFINE) SUGAR

300ml | ½ pint | 1¼ cups WATER

1 LEMON, well scrubbed

45ml | 3 tbsp EARL GREY TEA LEAVES

450ml | ¾ pint | 2 cups BOILING WATER

1 EGG WHITE

30ml | 2 tbsp chopped fresh MINT LEAVES

FRESH MINT SPRIGS OR FROSTED MINT, to decorate

1 Put the sugar and water into a pan and bring the mixture to the boil, stirring until the sugar has completely dissolved.

2 Thinly pare the rind from the lemon so that it falls straight into the pan of syrup. Simmer for 2 minutes then pour into a bowl. Cool, then chill.

3 Put the tea into a pan and pour on the boiling water. Cover and leave to stand for 5 minutes, then strain into a bowl. Cool, then chill.

4 Remove the lemon rind from the syrup, add the tea and churn in an ice cream maker until thick.

5 Add the mint to the mixture. Lightly whisk the egg white until just frothy, then tip it into the ice cream maker and continue to churn until firm enough to scoop.

6 Serve in scoops, decorated with a few fresh or frosted mint leaves.

COOK'S TIP *If you only have Earl Grey tea bags these can be used instead, but add enough to make 450ml | ¾ pint | scant 2 cups strong tea. Make frosted mint leaves by dipping the leaves in egg white and sprinkling them with caster (superfine) sugar.*

Sorbets on Sticks

Almost any firm-textured sorbet can be frozen in ice lolly moulds, making a convenient and "fun" presentation.

For summer entertaining, a splash of alcohol in the sorbet gives added appeal for adults,

but this can easily be omitted if an alcohol-free version is preferred.

MAKES ABOUT 24

DEPENDING ON THE SIZE
OF THE MOULDS

INGREDIENTS

**For the pineapple and
kirsch lollies (popsicles)**

1 medium PINEAPPLE,
about 1.2kg | 2½lb

115g | 4oz | ½ cup CASTER
(SUPERFINE) SUGAR

300ml | ½ pint | 1¼ cups WATER

30ml | 2 tbsp LIME JUICE

60ml | 4 tbsp KIRSCH

**For the pink grapefruit and
Campari lollies (popsicles)**

3 PINK GRAPEFRUIT, plus a little
extra GRAPEFRUIT or
ORANGE JUICE

115g | 4oz | ½ cup CASTER
(SUPERFINE) SUGAR

150ml | ¼ pint | ⅔ cup WATER

75ml | 5 tbsp CAMPARI

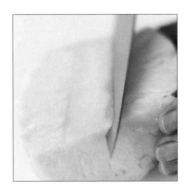

1 For the pineapple lollies, slice
the pineapple top and base,
then cut away the skin. Cut the
pineapple in half lengthways and
cut away the core. Roughly chop
the flesh and blend it in a food
processor until smooth. Press the
pulp through a sieve placed over
a bowl to extract as much juice
as possible.

2 Heat the sugar and water in a
heavy-based saucepan until the
sugar dissolves. Bring to the boil
and boil for 3 minutes, without
stirring, to make a syrup. Remove
from the heat and leave to cool.
Stir in the lime juice and kirsch.

3 Stir the pineapple juice into the
syrup, then chill until very cold.
Churn in an ice cream maker until
the sorbet just holds its own shape
but is not firm.

4 Spoon into 12 ice lolly moulds.
Press a wooden lolly stick into
the centre of each sorbet. Freeze
overnight until firm.

5 To make the pink grapefruit and
Campari lollies, cut away the skins
from the grapefruit using a sharp
knife. Slice the flesh, discarding
any pips, and blend in a food
processor until smooth, then press
through a sieve placed over a bowl
to extract as much juice as possible.

6 Measure the juice. You will
need 450ml | ¾ pint | scant 2 cups
for the sorbet. If there is not
enough, make it up with a little
grapefruit or orange juice.

7 Heat the sugar and water in
a heavy pan until the sugar has
dissolved. Bring to the boil and
boil for 3 minutes, without stirring,
to make a syrup.

8 Leave to cool completely, then
stir in the grapefruit juice and
Campari.. Chill until very cold.

9 Churn the mixture in an ice
cream maker until the sorbet just
holds its shape but is not firm.
Spoon into 12 ice lolly moulds,
position the sticks as in Step 4,
and freeze overnight until firm.

10 To serve the lollies, dip the
moulds in very hot water for
1–2 seconds, then carefully pull
each lolly from the mould.

COOK'S TIP *Don't let the fact that you
haven't any ice lolly (popsicle) moulds
deter you from making this delicious
dessert. Use wooden lolly sticks and
make use of small plastic cups or even
ice cube trays for miniature ice lollies.*

VARIATION *Other variations that are
just as delicious include orange sorbet
with a dash of Cointreau, or lemon sorbet
with gin. But don't be tempted to add too
much alcohol or the sorbet will not freeze.*

VARIATION *Yellow-fleshed grapefruit
can be used instead of ruby grapefruit.*

Damson Water Ice

Use ripe fruits to make the most of their natural sweetness. If you can't find damsons, use another

deep-red variety of plum or extra-juicy Victoria plums.

SERVES SIX

INGREDIENTS

500g | 1¼lb RIPE DAMSONS, washed

450ml | ¾ pint | scant 2 cups WATER

150g | 5oz | ⅔ cup CASTER
(SUPERFINE) SUGAR

1 Put the damsons into a pan and add 150ml | ¼ pint | ⅔ cup of the water. Cover and simmer for 10 minutes or until the damsons are tender.

2 Pour the remaining water into a second pan. Add the sugar and bring to the boil, stirring until the sugar has dissolved. Pour the syrup into a bowl, leave to cool, then chill.

3 Break up the cooked damsons in the pan with a wooden spoon and scoop out any free stones (pits). Pour the fruit and juices into a large sieve set over a bowl. Press the fruit through the sieve and discard the skins and any remaining stones from the sieve.

4 Mix the damson purée with the syrup. Chill, then churn in an ice cream maker until firm enough to scoop.

5 Spoon into tall glasses or dishes and serve with wafers.

VARIATIONS *Apricot water ice can be made in the same way. Flavour the water ice with a little lemon or orange rind or add a broken cinnamon stick to the pan when poaching the fruit.*

Apple and Cider Water Ice

This very English combination has a subtle apple flavour with just a hint of cider. As the apple purée is very pale, you could add a few drops of green food colouring to echo the pale green skin of the Granny Smith apples.

SERVES SIX

INGREDIENTS

500g | 1¼lb GRANNY
SMITH APPLES

150g | 5oz | ¾ cup CASTER
(SUPERFINE) SUGAR

300ml | ½ pint | 1¼ cups WATER

250ml | 8fl oz | 1 cup
STRONG DRY (HARD) CIDER

few drops of GREEN FOOD
COLOURING (optional)

strips of thinly pared
LIME RIND, to decorate

1 Quarter, core and roughly chop
the apples. Put them into a pan.
Add the sugar and half the water.
Cover and simmer for 10 minutes,
shaking the pan occasionally, until
the apples are soft.

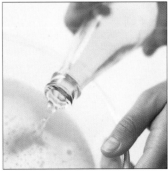

2 Press the mixture through a
sieve placed over a bowl. Discard
the apple skins and seeds. Stir the
cider and the remaining water into
the apple purée and add a little
colouring, if you like.

3 Chill, then churn in an ice cream
maker until firm enough to scoop.

4 Scoop into dishes and decorate
with twists of thinly pared lime rind.

COOK'S TIP *Add the food colouring
gradually, making the mixture a little
darker than you would like the finished
sorbet to be, as freezing lightens the
colour slightly.*

Rhubarb and Ginger Beer Sorbet

Rhubarb and ginger complement each other perfectly, and this pretty pastel-coloured sorbet packs a strong gingery punch. Serve with dainty ginger biscuits to heighten the ginger experience.

SERVES SIX

INGREDIENTS

500g | 1¼lb | 5 cups trimmed RHUBARB, washed and thickly sliced

350ml | 12fl oz | 1½ cups GINGER BEER

150g | 5oz | ¾ cup CASTER (SUPERFINE) SUGAR

few drops PINK FOOD COLOURING (optional)

1 EGG WHITE

To decorate

lightly poached and sweetened RHUBARB

strips of PRESERVED STEM GINGER

2 Put the remaining ginger beer into a pan with the sugar and bring to the boil, stirring until the sugar has completely dissolved. Pour the syrup into a bowl and leave to cool.

3 Pour the rhubarb and sugar syrup into an ice cream maker, mix in a few drops of pink food colouring, if using and churn until thick. Add the egg white and continue churning until firm enough to scoop.

4 Transfer to a freezer container and freeze until required.

5 Scoop into shallow bowls and serve decorated with the lightly poached rhubarb and strips of stem ginger.

COOK'S TIP *Try to use supple stems of young, forced rhubarb for this recipe as they have a more subtle flavour than the tougher stems of maincrop rhubarb.*

1 Put the rhubarb and 90ml | 6 tbsp ginger beer into a pan, cover and cook gently until the rhubarb is tender and still bright pink. Cool slightly then purée until smooth.

Espresso Sorbet

The perfect finalé for those guests who usually decline dessert. Light, refreshing, yet with the full mature depth of a strongly roasted cup of coffee. Serve with crisp biscuits, a drizzle of cream or spoonful of crème fraîche.

SERVES SIX

INGREDIENTS

90ml | 6 tbsp good-quality
ESPRESSO GROUND
FILTER COFFEE

1 litre | 1¾ pints | 4 cups
boiling WATER

115g | 4oz | ½ cup light
MUSCOVADO (BROWN) SUGAR

1 EGG WHITE

dainty CHOCOLATE BISCUITS
(COOKIES), to serve

1 Spoon the coffee into a cafetière (press pot) or jug (pitcher), pour on 750ml | 1¼ pints | 3 cups of the boiling water and leave to stand for 5 minutes.

2 Pour the remaining boiling water into a pan, add the sugar and heat until all of the sugar has dissolved. You can test for this by checking a spoonful of the liquid. Once the sugar has dissolved, bring the mixture to the boil.

3 Simmer the sugar mixture for 2 minutes. Allow the liquid to cool slightly and then pour it into a large bowl.

COOK'S TIP *For a special occasion you could add a dash of coffee liqeur to the mixture before you churn it.*

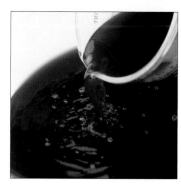

4 Plunge the cafetière or strain the coffee from the jug. Pour the coffee into a the bowl containing the sugar syrup, leave to cool then chill well.

5 Once the coffee mixture is completely chilled, pour into an ice cream maker and churn until starting to thicken.

6 Add the egg white and continue churning until the mixture is firm enough to scoop.

7 Spoon into glasses or attractive espresso cups and serve at once with dainty chocolate biscuits, if liked. If you don't want to serve the sorbet immediately, transfer it to a freezer container and freeze until required.

classic
vanilla, chocolate & coffee ice creams

This chapter provides the best classic vanilla ice cream recipes plus some imaginative variations using ingredients such as brandied fruits, crumbled cookies, saffron and cinnamon. The principal flavours of chocolate, coffee and toffee ice cream are many people's favourites, making this selection the ultimate collection of everyday ice creams.

Classic Vanilla Ice Cream

Nothing beats the creamy simplicity of true vanilla ice cream. Vanilla pods are expensive, but they are well worth buying for the superb flavour they impart.

SERVES FOUR

INGREDIENTS

1 VANILLA POD (BEAN)

300ml | ½ pint | 1¼ cups SEMI-SKIMMED (LOW-FAT) MILK

4 EGG YOLKS

75g | 3oz | 6 tbsp CASTER (SUPERFINE) SUGAR

5ml | 1 tsp CORNFLOUR (CORNSTARCH)

300ml | ½ pint | 1¼ cups DOUBLE (HEAVY) CREAM

1 Slit the vanilla pod lengthways. Pour the milk into a heavy pan, add the vanilla pod and bring to the boil. Remove from the heat and leave to infuse for 15 minutes.

2 Lift the vanilla pod up. Holding it over the pan, scrape the black seeds out of the pod into the milk.

3 Set the vanilla pod aside and bring the milk back to the boil.

4 Whisk the egg yolks, sugar and cornflour in a bowl until thick and foamy. Gradually pour on the hot milk, whisking constantly. Return to the pan and cook over a gentle heat, stirring all the time.

5 When the custard thickens and is smooth, pour it back into the bowl. Cool it, then chill.

6 Whip the cream until it has thickened but still falls from a spoon. Stir the cream into the custard and churn the mixture in an ice cream maker until thick.

7 Scoop the ice cream into dishes, bowls or cones – or eat straight from the tub.

COOK'S TIP *Don't throw the vanilla pod (bean) away after use. Instead, rinse it in cold water, dry and store in the sugar jar. After a week or so the sugar will take on the wonderful aroma and flavour of the vanilla and will be delicious sprinkled over summer fruits. Use it to sweeten whipped cream, custard, cookies and shortbread.*

Brown Bread Ice Cream

This very English ice cream consists of creamy vanilla ice cream flecked with tiny clusters of crisp, crunchy caramelized brown breadcrumbs and tastes similar to cookies-and-cream ice cream.

SERVES FOUR TO SIX

INGREDIENTS

4 EGG YOLKS

75g | 3oz | 6 tbsp CASTER (SUPERFINE) SUGAR

5ml | 1 tsp CORNFLOUR (CORNSTARCH)

300ml | ½ pint | 1¼ cups SEMI-SKIMMED (LOW-FAT) MILK

40g | 1½oz | 3 tbsp BUTTER

75g | 3oz | 1½ cups FRESH BROWN BREADCRUMBS

50g | 2oz | ¼ cup SOFT LIGHT MUSCOVADO (BROWN) SUGAR

5ml | 1 tsp NATURAL VANILLA ESSENCE (EXTRACT)

300ml | ½ pint | 1¼ cups DOUBLE (HEAVY) CREAM

1 Whisk the egg yolks, sugar and cornflour together in a bowl until thick and pale. Bring the milk just to the boil in a heavy pan, then gradually pour it on to the egg yolk mixture, whisking constantly.

2 Return the mixture to the pan and cook over a gentle heat, stirring constantly until the custard thickens and is smooth. Pour it back into the bowl, leave to cool, then chill.

3 Melt the butter in a large frying pan. Add the breadcrumbs, stir until evenly coated in butter, then sprinkle the sugar over.

4 Fry gently for 4–5 minutes, stirring until lightly browned. Remove from the heat and leave until cool and crisp.

5 Add the vanilla essence to the custard and mix well. Stir in the cream. Transfer to an ice cream maker and churn until thick.

6 Rub the fried breadcrumbs between your fingers to break up any lumps.

7 Stir the breadcrumbs into the mixture, then churn for 5–10 minutes more until ready to serve in scoops.

COOK'S TIP *Watch the breadcrumbs carefully when frying. Like almonds, they have a habit of burning if you turn your back on them for a moment, and burnt crumbs will give the ice cream a bitter taste. The crumbs should darken only slightly.*

Crème Fraîche and Honey Ice Cream

This delicately flavoured vanilla ice cream is naturally sweetened with fragrant flower honey and is absolutely delicious either on its own or with hot apple or cherry pie.

SERVES FOUR

INGREDIENTS

4 EGG YOLKS

60ml | 4 tbsp CLEAR
FLOWER HONEY

5ml | 1 tsp CORNFLOUR
(CORNSTARCH)

300ml | ½ pint | 1¼ cups
SEMI-SKIMMED
(LOW-FAT) MILK

7.5ml | 1½ tsp NATURAL
VANILLA ESSENCE (EXTRACT)

250g | 9oz | generous 1 cup
CRÈME FRAÎCHE

NASTURTIUM, PANSY or HERB
FLOWERS, to decorate

1 Whisk the egg yolks, honey and cornflour in a bowl until thick and foamy. Bring the milk just to the boil in a heavy pan, then gradually pour on to the yolk mixture, whisking constantly.

2 Return to the pan and cook over a gentle heat, stirring all the time until the custard thickens.

3 Pour the honey custard into a jug (pitcher) and then chill until it is completely cold.

4 Stir the vanilla essence and crème fraîche into the custard mix, pour into an ice cream maker and churn until thick and firm enough to scoop.

5 Serve in glass dishes. Decorate with nasturtiums, pansies or edible herb flowers.

COOK'S TIP *Measure the honey carefully and use level spoonfuls; if you are over generous, the honey flavour will dominate and the ice cream will be too sweet.*

Tutti Frutti Ice Cream

This Italian ice cream takes its name from an expression meaning "all the fruits". Four fruits have been used here, but you can create your own blend of candied or glacé fruits, including exotics such as papaya or mango.

SERVES FOUR TO SIX

INGREDIENTS

300ml | ½ pint | 1¼ cups
SEMI-SKIMMED
(LOW-FAT) MILK

1 VANILLA POD (BEAN)

4 EGG YOLKS

75g | 3oz | 6 tbsp CASTER
(SUPERFINE) SUGAR

5ml | 1 tsp CORNFLOUR
(CORNSTARCH)

300ml | ½ pint | 1¼ cups
WHIPPING CREAM

150g | 5oz | ⅔ cup
MULTICOLOURED GLACÉ
(CANDIED) CHERRIES

50g | 2oz | ⅓ cup
SLICED CANDIED LIME and
ORANGE PEEL

50g | 2oz | ⅓ cup
CANDIED PINEAPPLE

1 Pour the milk into a heavy pan. Using a small, sharp knife, slit the vanilla pod lengthways, add it to the pan and bring the milk to the boil. Immediately remove the pan from the heat and leave the milk for 15 minutes to allow the vanilla flavour to infuse.

2 Lift the vanilla pod up out of the milk. Holding it over the pan of infused milk, scrape out the small black seeds so that they fall into the pan. Bring the flavoured milk back to a gentle boil over a low heat.

3 Meanwhile, whisk the egg yolks, sugar and cornflour in a bowl until the mixture is thick and foamy. Gradually pour in the flavoured milk, whisking all the time.

4 Pour the custard mixture back into the pan. Cook over a gentle heat, stirring constantly until the custard thickens and is smooth. Pour it back into the bowl and cover. Cool, then chill.

5 Mix the thickened custard with the cream. There is no need to whip the cream first. Churn the custard and cream mixture in a food processor until it is thick.

6 Finely chop the glacé cherries, candied peel and pineapple and fold into the ice cream. Churn in the ice cream maker for 5–10 minutes or return to the freezer for 2–3 hours, until firm enough to scoop.

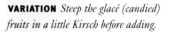

VARIATION *Steep the glacé (candied) fruits in a little Kirsch before adding.*

Cookies and Cream Ice Cream

This wickedly indulgent ice cream is a favourite in the USA. To make the result even more luxurious,

use freshly baked home-made cookies with large chunks of chocolate and nuts.

SERVES FOUR TO SIX

INGREDIENTS

4 EGG YOLKS

75g | 3oz | 6 tbsp CASTER (SUPERFINE) SUGAR

5ml | 1 tsp CORNFLOUR (CORNSTARCH)

300ml | ½ pint | 1¼ cups SEMI-SKIMMED (LOW-FAT) MILK

5ml | 1 tsp NATURAL VANILLA ESSENCE (EXTRACT)

300ml | ½ pint | 1¼ cups WHIPPING CREAM

150g | 5oz CHUNKY CHOCOLATE AND HAZELNUT COOKIES, crumbled into chunky pieces

1 Whisk the egg yolks, sugar and cornflour in a bowl until the mixture is thick and foamy. Pour the milk into a heavy pan, bring it just to the boil, then pour it on to the yolk mixture in the bowl, whisking constantly.

2 Return to the pan and cook over a gentle heat, stirring until the custard thickens and is smooth. Pour it back into the bowl and cover closely. Leave to cool, then chill.

COOK'S TIP *Experiment with different types of cookie to find the type that gives the best results.*

3 Stir the vanilla essence into the custard. Stir in the whipping cream and churn in an ice cream maker until thick.

4 Scrape the ice cream into a freezerproof container. Fold in the cookie chunks and freeze for 2–3 hours until firm.

Brandied Fruit and Rice Ice Cream

Based on a favourite Victorian rice ice cream, this rich dessert combines spicy rice pudding with a creamy egg custard flecked with brandy-soaked fruits. The mixture is then frozen until it is just firm enough to scoop.

SERVES FOUR TO SIX

INGREDIENTS

50g | 2oz | ⅓ cup READY-TO-EAT STONED (PITTED) PRUNES

50g | 2oz | ⅓ cup READY-TO-EAT DRIED APRICOTS

50g | 2oz | ¼ cup GLACÉ (CANDIED) CHERRIES

30ml | 2 tbsp BRANDY

150ml | ¼ pint | ⅔ cup SINGLE (LIGHT) CREAM

For the rice mixture

40g | 1½oz | generous ¼ cup SHORT-GRAIN RICE

450ml | ¾ pint | scant 2 cups FULL-CREAM (WHOLE) MILK

1 CINNAMON STICK, halved, plus extra CINNAMON STICKS, to decorate

4 CLOVES

For the custard

4 EGG YOLKS

75g | 3oz | 6 tbsp CASTER (SUPERFINE) SUGAR

5ml | 1 tsp CORNFLOUR (CORNSTARCH)

300ml | ½ pint | 1¼ cups FULL-CREAM (WHOLE) MILK

1 Chop the prunes, apricots and glacé cherries finely and put them in a bowl. Pour over the brandy. Cover the bowl and leave the fruit to soak for 3 hours or overnight if possible.

2 Put the rice, milk and whole spices in a pan. Bring the mixture to the boil, then simmer gently for 30 minutes, stirring occasionally until most of the milk has been absorbed by the rice.

3 Lift out the spices and leave the rice to cool. Chill until required.

4 Whisk the egg yolks, sugar and cornflour in a bowl until thick and foamy. Heat the milk in a heavy pan, then gradually pour it on to the yolks, whisking constantly.

5 Pour back into the pan and cook over a gentle heat, stirring until the custard thickens. Leave to cool, then chill.

6 Mix the chilled custard, rice and cream together. Churn in an ice cream maker until thick.

7 Spoon the ice cream into a freezerproof container and fold in the fruits. Freeze for 2–3 hours until firm.

8 Serve the ice cream in scoops decorated with cinnamon sticks.

COOK'S TIP *As the brandy-soaked fruits are very soft, it is better to remove the ice cream from the ice cream maker, fold in the fruits and then freeze the mixture in a tub until firm enough to scoop, rather than adding the soaked fruits to the machine. This way, the fruits do not disintegrate and their colours are preserved.*

Chunky Coffee Bean and Kahlúa Ice Cream

A wonderful combination of creamy dark coffee with a hint of coffee liqueur, peppered with crunchy chocolate-covered coffee beans. The beans used here have been coated with white, dark and milk chocolate, but all dark chocolate-covered beans would work just as well.

SERVES SIX

INGREDIENTS

4 EGG YOLKS

75g | 3oz | 6 tbsp CASTER (SUPERFINE) SUGAR

5ml | 1 tsp CORNFLOUR (CORNSTARCH)

300ml | ½ pint | 1¼ cups SEMI-SKIMMED (LOW-FAT) MILK

30ml | 2 tbsp instant COFFEE GRANULES OR POWDER

300ml | ½ pint | 1¼ cups DOUBLE (HEAVY) CREAM

120ml | 4fl oz | ½ cup KAHLÚA

115g | 4oz assorted CHOCOLATE-COVERED COFFEE BEANS

a little sifted COCOA POWDER (UNSWEETENED), to decorate

1 Whisk the egg yolks, sugar and cornflour in a bowl until the mixture is thick and pale. Heat the milk in a pan then gradually whisk into the yolk mixture. Return the custard to the pan and cook over a gentle heat, stirring constantly so that it does not catch on the bottom and burn.

2 When the custard has thickened and is smooth, pour it back into the bowl and mix in the instant coffee granules or powder, stirring continuously until all of the coffee has completely dissolved. Cover the custard with clear film (plastic wrap) to prevent a skin from forming, leave to cool then chill well before churning.

3 Stir the cream and Kahlúa into the coffee custard then pour into an ice cream maker. Churn until thick. Roughly chop 75g | 3oz of the chocolate-covered coffee beans, add to the ice cream and churn until firm enough to scoop. Transfer to a freezer container and freeze until required.

4 Scoop the ice cream into coffee cups and decorate with the remaining chocolate-covered coffee beans and a light dusting of cocoa powder.

Double White Chocolate Ice Cream

Crunchy chunks of white chocolate are a bonus in this delicious ice cream. Serve it scooped in waffle cones dipped in dark (bittersweet) chocolate, for a sensational treat.

SERVES EIGHT

INGREDIENTS

4 EGG YOLKS

75g | 3oz | 6 tbsp CASTER (SUPERFINE) SUGAR

5ml | 1 tsp CORNFLOUR (CORNSTARCH)

300ml | ½ pint | 1¼ cups SEMI-SKIMMED (LOW-FAT) MILK

250g | 9oz WHITE CHOCOLATE, chopped

10ml | 2 tsp NATURAL VANILLA ESSENCE (EXTRACT)

300ml | ½ pint | 1¼ cups WHIPPING CREAM

8 CHOCOLATE-DIPPED CONES, to serve

1 Whisk the egg yolks, sugar and cornflour in a bowl until the mixture is thick and foamy. Pour the milk into a heavy pan, bring it to the boil, then gradually pour the hot milk on to the yolk mixture, whisking constantly.

2 Return the custard mixture to the pan and cook over a gentle heat, stirring constantly until the custard thickens and is smooth. Pour the hot custard back into the same bowl.

3 Add 150g | 5oz of the chopped white chocolate to the hot custard, with the vanilla essence. Gently stir until the chocolate has melted, leave to cool, then chill.

4 Stir the cream into the custard, then churn the mixture until thick. Add the remaining chocolate and churn for 5–10 minutes until firm. Serve in chocolate-dipped cones.

VARIATION *If you prefer, scoop the ice cream into glass dishes and decorate with white chocolate curls or extra diced chocolate. Ice cream served this way won't go quite as far, so will only serve 4–6.*

Classic Dark Chocolate Ice Cream

Rich, dark and wonderfully luxurious, this ice cream can be served solo or drizzled with warm chocolate sauce. If you are making it in advance, don't forget to soften the ice cream before serving so that the full flavour of the chocolate comes through.

SERVES FOUR TO SIX

INGREDIENTS

4 EGG YOLKS

75g | 3oz | 6 tbsp CASTER (SUPERFINE) SUGAR

5ml | 1 tsp CORNFLOUR (CORNSTARCH)

300ml | ½ pint | 1¼ cups SEMI-SKIMMED (LOW-FAT) MILK

200g | 7oz DARK (BITTERSWEET) CHOCOLATE

300ml | ½ pint | 1¼ cups WHIPPING CREAM

SHAVED CHOCOLATE, to decorate

1 Whisk the egg yolks, sugar and cornflour in a bowl until thick and foamy. Pour the milk into a pan, bring it just to the boil, then gradually whisk it into the yolk mixture.

2 Return the mixture to the pan and cook over a gentle heat, stirring constantly until the custard thickens and is smooth. Take the pan off the heat.

3 Break the chocolate into small pieces and stir into the hot custard until it has melted. Leave to cool, then chill.

4 Whip the cream, and mix with the cool chocolate custard.

5 Place in an ice cream maker and churn until firm enough to scoop. Serve the ice cream in scoops, decorated with chocolate shavings.

COOK'S TIP *For the best flavour use a good quality chocolate with at least 75 per cent cocoa solids, such as top-of-the-range Belgian dark (bittersweet) chocolate or Continental-style dark (bittersweet) cooking chocolate.*

Chocolate Double Mint Ice Cream

Full of body and flavour, this creamy, smooth ice cream combines the sophistication of dark chocolate with the satisfying coolness of fresh chopped mint. Crushed peppermints provide extra crunch, and this classic combination of flavours will be loved by children and adults alike.

SERVES FOUR

INGREDIENTS

4 EGG YOLKS

75g | 3oz | 6 tbsp CASTER (SUPERFINE) SUGAR

5ml | 1 tsp CORNFLOUR (CORNSTARCH)

300ml | ½ pint | 1¼ cups SEMI-SKIMMED (LOW-FAT) MILK

200g | 7oz DARK (BITTERSWEET) CHOCOLATE, broken into squares

40g | 1½oz | ¼ cup PEPPERMINTS

60ml | 4 tbsp CHOPPED FRESH MINT

300ml | ½ pint | 1¼ cups WHIPPING CREAM

sprigs of FRESH MINT dusted with ICING (CONFECTIONERS') SUGAR, to decorate

1 Put the egg yolks, sugar and cornflour in a bowl and whisk until thick and foamy. Pour the milk into a heavy pan, bring to the boil, then gradually whisk into the yolk mixture.

2 Scrape the mixture back into the pan and cook over a gentle heat, stirring constantly until the custard thickens and is smooth. Scrape it back into the bowl, add the chocolate, a little at a time, and stir until melted. Cool, then chill.

3 Put the peppermints in a strong plastic bag and crush them with a rolling pin. Stir them into the custard with the chopped mint.

4 Mix the custard and cream together and churn the mixture in an ice cream maker until firm enough to scoop.

5 Serve the ice cream in scoops and then decorate with mint sprigs dusted with sifted icing sugar.

COOK'S TIP *If you freeze the ice cream in a tub, don't beat it in a food processor when breaking up the ice crystals, or the crunchy texture of the crushed peppermints will be lost.*

Chocolate and Hazelnut Brittle Ice Cream

For nut lovers and chocoholics everywhere, this luxurious ice cream is the ultimate indulgence. Rich, smooth dark chocolate is combined with crisp little chunks of sweet hazelnut brittle that provide a satisfying contrast. For a change, use other types of nuts, such as almonds, walnuts or pecan nuts.

SERVES FOUR TO SIX

INGREDIENTS

4 EGG YOLKS

175g | 6oz | scant 1 cup SUGAR

5ml | 1 tsp CORNFLOUR (CORNSTARCH)

300ml | ½ pint | 1¼ cups SEMI-SKIMMED (LOW-FAT) MILK

150g | 5oz DARK (BITTERSWEET) CHOCOLATE, broken into squares

115g | 4oz | 1 cup HAZELNUTS

60ml | 4 tbsp WATER

300ml | ½ pint | 1¼ cups WHIPPING CREAM

1 Whisk the egg yolks, sugar and cornflour in a bowl until thick and foamy. Pour the milk into a pan, bring it just to the boil, then gradually whisk it into the yolk mixture.

2 Scrape back into the pan and cook over a gentle heat, stirring constantly, until the custard has thickened and is smooth.

3 Take the pan off the heat and stir the chocolate into the hot custard, a few squares at a time. Cool, then chill. Brush a baking sheet with oil and set it aside.

4 Meanwhile put the hazelnuts, remaining sugar and measured water in a large, heavy frying pan. Place over a gentle heat and heat without stirring until all the sugar has dissolved.

5 Increase the heat slightly and cook until the syrup surrounding the nuts has turned pale golden. Quickly pour the mixture on to the oiled baking sheet and leave to stand at room temperature until the hazelnut brittle (praline) cools and hardens.

6 Pour the chocolate custard into the ice cream maker and add the cream. Churn for 25 minutes or until it is thick and firm enough to scoop.

7 Break the nut brittle into pieces. Reserve a few pieces for decoration and finely chop the rest. Scrape the ice cream into a tub and stir in the nut brittle. Freeze for 2–3 hours or until firm enough to scoop.

8 Scoop on to plates and decorate with the reserved praline.

Classic Triple Chocolate Terrine

This variation on the popular Neapolitan layered ice cream is made with smooth, dark,

milk and white chocolate. Serve it in slices, sandwiched between rectangular wafer biscuits

or in a pool of warm dark chocolate sauce.

SERVES EIGHT TO TEN

INGREDIENTS

6 EGG YOLKS

115g | 4oz | ½ cup CASTER (SUPERFINE) SUGAR

5ml | 1 tsp CORNFLOUR (CORNSTARCH)

450ml | ¾ pint | scant 2 cups SEMI-SKIMMED (LOW-FAT) MILK

115g | 4oz DARK (BITTERSWEET) CHOCOLATE, broken into squares

115g | 4oz MILK CHOCOLATE, broken into squares

115g | 4oz WHITE CHOCOLATE, broken into squares

2.5ml | ½ tsp NATURAL VANILLA ESSENCE (EXTRACT)

450ml | ¾ pint | scant 2 cups WHIPPING CREAM

1 Whisk the egg yolks, sugar and cornflour until thick. Pour the milk into a heavy pan and bring it to the boil. Gradually pour it on to the yolk mixture, whisking constantly, then return the mixture to the pan and simmer, stirring constantly until the custard thickens and is smooth.

2 Divide the custard among three bowls. Add the dark chocolate to one, the milk chocolate to another and the white chocolate and vanilla essence to the third.

3 Stir with separate spoons until the chocolate has completely melted. Cool, then chill. Line a 25 x 7.5 x 7.5cm | 10 x 3 x 3in terrine or large loaf tin (pan) with clear film (plastic wrap).

4 Stir a third of the cream into each bowl, then churn the milk chocolate custard mixture until thick. Return the remaining bowls of flavoured custard and cream mixture to the refrigerator.

COOK'S TIP *Make sure each layer of ice cream is firm before adding another, or the layers may merge. The dark (bittersweet) chocolate layer may need to be softened at room temperature before spreading.*

5 Spoon the milk chocolate ice cream into the lined terrine or loaf tin, level the surface using the back of a spoon and freeze the ice cream until it is firm.

6 Churn the white chocolate ice cream in an ice cream maker until it is thick and smooth, then spoon it into the tin. Level the surface and freeze the ice cream until it is firm.

7 Finally, churn the dark chocolate ice cream and spread it in the tin to form the top layer, making sure the surface is smooth and level.

8 Cover the terrine with clear film, then freeze it overnight. To serve, remove the clear film cover, then invert on to a plate. Peel off the clear film and serve in slices.

Chunky Chocolate Ice Cream

This creamy milk chocolate ice cream, topped with delicious chunks of milk, dark and white chocolate will satisfy even the sweetest tooth and will be a hit with adults as well as children.

SERVES FOUR TO SIX

INGREDIENTS

4 EGG YOLKS

75g | 3oz | 6 tbsp CASTER (SUPERFINE) SUGAR

5ml | 1 tsp CORNFLOUR (CORNSTARCH)

300ml | ½ pint | 1¼ cups SEMI-SKIMMED (LOW-FAT) MILK

200g | 7oz MILK CHOCOLATE

50g | 2oz DARK (BITTERSWEET) CHOCOLATE, plus extra, to decorate

50g | 2oz WHITE CHOCOLATE

300ml | ½ pint | 1¼ cups WHIPPING CREAM

1 Whisk the egg yolks, caster sugar and cornflour in a bowl until the mixture is thick and foamy. Pour the milk into a large, heavy pan. Heat the milk and bring it just to the boil, then gradually pour it on to the egg yolk mixture, whisking constantly.

2 Return the custard mixture to the pan and cook over a gentle heat, stirring constantly with a wooden spoon until the custard thickens and is smooth.

3 Pour the custard back into the bowl. Break 150g | 5oz of the milk chocolate into squares, stir these into the hot custard, then cover closely. Leave to cool, then chill.

4 Chop the remaining milk, dark and white chocolate finely and keep on one side.

5 Mix the chocolate custard and the whipping cream and churn in an ice cream maker for 25–30 minutes until thick.

6 Scoop the churned ice cream out of the machine and into a plastic tub. Fold in the pieces of chocolate and freeze for 2–3 hours until firm enough to scoop.

7 Scoop into glasses or bowls and decorate with more pieces of chopped chocolate.

COOK'S TIP *For maximum flavour, use good quality Belgian chocolate or your favourite chocolate bar; avoid using dark, milk or white cake covering.*

Chocolate Ripple Ice Cream

This creamy, dark chocolate ice cream, unevenly rippled with wonderful swirls of rich chocolate sauce, will stay deliciously soft even after freezing. Not that it will remain in the freezer for long!

SERVES FOUR TO SIX

INGREDIENTS

4 EGG YOLKS

75g | 3oz | 6 tbsp CASTER (SUPERFINE) SUGAR

5ml | 1 tsp CORNFLOUR (CORNSTARCH)

300ml | ½ pint | 1¼ cups SEMI-SKIMMED (LOW-FAT) MILK

250g | 9oz DARK (BITTERSWEET) CHOCOLATE, broken into squares

25g | 1oz | 2 tbsp BUTTER, diced

30ml | 2 tbsp GOLDEN SYRUP or LIGHT CORN SYRUP

90ml | 6 tbsp SINGLE CREAM or CREAM and MILK MIXED

300ml | ½ pint | 1¼ cups WHIPPING CREAM

ICE CREAM WAFERS, to serve

1 Whisk the egg yolks, sugar and cornflour until thick and frothy. Bring the milk just to the boil in a heavy pan, then gradually pour it on to the yolk mixture, whisking constantly. Return to the pan and simmer, stirring until the custard thickens and is smooth.

2 Pour the chocolate custard back into the bowl and stir in 150g | 5oz of the chocolate, until melted. Cover the custard closely, leave it to cool, then chill.

3 Put the remaining chocolate into a pan and add the butter and syrup.

4 Heat gently, stirring, until the chocolate and butter have melted.

5 Stir in the single cream or cream and milk mixture. Heat gently, stirring, until smooth then leave the chocolate sauce to cool.

6 Stir the cream into the custard and churn the mixture in an ice cream maker for 20–25 minutes until thick.

7 Add alternate spoonfuls of ice cream and chocolate sauce to a 1.5 litre | 2½ pint | 6 cup plastic container. Marble together by roughly running a knife through the mixture.

8 Cover and freeze the ice cream for 5–6 hours until it is firm enough to scoop. Serve in scoops in bowls or plates.

COOK'S TIP *For the ultimmate indulgence make more chocolate sauce than is required in the recipe and spoon the extra over the top of the chocolate ripple ice cream.*

Choca Mocha Sherbet

This dark chocolate sherbet is a cross between a water ice and a light cream-free ice cream, and is ideal for chocoholics who are trying to count calories.

SERVES FOUR TO SIX

INGREDIENTS

600ml | 1 pint | 2½ cups
SEMI-SKIMMED (LOW-FAT) MILK

40g | 1½oz | ⅓ cup GOOD QUALITY
(UNSWEETENED) COCOA POWDER

115g | 4oz | ½ cup CASTER
(SUPERFINE) SUGAR

5ml | 1 tsp INSTANT COFFEE
GRANULES

CHOCOLATE-COVERED RAISINS,
to decorate

COOK'S TIP *Use good quality cocoa and don't overheat the milk mixture or the finished ice may taste bitter. If there are any lumps of cocoa in the milk, beat the mixture with a balloon whisk to remove them.*

1 Heat the milk in a pan. Meanwhile, put the cocoa in a bowl. Add a little of the hot milk to the cocoa and mix to a paste.

2 Add the remaining milk to the cocoa mixture, stirring all the time, then pour the chocolate milk back into the pan. Bring to the boil, stirring continuously.

3 Take the pan off the heat and stir in the sugar and the coffee granules. Pour into a jug (pitcher), leave to cool, then chill well.

4 Churn the chilled mixture in an ice cream maker until it is very thick. Scoop into dishes. Sprinkle each portion with a few chocolate-covered raisins.

Iced Tiramisu

This favourite Italian combination makes a marvellous ice cream. Like the more traditional version, it tastes very rich, despite the fact that virtually fat-free fromage frais is a major ingredient.

SERVES FOUR

INGREDIENTS

150g | 5oz | ¾ cup CASTER (SUPERFINE) SUGAR

150ml | ¼ pint | ⅔ cup WATER

250g | 9oz | generous 1 cup MASCARPONE

200g | 7oz | scant 1 cup VIRTUALLY FAT-FREE FROMAGE FRAIS or CREAM CHEESE

5ml | 1 tsp NATURAL VANILLA ESSENCE (EXTRACT)

10ml | 2 tsp INSTANT COFFEE, dissolved in 30ml | 2 tbsp BOILING WATER

30ml | 2 tbsp COFFEE LIQUEUR

75g | 3oz SPONGE FINGER BISCUITS (LADY FINGERS)

(UNSWEETENED) COCOA POWDER, for dusting

CHOCOLATE CURLS, to decorate

1 Put 115g | 4oz | ½ cup of the sugar into a small pan. Add the water and bring to the boil, stirring until the sugar has dissolved. Leave the syrup to cool, then chill it.

2 Put the mascarpone into a bowl. Beat it with a spoon until it is soft, then stir in the fromage frais. Add the chilled sugar syrup, a little at a time, then stir in the vanilla essence.

3 Spoon the mascarpone mixture into an ice cream maker and churn until it is thick but too soft to scoop.

COOK'S TIP *You can make chocolate curls from milk, dark (bittersweet) or white chocolate. Simply hold the bar of chocolate over a plate and pare curls away from the edge of the bar using a swivel-blade vegetable peeler. Lift the pared curls with a flat blade, a palette knife or a spatula rather than your fingers, and arrange as desired on top of the ice cream.*

4 Meanwhile, put the instant coffee mixture in a small bowl, sweeten with the remaining sugar, then add the liqueur. Stir well and leave to cool.

5 Crumble the sponge finger biscuits into small pieces and toss them in the coffee mixture.

6 Spoon a third of the ice cream into a 900ml | 1½ pint | 3¾ cup plastic container, spoon over half the biscuits then top with half the remaining ice cream.

7 Sprinkle over the last of the coffee-soaked biscuits, then cover with the remaining ice cream. Freeze for 2–3 hours until firm enough to scoop. Dust with cocoa powder and spoon into glass dishes. Decorate with chocolate curls, and serve.

Classic Coffee Ice Cream

This bittersweet blend is a must for those who like their coffee strong and dark with just a hint of cream.
When serving, decorate with the chocolate-covered coffee beans that are available from some larger
supermarkets and good confectioners.

4 Mix the coffee and cream with the chilled custard, then churn the mixture in an ice cream maker until firm enough to scoop.

5 Scoop the ice cream into glass dishes, sprinkle with chocolate-covered coffee beans and serve.

COOK'S TIP *If you only have coffee beans, put 50g | 2oz | ¼ cup in a mortar and crush with a pestle. Bring 300ml | ½ pint | 1¼ cups semi-skimmed milk to the boil, and infuse the crushed beans for 15 minutes. Strain and use the flavoured milk to make the custard.*

SERVES FOUR TO SIX

INGREDIENTS

90ml | 6 tbsp FINE FILTER COFFEE

250ml | 8fl oz | 1 cup
BOILING WATER

4 EGG YOLKS

75g | 3oz | 6 tbsp CASTER
(SUPERFINE) SUGAR

5ml | 1 tsp CORNFLOUR
(CORNSTARCH)

300ml | ½ pint | 1¼ cups
SEMI-SKIMMED (LOW-FAT) MILK

150ml | ¼ pint | ⅔ cup
DOUBLE (HEAVY) CREAM

1 Put the coffee in a cafetière (press pot) and pour on the boiling water. Leave to cool, then strain and chill until required.

2 Whisk the egg yolks, sugar and cornflour in a bowl until the mixture is thick and foamy. Pour the milk into a heavy pan, bring to the boil, then gradually pour on to the yolk mixture in the bowl, whisking constantly.

3 Return the mixture to the pan and cook over a gentle heat, stirring all the time until the custard thickens and is smooth. Pour it back into the bowl and cover closely with clear film (plastic wrap). Cool, then chill.

Coffee Toffee Swirl Ice Cream

A wonderful combination of creamy vanilla, marbled with coffee-flavoured toffee. Serve on its own as an impressive grand finale to a dinner party, or on a hot day as an ice cream sundae with classic coffee and chocolate ice cream.

SERVES FOUR TO SIX

INGREDIENTS

For the toffee sauce

10ml | 2 tsp CORNFLOUR (CORNSTARCH)

170g | 5¾oz can EVAPORATED MILK

75g | 3oz | 6 tbsp LIGHT MUSCOVADO (BROWN) SUGAR

20ml | 4 tsp INSTANT COFFEE GRANULES

15ml | 1tbsp BOILING WATER

For the ice cream

4 EGG YOLKS

75g | 3oz | 6 tbsp CASTER (SUPERFINE) SUGAR

5ml | 1 tsp CORNFLOUR (CORNSTARCH)

300ml | ½ pint | 1¼ cups SEMI-SKIMMED (LOW-FAT) MILK

5ml | 1tsp VANILLA ESSENCE (EXTRACT)

300ml | ½ pint | 1¼ cups WHIPPING CREAM

1 For the sauce, put the cornflour and a little evaporated milk in a small, heavy pan and mix to a smooth paste. Add the sugar and remaining evaporated milk.

2 Cook over a gentle heat, stirring until the sugar has dissolved, then increase the heat and cook, stirring continuously, until slightly thickened and just beginning to darken in colour.

3 Take the pan off the heat. Mix the coffee with the boiling water and stir into the sauce. Cool the sauce quickly by plunging the base of the pan into cold water.

4 Whisk the egg yolks, sugar and cornflour together until thick and foaming. Bring the milk just to the boil in a heavy pan then gradually whisk into the yolk mixture. Return to the pan and cook over a gentle heat, stirring until thick and smooth. Pour back into the bowl, stir in the vanilla and leave to cool.

5 Mix the custard and cream together and churn in an ice cream maker until thick but not firm enough to scoop. Transfer the semi-frozen churned ice cream to a plastic container.

6 Beat the toffee sauce well and drizzle it thickly over the ice cream. Marble the two together by roughly running a knife through the mixture.

7 Cover and freeze the ice cream for 4–5 hours until it is firm enough to scoop. Serve in scoops in bowls or plates.

COOK'S TIP *If the sauce is too thick to drizzle, gently warm the base of the pan for a few seconds, stirring well.*

VARIATION *The sauce is also delicious drizzled over plain vanilla ice cream.*

classic fruit & nut ice creams

From traditional fruit-flavoured ice creams to those speckled with chopped toasted nuts, this chapter imaginatively introduces the most widely used ice cream flavours. Fresh fruit purées, liqueured dried fruits and satisfying, crunchy nuts transform a basic ice cream into something very special.

Simple Strawberry Ice Cream

Capture the essence of childhood summers with this easy-to-make ice cream. Whipping cream is better than double cream for this recipe as it doesn't overwhelm the taste of the fresh fruit. Serve with extra strawberries or other summer fruits such as raspberries or redcurrants.

SERVES FOUR TO SIX

INGREDIENTS

500g | 1¼lb | 4 cups
STRAWBERRIES, hulled

50g | 2oz | ½ cup ICING
(CONFECTIONERS') SUGAR

juice of ½ LEMON

300ml | ½ pint | 1¼ cups
WHIPPING CREAM

extra STRAWBERRIES,
to decorate

1 Purée the strawberries in a food processor or blender until smooth, then add the icing sugar and lemon juice and process again to mix. Press the purée through a sieve into a bowl. Chill until very cold.

2 Churn the purée in an ice cream maker until mushy, then pour in the cream and churn until thick enough to scoop. Scoop into dishes and decorate with a few extra strawberries.

COOK'S TIP *If possible, taste the strawberries before buying them. Halve large strawberries for decoration.*

VARIATION *Raspberry or any other berry fruit can be used to make this ice cream, in the same way as strawberry.*

Gooseberry and Clotted Cream Ice Cream

A rather neglected fruit, gooseberries can conjure up images of the tired grey-looking crumble that used to be served at school or in the work canteen. This indulgent ice cream puts gooseberries in a totally different class. Its delicious, slightly tart flavour goes particularly well with tiny, melt-in-the-mouth meringues.

SERVES FOUR TO SIX

INGREDIENTS

500g | 1¼lb | 4 cups
GOOSEBERRIES, trimmed

60ml | 4 tbsp WATER

75g | 3oz | 6 tbsp CASTER
(SUPERFINE) SUGAR

150ml | ¼ pint | ⅔ cup
WHIPPING CREAM

a few drops of GREEN FOOD
COLOURING (optional)

120ml | 4fl oz | ½ cup
CLOTTED CREAM

FRESH MINT SPRIGS,
to decorate

MERINGUES, to serve

1 Put the gooseberries in a pan and add the water and sugar. Cover and simmer for 10 minutes or until soft. Tip into a food processor or blender and process to a smooth purée. Press through a sieve placed over a bowl. Cool, then chill.

COOK'S TIP *Just a small amount of clotted cream adds a surprising richness to this simple ice cream. If the gooseberry purée is very tart, you can add extra sugar when mixing in the whipping cream.*

2 Mix the chilled purée with the whipping cream, add a few drops of green food colouring if using and churn in an ice cream maker until thickened and semi-frozen. Add the clotted cream and continue to churn until thick enough to scoop.

3 To serve, scoop the ice cream into dishes or small plates, decorate with fresh mint sprigs and add a few small meringues to each serving.

Blackberry Ice Cream

There could scarcely be fewer ingredients in this delicious, vibrant ice cream. If you make the ice cream in a machine, don't be tempted to add the cream with the fruit or the mixture will become buttery by the time it has been churned and is stiff enough to scoop.

SERVES FOUR TO SIX

INGREDIENTS

500g | 1¼lb | 5 cups BLACKBERRIES, hulled, plus extra, to decorate

75g | 3oz | 6 tbsp CASTER (SUPERFINE) SUGAR

30ml | 2 tbsp WATER

300ml | ½ pint | 1¼ cups WHIPPING CREAM

CRISP DESSERT BISCUITS (COOKIES), to serve

1 Simmer the blackberries with the sugar and water until just soft. Tip the fruit into a sieve placed over a bowl and press it through the mesh, using a wooden spoon. Leave to cool, then chill.

2 Churn the chilled purée in an ice cream maker for 10–15 minutes until it is thick, then gradually pour in the cream and continue to churn the ice cream until it is firm enough to scoop.

3 Scoop into dishes and decorate with extra blackberries. Serve with crisp dessert biscuits.

VARIATION *Frozen blackberries can be used for the purée. You will need to increase the cooking time to 10 minutes and stir occasionally. Blackcurrants can be used instead of blackberries. A combination of blackberries and peeled and sliced cooking apples also works well.*

Apricot and Amaretti Ice Cream

Prolong the very short season of fresh apricots by transforming them into this superb ice cream with crushed amaretti biscuits and whipped cream. If you want to make this ice cream when apricots are not available, you can use the canned variety instead.

SERVES FOUR TO SIX

INGREDIENTS

500g | 1¼lb FRESH APRICOTS, halved and stoned (pitted)

juice of 1 ORANGE

50g | 2oz | ¼ cup CASTER (SUPERFINE) SUGAR

300ml | ½ pint | 1¼ cups WHIPPING CREAM

50g | 2oz AMARETTI

1 Put the apricots, orange juice and sugar in a heavy pan. Cover and simmer for 5 minutes until the fruit is tender. Leave the mixture to cool.

2 Lift out one third of the fruit using a slotted spon and set it aside on a plate. Tip the remaining contents of the pan into a food processor or blender and process to a smooth purée.

3 Churn the apricot purée in an ice cream maker until the mixture is slushy, then gradually add the cream. Continue to churn until the ice cream is thick, but not firm enough to scoop.

4 Scrape the ice cream into a tub. Crumble the amaretti between your fingers so that the crumbs fall into the tub of ice cream.

5 Add the reserved apricots and gently fold them, and the amaretti crumbs, into the ice cream. Freeze for 2–3 hours until firm enough to scoop.

COOK'S TIP *It is better to chill the fruit purée if you have time, as this will speed up the churning or freezing process. If you have some amaretto liqueur, fold in 45ml | 3 tbsp with the biscuits for an alcoholic kick.*

Banana and Toffee Ice Cream

Smooth and creamy condensed milk replaces the sugar in this fabulous ice cream. Because it's made without a cooked egg custard base, it's incredibly easy and fast.

SERVES FOUR TO SIX

INGREDIENTS

150g | 5oz TOFFEES

3 RIPE BANANAS

juice of 1 LEMON

400g | 14oz SWEETENED
CONDENSED MILK

450ml | ¾ pint | scant 2 cups
WHIPPING CREAM

chopped TOFFEES, to decorate

COOK'S TIP *If making this ice cream for small children, you may prefer to use chopped chocolate instead of toffee.*

1 Unwrap the toffees and chop them as finely as possible, or if too firm to chop, put in a plastic bag and beat with a rolling pin or small hammer. (Make sure that the toffees are very finely crushed or they will make extremely hard lumps when they are frozen.)

2 Slice the bananas into a food processor, add the lemon juice and process until smooth. Pour in the condensed milk and process again to combine.

3 Mix the banana mixture with the cream and pour into the ice cream maker. Churn to a very soft scoop consistency and stir in the toffees.

4 Churn for 1–2 minutes to mix in. Transfer to a freezer container, cover and freeze for at least 2 hours before serving.

5 Scoop into bowls and serve scattered with extra toffees.

Rum and Raisin Ice Cream

For children this ice cream always seemed so much more sophisticated than mere vanilla. The longer you can leave the raisins to soak in the rum, the stronger the flavour will be.

SERVES FOUR TO SIX

INGREDIENTS

150g | 5oz | scant 1 cup
LARGE RAISINS

60ml | 4 tbsp DARK RUM

4 EGG YOLKS

75g | 3oz | 6 tbsp LIGHT
MUSCOVADO (MOLASSES) SUGAR

5ml | 1 tsp CORNFLOUR
(CORNSTARCH)

300ml | ½ pint | 1¼ cups
SEMI-SKIMMED (LOW-FAT) MILK

300ml | ½ pint | 1¼ cups
WHIPPING CREAM

DESSERT BISCUITS (COOKIES)

1 Put the raisins in a bowl, add the rum and mix together well. Cover the bowl and leave the raisins to soak for 3–4 hours or overnight.

2 Whisk the egg yolks, muscovado sugar and cornflour in a large bowl until the mixture is thick and foamy. Pour the milk into a heavy pan, and bring it to just below boiling point.

3 Gradually whisk the milk into the eggs, then pour the mixture back into the pan.

4 Cook over a gentle heat, stirring constantly until the custard thickens and is smooth. Take the pan off the heat and leave to cool.

5 Pour the cream into the custard, then churn until thick. Transfer to a plastic container.

6 Fold the soaked raisins into the ice cream, cover and freeze for 2–3 hours or until firm enough to scoop.

7 Serve in bowls or tall glasses with dessert biscuits.

COOK'S TIP *If you prefer, scoop the ice cream into cones. It will serve 6–8 people. If you haven't any dark rum, white rum, brandy or even whisky can be used instead.*

Mango and Passion Fruit Gelato

Fresh and fruity, this tropical ice cream has a delicate perfume and a delectable flavour and makes a refreshing dessert or snack during the hot summer months. Passion fruit tend to vary in size; if you can locate the large ones, four will be plenty for this dish.

2 Turn the slices inside out so that the pieces of mango stand proud of the skin, then scoop them into a food processor or blender, using a spoon. Finally, cut the remaining flesh away from the stones and add it to the rest.

3 Process the mango flesh until smooth, then add the grated lime rind, lime juice and caster sugar and process briefly.

4 Churn the fruit mixture in an ice cream maker for 10–15 minutes, then add the cream and continue to churn until the mixture is thick but still too soft to scoop. Scrape it into a plastic tub.

5 Cut the passion fruit in half and scoop the seeds and pulp into the ice cream mixture, mix well and freeze for 2 hours until firm enough to scoop.

SERVES FOUR

INGREDIENTS

4 LARGE MANGOES

grated rind and juice of 1 LIME

50g | 2oz | ¼ cup CASTER (SUPERFINE) SUGAR

300ml | ½ pint | 1¼ cups WHIPPING CREAM

4–6 PASSION FRUIT

1 Cut a thick slice from either side of the stone (pit) on each unpeeled mango. Using a sharp knife, make criss-cross cuts in the mango flesh, cutting down as far as the skin.

Apricot Parfait

Dried apricot purée adds a lively, fruity flavour to a creamy smooth ice cream, particularly when it is laced with orange liqueur. The caramelized sugar decoration isn't, of course, essential but it sets off the delicate colour of the ice cream.

SERVES SIX

INGREDIENTS

75g | 3oz | scant 1 cup DEMERARA (RAW) SUGAR

200g | 7oz | scant 1 cup DRIED APRICOTS

250ml | 8fl oz | 1 cup APPLE JUICE

60ml | 4 tbsp COINTREAU or GRAND MARNIER

4 EGG YOLKS

75g | 3oz | 6 tbsp CASTER (SUPERFINE) SUGAR

5ml | 1tsp CORNFLOUR (CORNSTARCH)

300ml | ½ pint | 1¼ cups FULL CREAM (WHOLE) MILK

300ml | ½ pint | 1¼ cups DOUBLE (HEAVY) CREAM

grated rind and juice of ½ LEMON

1 Preheat the grill (broiler) to its lowest setting. Line a baking sheet with foil and mark six 10cm | 4in circles on to the foil. Sprinkle the demerara sugar into the circles. Heat under the grill for about 3–4 minutes, watching closely, until the sugar has caramelized. Leave to cool.

2 Finely chop 50g | 2oz | ¼ cup of the apricots and reserve on one side. Roughly chop the remainder and put in a pan with the apple juice.

3 Simmer the apricots and apple juice for 10 minutes until the apricots are soft and plump. Leave to cool then blend until smooth and stir in the liqueur.

4 Whisk the egg yolks, sugar and cornflour in a bowl until light and frothy. Bring the milk just to the boil in a heavy pan. Pour the milk over the whisked mixture, whisking well to combine.

5 Pour the custard back into the pan and cook over a very gentle heat, stirring until slightly thickened. Pour into a bowl and leave to cool completely.

6 Stir the cream and apricot purée into the custard, pour into the ice cream maker and churn until thick. Tip in the chopped apricots and churn lightly to mix in. Turn into a freezer container and freeze until ready to serve.

7 Scoop the ice cream into small bowls. Break the caramelized sugar into chunky pieces and use to decorate.

COOK'S TIP *The sugared decorations will slowly soften if left exposed. If making them in advance, loosen them from the foil and cover with very lightly oiled clear film (plastic wrap). Store in a cool place.*

Pineapple Crush

Look out for pineapples that are labelled "extra sweet". This variety has bright sunflower-yellow flesh that is naturally sweet and juicy. It is ideal for making the most wonderful ice cream.

SERVES FOUR TO SIX

INGREDIENTS

2 EXTRA-SWEET PINEAPPLES

300ml | ½ pint | 1¼ cups
WHIPPING CREAM

50g | 2oz | ¼ cup CASTER
(SUPERFINE) SUGAR

1 Slice one pineapple in half through the leafy top, then scoop out the flesh from both halves, keeping the shells intact. Drain them upside down, wrap in clear film (plastic wrap) and chill.

2 Trim the top off the remaining pineapple, cut the flesh into slices, then cut away the skin and any "eyes". Remove the core from each slice, then finely chop the flesh from both pineapples.

3 Purée 300g | 11oz of the pineapple in a food processor or blender. Set aside the remaining chopped pineapple.

4 Churn the pineapple purée with the sugar for 15–20 minutes. Mix in the cream and churn until thick but still too soft to scoop.

5 Add the pineapple to the ice cream maker and continue to churn the ice cream until it is stiff enough to serve in scoops.

6 Serve the ice cream in scoops in the pineapple shells. Offer any remaining pineapple separately. Fold in 175g | 6oz | 1½ cups of the chopped pineapple and freeze for 2–3 hours before serving.

VARIATION *This ice cream is also delicious mixed with meringues: crumble four meringue nests into the ice cream mixture when adding the finely chopped pineapple.*

Peach and Cardamom Yogurt Ice

SERVES FOUR

INGREDIENTS

8 CARDAMOM PODS

6 PEACHES,
total weight about 500g | 1¼lb,
halved, and stoned (pitted)

75g | 3oz | 6 tbsp CASTER
(SUPERFINE) SUGAR

30ml | 2 tbsp WATER

200ml | 7fl oz | scant 1 cup
NATURAL (PLAIN) YOGURT

The velvety texture of this smooth peach ice cream spiced with cardamom suggests it is made with cream, but the secret ingredient is actually natural yogurt; great for those watching their waistline.

1 Crush the cardamom pods with the bottom of a ramekin.

2 Chop the peaches roughly and put them in a pan. Add the crushed cardamom pods, with their black seeds, and the sugar and water. Cover the pan and simmer for 10 minutes or until the fruit is tender. Leave to cool.

3 Tip the peach mixture into a food processor or blender, process until smooth, then press through a sieve placed over a bowl.

4 Churn the purée in an ice cream machine until it is thick, then scrape it into a plastic tub and stir in the yogurt.

5 Freeze the purée and yogurt mixture until it is firm enough to scoop.

COOK'S TIP *Use bio natural (plain) yogurt for its extra mild taste. Greek yogurt or ordinary natural yogurt are both sharper and more acidic and tend to overwhelm the delicate taste of the peaches. You could use crème fraîche in place of the yogurt for a slightly richer, creamier flavour.*

6 Using a melon baller, scoop on to a large platter and serve at once.

Rhubarb and Ginger Ice Cream

This "fruit" was so highly favoured by Queen Victoria that two varieties were grown and named after her and her consort Prince Albert. The classic combination of gently poached rhubarb and chopped ginger is brought up to date by blending it with mascarpone to make this pretty blush-pink ice cream.

SERVES FOUR TO SIX

INGREDIENTS

5 pieces of PRESERVED
STEM GINGER

450g | 1lb trimmed RHUBARB, sliced

115g | 4oz | ½ cup CASTER
(SUPERFINE) SUGAR

30ml | 2 tbsp WATER

150g | 5oz | ⅔ cup MASCARPONE

150ml | ¼ pint | ⅔ cup
WHIPPING CREAM

WAFER CUPS, to serve (optional)

1 Using a sharp knife, roughly chop the stem ginger and set it aside. Put the rhubarb slices into a pan and add the sugar and water. Cover and simmer for 5 minutes until the rhubarb is just tender and still bright pink.

2 Tip the mixture into a food processor or blender, process until smooth, then leave to cool. Chill if time permits.

3 Churn the rhubarb purée in an ice cream maker for 15–20 minutes until it is thick.

VARIATION *If the rhubarb purée is rather pale, add a few drops of pink food colouring when you put the mixture in the blender.*

4 Put the mascarpone into a bowl, soften it with a wooden spoon, then gradually beat in the cream. Add the chopped ginger, then transfer to the ice cream maker and churn until the ice cream is firm. Serve as scoops in bowls or wafer baskets.

Nougat Ice Cream

Flavoured with traditional nougat ingredients – nuts, candied peel and orange flower water, this ice cream also imitates nougat in the way it's sandwiched between layers of rice paper. For convenience, let the ice cream freeze until firm, then cut it up and return to the freezer so it's ready to serve.

SERVES SIX

INGREDIENTS

50g | 2oz | ½ cup HAZELNUTS

50g | 2oz | ½ cup PISTACHIO NUTS

50g | 2oz | ⅓ cup CANDIED PEEL

4-6 sheets RICE PAPER

3 EGG YOLKS

30ml | 2 tbsp ORANGE FLOWER WATER

75g | 3oz | 6 tbsp CASTER (SUPERFINE) SUGAR

5ml | 1tsp CORNFLOUR (CORNSTARCH)

300ml | ½ pint | 1¼ cups FULL CREAM (WHOLE) MILK

300ml | ½ pint | 1¼ cups EXTRA THICK DOUBLE (HEAVY) CREAM

3 Whisk together the egg yolks, orange flower water, sugar and cornflour in a bowl until light and frothy. Bring the milk just to the boil in a heavy pan.

4 Pour the boiling milk over the yolk mixture, whisking together well to combine.

5 Pour the custard back into the pan and cook it over a very gentle heat, stirring continuously until the mixture has slightly thickened. Take off the heat.

6 Pour the custard back into the bowl, cover with a circle of baking parchment and leave to cool completely.

7 Stir in both types of cream, pour into the ice cream maker and churn until thick. Sprinkle in the nuts and churn again until just mixed. Spoon the ice cream into the paper-lined tin, spreading it in an even layer. Cover with another layer of rice paper. Freeze for at least 4 hours, or overnight, until firm.

8 To serve, invert the tin on to a board and remove the clear film. Cut the ice cream into squares or triangles, pile up on a plate and serve.

VARIATION *Use toasted blanched almonds instead of pistachios if you prefer. The meringue can be flavoured with rose water or grated lemon rind instead of orange flower water.*

1 Spread out the hazelnuts on a baking sheet and brown them lightly under a hot grill (broiler). Mix with the pistachio nuts and roughly chop. Chop the candied peel.

2 Line the base and sides of a 28 x 18 x 4cm | 11 x 7 x 1½in shallow baking tin (pan) with clear film (plastic wrap), then with a layer of rice paper, making sure you overlap the sheets slightly.

Maple and Pecan Nut Ice Cream

This all-American ice cream is even more delicious when it is served with extra maple syrup and topped with whole pecan nuts.

SERVES FOUR TO SIX

INGREDIENTS

115g | 4oz | 1 cup PECAN NUTS

4 EGG YOLKS

50g | 2oz | ¼ cup CASTER
(SUPERFINE) SUGAR

5ml | 1 tsp CORNFLOUR
(CORNSTARCH)

300ml | ½ pint | 1¼ cups
SEMI-SKIMMED (LOW-FAT) MILK

60ml | 4 tbsp MAPLE SYRUP

300ml | ½ pint | 1¼ cups
WHIPPING CREAM

extra MAPLE SYRUP AND PECAN
NUTS, to serve

1 Cut the pecan nuts in half lengthways, spread them out on a baking sheet and grill (broil) them under a moderate heat for 2–3 minutes until lightly browned. Remove the pecan nuts from the heat and leave to cool.

2 Place the egg yolks, sugar and cornflour in a bowl and whisk until thick and foamy. Pour the milk into a heavy pan, bring to the boil, then gradually whisk it into the yolk mixture.

3 Return the mixture to the pan and cook over a gentle heat, stirring constantly until the custard thickens and is smooth.

4 Pour the custard back into the bowl, and stir in the maple syrup.

5 Leave the mixture to cool in the bowl, then chill in the refrigerator until it is completely cold.

6 Stir the cream into the custard, then churn the mixture in an ice cream maker until thick. Scrape into a plastic container.

7 Fold in the nuts. Freeze for 2–3 hours until firm enough to scoop into dishes. Pour extra maple syrup over each portion and top with extra pecan nuts.

COOK'S TIP *Avoid "maple-flavoured" syrup, which can taste harsh and have a rather synthetic flavour. Look out for "pure maple syrup" on the label.*

Rocky Road Ice Cream

This American classic ice cream is a mouth-watering combination of roughly crushed nut brittle, rich vanilla custard and whipping cream.

SERVES FOUR TO SIX

INGREDIENTS

4 EGG YOLKS

5ml | 1 tsp CORNFLOUR (CORNSTARCH)

225g | 8oz | generous 1 cup SUGAR

300ml | ½ pint | 1¼ cups SEMI-SKIMMED (LOW-FAT) MILK

10ml | 2 tsp NATURAL VANILLA ESSENCE (EXTRACT)

OIL, for greasing

50g | 2oz | ½ cup MACADAMIA NUTS

50g | 2oz | ½ cup HAZELNUTS

50g | 2oz | ½ cup FLAKED (SLICED) ALMONDS

60ml | 4 tbsp WATER

300ml | ½ pint | 1¼ cups WHIPPING CREAM

1 Put the egg yolks in a bowl and stir in the cornflour, with 75g | 3oz | 6 tbsp of the sugar. Whisk until the mixture has turned thick and foamy. Pour the milk into a heavy pan, bring it to the boil, then gradually whisk it into the yolk mixture in the bowl.

2 Return the mixture to the pan. Cook over a gentle heat, stirring constantly until the custard thickens and is smooth.

3 Pour it back into the bowl and stir in the natural vanilla essence. Leave to cool, then chill.

COOK'S TIP *If the nuts fail to brown evenly when you are making the nut brittle (praline) in the frying pan, don't stir the syrup. Instead, tilt the pan first one way then the other.*

4 Grease a large baking sheet with oil. Put the remaining sugar in a large, heavy frying pan, sprinkle the nuts on top and pour over the water.

5 Heat gently, without stirring, until the sugar has dissolved completely, then boil the syrup for 3–5 minutes until it is just beginning to turn golden.

6 Quickly pour the nut mixture on to the oiled baking sheet and leave it to cool and harden.

7 Stir the cream into the custard and churn in an ice cream maker until stiff but too soft to scoop. Scrape into a tub.

8 Smash the nut brittle with a rolling pin to break off about a third. Reserve this for the decoration.

9 Put the rest of the praline into a strong plastic bag and hit it several times with a rolling pin until it breaks into bite-size pieces.

10 Fold the crushed praline into the ice cream and freeze it for 2–3 hours until firm.

11 Scoop the ice cream into glasses and decorate with the reserved praline, broken into large pieces.

Cashew and Orange Flower Ice Cream

Delicately perfumed with orange flower water and a little orange rind, this nutty, lightly sweetened ice cream evokes images of puddings that are popular in the Middle East.

SERVES FOUR TO SIX

INGREDIENTS

4 EGG YOLKS

75g | 3oz | 6 tbsp CASTER (SUPERFINE) SUGAR

5ml | 1 tsp CORNFLOUR (CORNSTARCH)

300ml | ½ pint | 1¼ cups SEMI-SKIMMED (LOW-FAT) MILK

300ml | ½ pint | 1¼ cups WHIPPING CREAM

150g | 5oz | 1¼ cups CASHEW NUTS, finely chopped

15ml | 1 tbsp ORANGE FLOWER WATER

grated rind of ½ ORANGE, plus CURLS OF THINLY PARED ORANGE RIND, to decorate

1 Whisk the egg yolks, caster sugar and cornflour in a bowl until the mixture is thick and foamy. Pour the semi-skimmed milk into a heavy pan, gently bring it to the boil, then gradually whisk it into the egg yolk mixture.

2 Return to the pan and cook over a gentle heat, stirring constantly until smooth. Pour back into the bowl. Cool, then chill.

3 Heat the cream in a small pan. When it boils, stir in the chopped cashew nuts. Leave to cool.

4 Stir the orange flower water and grated orange rind into the chilled custard. Process the nut cream in a food processor or blender until it forms a fine paste, then stir it into the custard mixture.

5 Churn the mixture until it is firm enough to scoop.

6 Thinly pare the orange rind, then wrap each strip in turn around a cocktail stick (toothpick) and leave it for a minute or two.

7 To serve, scoop the ice cream into dishes and decorate each portion with an orange rind curl.

Pistachio Ice Cream

SERVES FOUR TO SIX

This continental favourite owes its enduring popularity to its delicate pale green colour and distinctive yet subtle flavour. Buy the pistachio nuts as you need them, as they quickly go stale if left in the cupboard.

INGREDIENTS

4 EGG YOLKS

75g | 3oz | 6 tbsp CASTER (SUPERFINE) SUGAR

5ml | 1 tsp CORNFLOUR (CORNSTARCH)

300ml | ½ pint | 1¼ cups SEMI-SKIMMED (LOW-FAT) MILK

115g | 4oz | 1 cup PISTACHIOS, plus a few extra, to decorate

300ml | ½ pint | 1¼ cups WHIPPING CREAM

a little GREEN FOOD COLOURING

CHOCOLATE-DIPPED WAFFLE CONES, to serve (optional)

1 Place the egg yolks, sugar and cornflour in a bowl and whisk until the mixture is thick and foamy.

2 Pour the milk into a heavy pan, gently bring it to the boil, then gradually whisk it into the egg yolk mixture.

3 Return the mixture to the pan and cook it over a gentle heat, stirring constantly until the custard thickens and is smooth. Pour it back into the bowl, set aside to cool, then chill in the refrigerator until required.

4 Shell the pistachios and put them in a food processor or blender. Add 30ml | 2 tbsp of the cream and grind the mixture to a coarse paste.

5 Pour the rest of the cream into a small pan. Bring it to the boil, stir in the coarsely ground pistachios, then leave to cool.

6 Mix the chilled custard and pistachio cream together and tint the mixture delicately with a few drops of food colouring.

COOK'S TIP *Bought waffle cones can be decorated by dipping them in melted chocolate and sprinkling them with extra chopped pistachios.*

7 Churn the mixture in an ice cream maker until firm enough to scoop. Serve in cones or dishes, sprinkled with extra pistachios.

modern
favourites

From rich, gooey chocolate brownies to crunchy, tangy strawberry pavlova, this chapter incorporates all of the family favourites, transforming hot and cold puddings and teatime cakes into delicious ice creams. This modern twist on classic treats will be loved by young and old alike.

White Chocolate and Brownie Ice Cream

This recipe combines an irresistible contrast between creamy white chocolate ice cream and chocolate brownie pieces. Use good quality, bought chocolate brownies, or better still, make your own.

SERVES SIX

INGREDIENTS

4 EGG YOLKS

2.5ml | ½tsp CORNFLOUR (CORNSTARCH)

300ml | ½ pint | 1¼ cups FULL CREAM (WHOLE) MILK

200g | 7oz WHITE CHOCOLATE, CHOPPED

200g | 7oz CHOCOLATE BROWNIES

300ml | ½ pint | 1¼ cups WHIPPING CREAM

1 Put the egg yolks and cornflour in a bowl and whisk lightly to combine. Bring the milk to the boil in a heavy pan. Pour the milk over the whisked mixture, whisking well to combine.

2 Pour the custard back into the pan and cook over a very gentle heat, stirring continually until slightly thickened.

3 Pour into a bowl and add the chopped chocolate. Leave until the chocolate has melted, stirring frequently. Leave to cool.

4 Crumble the brownies into small pieces. Stir the cream into the chocolate custard and pour into the ice cream maker. Churn the mixture until it is thick.

5 Sprinkle the crumbled brownies over the custard and churn until just mixed. Scoop into glasses or transfer to a freezer container and freeze until ready to serve.

VARIATION *As an alternative, you could use chopped dark (bittersweet) chocolate in place of the white chocolate, and white chocolate brownies or "blondies" in place of the dark chocolate brownies.*

Apple Crumble Ice Cream

The flavours of this tangy buttery apple crumble flavoured ice cream are so like the recipe it is based on

that it provides a perfect refreshing alternative to the hot pudding on a summer's day.

SERVES SIX

INGREDIENTS

4 EGG YOLKS

90g | 3½oz | ½ cup CASTER
(SUPERFINE) SUGAR

2.5ml | ½ tsp CORNFLOUR
(CORNSTARCH)

1.5ml | ¼ tsp GROUND CLOVES

300ml | ½ pint | 1¼ CUPS FULL
CREAM (WHOLE) MILK

65g | 2½oz | 9 tbsp PLAIN
(ALL-PURPOSE) FLOUR

40g | 1½oz | 3 tbsp UNSALTED
(SWEET) BUTTER, diced

4 EATING APPLES, peeled, cored
and chopped

300ml | ½ pint | 1¼ cups
WHIPPING CREAM

1 Whisk the egg yolks, 75g | 3oz | scant ½ cup of the sugar, the cornflour and ground cloves in a bowl. Bring the milk just to the boil in a heavy pan.

2 Pour the milk over the whisked mixture, whisking well to combine. Pour the custard back into the pan and cook over a very gentle heat, stirring until slightly thickened. Tip into a bowl and leave to cool completely.

3 Preheat the oven to 200°C | 400°F | Gas 6. Lightly grease a baking sheet. Put the flour in a food processor with the butter and blend until it resembles breadcrumbs.

4 Add the remaining sugar and blend lightly until beginning to bind together. Tip out on to a baking sheet and spread in a thin layer. Bake in the oven for 15–20 minutes until golden. Leave to cool.

5 Put the apples in a heavy pan with 60ml | 4 tbsp of water. Cover with a lid and cook very gently for 10 minutes or until the apples have softened. Tip the cooked apples into a food processor and blend until smooth.

6 Stir the whipping cream into the custard and pour into the ice cream maker. Churn until it has a soft set consistency.

7 Reserve 30ml | 2 tbsp of the crumble mixture and add the remainder to the ice cream maker. Churn very lightly until mixed.

8 Spoon one third of the ice cream into a freezer container and spoon over half the apple purée. Add half the remaining ice cream and the remaining apple puree. Add the rest of the ice cream.

9 Using a knife, very lightly swirl the ingredients together so that the apple is partially mixed into the ice cream. Freeze for at least 2 hours or until ready to serve.

Strawberry Pavlova Ice Cream

This ice cream contains all the ingredients of a pavlova dessert and is equally as good. For best results serve when strawberries are in season and at their sweetest and most delicious.

SERVES SIX

INGREDIENTS

3 EGG YOLKS plus 2 EGG WHITES

150g | 5oz | ¾ cup CASTER (SUPERFINE) SUGAR

5ml | 1tsp VANILLA ESSENCE (EXTRACT)

2.5ml | ½ tsp CORNFLOUR (CORNSTARCH)

300ml | ½ pint | 1¼ cups MILK

300g | 11oz | 2¾ cups STRAWBERRIES

300ml | ½ pint | 1¼ cups DOUBLE (HEAVY) CREAM

STRAWBERRIES, to decorate

VARIATION *You could make this crunchy ice cream using any puréed summer fruits, such as raspberries, redcurrants and blackcurrants or even peaches or nectarines.*

1 Preheat the oven to 140°C | 275°F | Gas 1. Line a baking sheet with baking parchment. Whisk the egg whites thoroughly in a clean bowl until stiff.

2 Gradually whisk in 90g | 3½oz | ½ cup of the sugar, a little at a time, whisking well after each addition until the meringue is stiff and glossy. Whisk in the vanilla with the last of the sugar.

3 Place 8–10 spoonfuls of the mixture on the baking sheet. Bake for about 1 hour or until crispy on the outside. Leave to cool.

4 Mix the remaining sugar in a bowl with the egg yolks and cornflour. Bring the milk just to the boil in a heavy pan. Pour the milk over the whisked mixture, whisking well to combine.

5 Pour the custard back into the pan and cook over a very gentle heat, stirring until slightly thickened. Pour into a bowl and leave to cool completely.

6 Purée the strawberries in a food processor or blender until smooth.

7 Roughly break the meringues into small pieces using your hands. Stir the cream into the custard and pour the mixture into the ice cream maker. Churn until it has a softly set consistency.

8 Scatter a layer of the broken meringues into a freezer container and spoon over a little of the ice cream, spreading it to the edges. Spoon over a little of the strawberry purée.

9 Repeat the layering until all the ingredients are used then press the surface down lightly to level it. Freeze for at least 2 hours or until ready to serve.

10 Scoop the ice cream into glasses and serve decorated with the extra strawberries.

Raspberry Cheesecake Ice Cream

This is a very quick and easy ice cream that looks stunning and tastes gorgeous.

SERVES SIX

INGREDIENTS

300g | 11oz | 2 cups RASPBERRIES

90g | 3½oz | scant 1 cup ICING
(CONFECTIONER'S) SUGAR,
plus 15ml | 1tbsp

200g | 7oz | scant 1 cup CREAM
CHEESE

250g | 9oz | generous 1 cup
MASCARPONE CHEESE

5ml | 1tsp VANILLA ESSENCE
(EXTRACT)

300ml | ½ pint | 1¼ cups DOUBLE
(HEAVY) CREAM

150ml | ¼ pint | ⅔ cup FULL CREAM
(WHOLE) MILK

RASPBERRIES, to decorate

1 Thoroughly blend the raspberries in a food processor or blender until they form a smooth purée. Press the purée through a sieve set over a bowl (to remove any seeds) and stir in 15ml | 1tbsp of the icing sugar. Chill the raspberry purée until it is needed.

2 Beat the cream cheese in a bowl to soften, then beat in the mascarpone, vanilla, cream, milk and remaining icing sugar until smooth. Stir in 60ml | 4 tbsp of the fruit purée. Scrape into the ice cream maker and churn until thick.

3 Transfer one third of the ice cream into a freezer container, spreading it in a thin layer, and spoon over half of the remaining purée. Top with half of the remaining ice cream and the remaining purée. Add the rest of the ice cream.

4 Using a knife, stir through the ice cream two or three times to ripple the flavours together. Freeze for at least 2 hours until set.

5 Serve scooped into glasses, decorated with fresh raspberries.

VARIATION *As an alternative, use really full-flavoured strawberries instead of raspberries to ripple the cheesecake cream.*

Lemon Meringue Ice Cream

This ice cream contains the delicious combination of tangy lemon and sweet, crunchy pieces of meringue.

SERVES SIX

INGREDIENTS

4 EGG YOLKS, plus 2 EGG WHITES

150g | 5oz | ¾ cup CASTER (SUPERFINE) SUGAR

finely grated rind of 2 LEMONS, plus 60ml | 4 tbsp JUICE

2.5ml | ½ tsp CORNFLOUR (CORNSTARCH)

300ml | ½ pint | 1¼ cups MILK

130g | 4½oz LEMON CURD

300ml | ½ pint | 1¼ CUPS WHIPPING CREAM

1 Preheat the oven to 140°C | 275°F | Gas 1. Line a baking sheet with baking parchment.

2 Whisk the egg whites in a clean bowl until stiff. Gradually whisk in 90g | 3½oz | ½ cup of the sugar, a little at a time, whisking well after each addition until the meringue is stiff and glossy. Whisk in the lemon rind with the last of the sugar.

3 Place small spoonfuls of the meringue on the baking sheet.

4 Bake in the oven for about 1–1½ hours or until the meringues are crisp. Leave to cool.

5 Mix the remaining sugar in a bowl with the egg yolks and the cornflour. Bring the milk just to the boil in a heavy pan. Pour the milk over the whisked egg yolk and sugar mixture, whisking well to combine.

6 Pour the custard back into the pan and cook over a very gentle heat, stirring continuously until slightly thickened. Turn into a bowl and leave the mixture to cool completely.

7 Lightly crush the cooled meringues. Tip the lemon curd into a bowl and stir in the lemon juice. Add the cream to the custard and pour into the ice cream maker. Churn until the ice cream has a soft set consistency.

8 Spoon a third of the ice cream into a freezer container and scatter with a third of the crushed meringues. Spoon over one third of the lemon sauce. Repeat the layering process, finishing with a layer of sauce.

9 Lightly swirl the mixture together and level the surface. Freeze for at least 2 hours before serving, scooped into glasses.

Black Forest and Kirsch Ice Cream

All the flavours of boozy soaked dark cherries, cream and chocolate sponge combined

in a light ice cream dessert – wicked!

SERVES SIX

INGREDIENTS

425g | 15oz can BLACK CHERRIES

90ml | 6 tbsp KIRSCH

4 EGG YOLKS

75g | 3oz | 6 tbsp CASTER
(SUPERFINE) SUGAR

5ml | 1 tsp CORNFLOUR
(CORNSTARCH)

300ml | ½ pint | 1¼ cups SEMI-
SKIMMED (LOW-FAT) MILK

300ml | ½ pint | 1¼ cups DOUBLE
(HEAVY) CREAM

6 DOUBLE CHOCOLATE
MUFFINS, each one weighing about
75g | 3oz

To decorate

FRESH CHERRIES, on stalks

a little sifted COCOA POWDER
(UNSWEETENED)

1 Drain the cherries, discarding the juice then put into a bowl and spoon over 30ml | 2 tbsp of the Kirsch. Leave to soak for 2 hours or overnight.

2 Whisk the egg yolks, sugar and cornflour together in a bowl until thick and pale. Pour the milk into a heavy pan, bring it just to the boil, then gradually pour it on to the egg yolk mixture, whisking constantly.

3 Return the mixture to the pan and cook over a gentle heat, stirring constantly until the custard thickens and is smooth. Pour it back into the bowl, cover, leave to cool, then chill well.

4 Stir the cream into the custard then pour into an ice cream maker. Churn until thick.

5 Gradually mix in the soaked cherries and any kirsch juices and gently churn together.

6 Meanwhile, cut each muffin into three horizontal slices and drizzle with the remaining Kirsch.

7 To serve, sandwich the muffin slices back together with ice cream, arrange on serving plates and decorate with the fresh cherries and a light dusting of cocoa powder.

COOK'S TIP *The juices from the cherries could be made into a sauce by flavouring with a little extra Kirsch and thickening with a little cornflour (cornstarch).*

Minty Madness Ice Cream

This creamy smooth peppermint ice cream is speckled with crushed peppermints and shards of chocolate-covered peppermint crisps, and looks particularly good served scooped in fine chocolate baskets.

SERVES SIX

INGREDIENTS

4 EGG YOLKS

75g | 3oz | 6 tbsp CASTER (SUPERFINE) SUGAR

5ml | 1 tsp CORNFLOUR (CORNSTARCH)

300ml | ½ pint | 1¼ cups SEMI-SKIMMED (LOW-FAT) MILK

250ml | 8fl oz | 1 cup CRÈME FRAÎCHE

5ml | 1 tsp PEPPERMINT EXTRACT

50g | 2oz MINT IMPERIALS or OTHER HARD MINTS

75g | 3oz CHOCOLATE-COVERED PEPPERMINT CRISPS

CHOCOLATE CASES to serve (see cook's tip)

1 Whisk the egg yolks, sugar and cornflour together in a bowl until thick and pale. Pour the milk into a heavy pan, bring it just to the boil, then gradually pour it on to the yolk mixture, whisking constantly.

2 Return the mixture to the pan and cook over a gentle heat, stirring constantly until the custard thickens and is smooth. Pour it back into the bowl, cover, cool then chill.

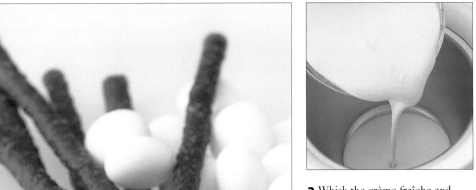

3 Whisk the crème fraîche and peppermint essence into the chilled custard. Pour into an ice cream maker and churn until thick.

VARIATION *If you can't find or do not like mint Imperials you could substitute either more chocolate covered peppermint crisps or some plain chocolate chips for the mint sweets.*

4 Put the mint Imperials into a plastic bag and beat them with a rolling pin until roughly crushed. Roughly chop the chocolate-covered sweets with a knife.

5 Stir both into the ice cream and churn until firm enough to scoop. Transfer to a freezer container and freeze until required.

6 Scoop into glasses or chocolate cases and sprinkle with extra pieces of chocolate-covered peppermint crisps.

COOK'S TIP *To make the chocolate cases: Spread 175g | 6oz melted chocolate over 6 squares of baking parchment to make swirly edged circles about 13cm | 5in in diameter. Drape over upturned tumblers so that the chocolate is on the outside.*
Leave to cool and harden, transferring to the refrigerator if needed. Ease off the tumblers then gently peel away the paper from inside the cups.

Ginger Crunch Ice Cream

This ice cream features smooth mascarpone cheese mixed with vanilla custard and flavoured with hot peppery stem ginger and crunchy pieces of ginger nut biscuit. Serve on its own or on thin slices of gingerbread.

SERVES SIX

INGREDIENTS

4 EGG YOLKS

75g | 3oz | 6 tbsp CASTER (SUPERFINE) SUGAR

5ml | 1 tsp CORNFLOUR (CORNSTARCH)

300ml | ½ pint | 1¼ cups SEMI-SKIMMED (LOW-FAT) MILK

250g | 9 oz | generous 1 cup MASCARPONE CHEESE

5ml | 1 tsp VANILLA ESSENCE (EXTRACT)

50g | 2oz PRESERVED STEM GINGER, drained and finely chopped

75g | 3oz GINGER NUT BISCUITS (GINGERSNAPS), sliced

PRESERVED STEM GINGER, to decorate

1 Whisk the egg yolks, sugar and cornflour together in a bowl until thick and pale. Pour the milk into a heavy pan, bring it just to the boil, then gradually pour it on to the egg yolk mixture, whisking constantly.

2 Return the mixture to the pan and cook over a gentle heat, stirring constantly until the custard thickens and is smooth.

3 Pour it back into the bowl, add the mascarpone cheese and vanilla essence and whisk until the cheese has melted. Cover, leave to cool, then chill.

4 Mix the chopped ginger into the mascarpone custard then pour into an ice cream maker. Churn until softly spoonable.

COOK'S TIP *It is best to eat this ice cream soon after you have made it or else the biscuits may lose some of their crunch.*

5 Put the biscuits in a strong plastic bag and break into small pieces with a rolling pin, or snap into pieces by hand.

6 Spoon the ice cream into a freezer container, mix in the broken biscuits, cover and transfer to the freezer for 2 hours or until firm enough to scoop.

7 Scoop the ice cream into dishes and decorate with a little extra sliced stem ginger.

Rainbow Ice Cream

Speckled with roughly chopped sugar-coated sweets this will soon be a family favourite with youngsters and adults alike, and it is especially good at children's parties.

SERVES SIX

INGREDIENTS

4 EGG YOLKS

75g | 3oz | 6 tbsp CASTER (SUPERFINE) SUGAR

5ml | 1 tsp CORNFLOUR (CORNSTARCH)

300ml | ½ pint | 1¼ cups SEMI-SKIMMED (LOW-FAT) MILK

300ml | ½ pint | 1¼ cups DOUBLE (HEAVY) CREAM

5ml | 1 tsp VANILLA ESSENCE (EXTRACT)

115g | 4oz SUGAR-COATED CHOCOLATE SWEETS (M&M's or Smarties)

WHOLE SWEETS (CANDIES), to decorate

1 Whisk the egg yolks, sugar and cornflour together in a bowl until thick and pale. Pour the milk into a heavy pan, bring it just to the boil, then gradually pour it on to the egg yolk mixture, whisking constantly.

COOK'S TIP *The sugar coating on the sweets will dissolved slightly into the ice cream, but this just adds to the swirly coloured effect.*

2 Return the mixture to the pan and cook over a gentle heat, stirring constantly until the custard thickens and is smooth.

3 Pour it back into the bowl, cover, leave to cool, then chill.

4 Mix the cream and vanilla essence into the cooled custard, then pour into an ice cream maker. Churn until thick.

5 Roughly chop the sweets, stir them into the ice cream and churn for a minute or two until firm enough to scoop. Transfer to a plastic container and freeze until it is required.

6 Scoop into glasses or cones and decorate with a few whole sweets.

Christmas Pudding Ice Cream

This ice cream is lighter than a traditional Christmas pudding, but with all the festive flavours.

SERVES SIX

INGREDIENTS

75g | 3oz | ½ cup MIXED DRIED FRUIT

50g | 2oz | ¼ cup DRIED APRICOTS, diced

50g | 2oz | ¼ CUP GLACÉ (CANDIED) CHERRIES, quartered

1.5ml | ¼ tsp GROUND CINNAMON

1 ORANGE, grated rind and juice

30ml | 2 tbsp SWEET SHERRY or BRANDY

4 EGG YOLKS

75g | 3oz | scant 1 cup CASTER (SUPERFINE) SUGAR

5ml | 1 tsp CORNFLOUR (CORNSTARCH)

300ml | ½ pint | 1¼ cups SEMI-SKIMMED (LOW-FAT) MILK

250ml | 8fl oz | 1 cup CRÈME FRAÎCHE

5ml | 1 tsp VANILLA ESSENCE (EXTRACT)

50g | 2oz | ½ cup PISTACHIO NUTS, HAZELNUTS or PECAN NUTS, or a mixture, roughly chopped

CHOCOLATE HOLLY LEAVES, to decorate (see Cook's tip)

THIN SHORTBREAD BISCUITS, to serve

1 Put the dried fruits, cherries, cinnamon, orange rind and juice and sherry or brandy in a small pan and bring the liquid just to the boil. Turn off the heat and leave to cool for 2 hours or overnight to allow the fruit to plump up.

3 When the custard thickens and is smooth, pour it back into the bowl. Cover, cool then chill.

4 Whisk the crème fraîche and vanilla essence into the chilled custard, pour into an ice cream maker and churn until thick.

2 Whisk the egg yolks, sugar and cornflour together in a bowl until the mixture is thick and pale. Heat the milk in a pan then gradually whisk into the yolk mixture. Return the mixture to the pan and cook over a gentle heat, stirring constantly.

5 Add the fruits and nuts and churn together briefly until just mixed. Spoon into a freezer container, cover and freeze for 2 hours or until firm enough to scoop.

6 Scoop into glasses, decorate with chocolate holly leaves and serve with thin shortbread biscuits.

COOK'S TIP *Decorate the ice cream with chocolate holly or bay leaves. Paint melted dark (bittersweet) chocolate over washed and dried leaves. Set aside to chill and set and then peel away the leaf to reveal the chocolate copy.*

herb,
spice &
flower ices

For those with an adventurous taste in ice cream, here is an intriguing repertoire of less predictable flavours such as Turkish delight, lavender and even chilli. The ices in the following collection are quick and easy to make, and will have everyone guessing the intrinsic ingredients.

Rosemary Ice Cream

Fresh rosemary has a lovely fragrance that works as well in sweet dishes as it does in savoury.

Serve this ice cream as an accompaniment to soft fruit or plum compote, or on its own,

with amaretti or ratafia biscuits.

SERVES SIX

INGREDIENTS

300ml | ½ pint | 1¼ cups MILK

4 large FRESH
ROSEMARY SPRIGS

3 EGG YOLKS

75g | 3oz | 6 tbsp CASTER
(SUPERFINE) SUGAR

10ml | 2 tsp CORNFLOUR
(CORNSTARCH)

400ml | 14fl oz | 1⅔ cups
CRÈME FRAÎCHE

about 15ml | 1 tbsp DEMERARA
(RAW) SUGAR

FRESH ROSEMARY SPRIGS
and HERB FLOWERS,
to decorate

RATAFIA BISCUITS (COOKIES),
to serve

1 Put the milk and rosemary sprigs in a heavy pan. Bring almost to the boil, remove from the heat and leave to infuse for about 20 minutes. Place the egg yolks in a bowl and whisk in the sugar and the cornflour.

2 Remove the rosemary sprigs. Return the pan to the heat and bring the milk almost to the boil. Gradually pour over the yolk mixture and mix well. Return to the pan and cook over a gentle heat, stirring constantly until it thickens. Do not let it boil.

3 Strain the custard through a sieve into a bowl. Cover the surface of the custard closely with baking parchment and leave the mixture to cool. Chill the custard until it is very cold, then stir in the crème fraîche, mixing well to combine thoroughly..

4 Churn the mixture in an ice cream maker until it is thick, then scrape it into a tub or similar freezerproof container. Freeze until ready to serve.

5 Soften the ice cream in the refrigerator for 30 minutes before serving. Scoop into dessert dishes, sprinkle lightly with demerara sugar and decorate with fresh rosemary sprigs and herb flowers. Serve with ratafia biscuits.

COOK'S TIP *For a stylish and attractive effect, use sprigs or petals of herb flowers that complement the colour of your dessert dishes.*

Lavender and Honey Ice Cream

Lavender and honey make a memorable partnership in this old-fashioned and elegant ice cream.

Serve scooped into glasses or set in little moulds and top with lightly whipped cream.

Pretty lavender flowers add the finishing touch.

SERVES SIX TO EIGHT

INGREDIENTS

90ml | 6 tbsp CLEAR HONEY

4 EGG YOLKS

10ml | 2 tsp CORNFLOUR
(CORNSTARCH)

8 LAVENDER SPRIGS,
plus extra, to decorate

450ml | ¾ pint | scant 2 cups MILK

450ml | ¾ pint | scant 2 cups
WHIPPING CREAM

DESSERT BISCUITS (COOKIES),
to serve

1 Put the honey, egg yolk, and cornflour in a bowl. Separate the lavender flowers and add them to the bowl, plus a little milk. Whisk lightly. In a heavy pan bring the remaining milk just to the boil. Add the hot milk to the egg yolk mixture, stirring well.

2 Return the mixture to the pan and cook very gently, stirring until the mixture thickens. Pour the custard into a bowl, cover the surface closely with a circle of baking parchment and leave to cool, then chill the mixture until it is very cold.

3 Stir the cream into the custard, then churn the mixture in an ice cream maker until it holds its shape. Transfer to a tub or similar freezerproof container and freeze until ready to serve.

4 Soften the ice cream in the refrigerator for 30 minutes before serving. Scoop into small dishes, decorate with lavender flowers and serve with dessert biscuits.

COOK'S TIP *For a stronger lavender flavour use lavender honey.*

Strawberry and Rose Water Ice Cream

A light, delicate ice cream made with strawberry purée, thick creamy Greek yogurt and just a hint of rose water

If you can't get fresh strawberries, then thawed frozen ones will work just as well.

SERVES FOUR TO SIX

INGREDIENTS

450g | 1lb | 4 cups STRAWBERRIES

2 EGG WHITES

75g | 3oz | 6 tbsp CASTER (SUPERFINE) SUGAR

300ml | ½ pint | 1¼ cups GREEK (US STRAINED PLAIN) YOGURT

15-20ml | 3–4 tsp ROSE WATER

To decorate

small STRAWBERRIES, halved

ROSE PETALS, washed and dried

tiny, CRISP BISCUITS (COOKIES)

1 Wash and hull the strawberries, then place them in a liquidiser or food processor and purée until smooth. Press the purée through a sieve into a bowl and discard the seeds.

2 Whisk the egg whites until they form stiff, moist-looking peaks. Gradually whisk in the sugar one teaspoon at a time and continue whisking for several more minutes until thick and glossy.

3 Fold the strawberry purée into the meringue mixture, then fold in the yogurt. Add enough rose water to taste (see Cook's Tip).

4 Pour into an ice cream maker and churn until thick enough to scoop. Transfer to a freezer container and freeze until required.

5 Spoon into dishes and decorate with halved strawberries and rose petals. Serve with tiny crisp biscuits.

COOK'S TIP *Rose water varies in strength, so add it drop by drop and taste the mixture as you go.*

If you happen to have pink roses in the garden, then decorate the scooped ice cream with a few pink petals for an extra special touch.

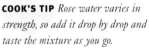

Peppermint Swirl Ice Cream

Delicately marbled with a pale green tinged syrup, this sophisticated yogurt ice cream is ideal for serving after a rich main course.

SERVES SIX

INGREDIENTS

75g | 3oz | 6 tbsp CASTER (SUPERFINE) SUGAR

60ml | 4 tbsp WATER

10 large FRESH PEPPERMINT SPRIGS

5ml | 1 tsp PEPPERMINT ESSENCE (EXTRACT)

450ml | ¾ pint | scant 2 cups DOUBLE (HEAVY) CREAM

a few drops of GREEN FOOD COLOURING

200ml | 7fl oz | scant 1 cup GREEK (US STRAINED PLAIN) YOGURT

To decorate

FRESH MINT LEAVES

sifted ICING (CONFECTIONER'S) SUGAR

1 Put the sugar, water and fresh peppermint sprigs in a small heavy pan and heat gently, stirring occasionally, until the sugar has dissolved. Bring to the boil and cook without stirring for about 3 minutes to make a syrup.

2 Strain the syrup into a medium bowl and stir in the peppermint essence then leave to cool.

3 Mix half the peppermint mixture with 30ml | 2 tbsp of the cream and a few drops of food colouring, then chill until required.

4 Mix the remaining mint syrup with the remaining cream and the yogurt. Pour into the ice cream maker and churn until thick.

5 Spoon into a freezer container, adding spoonfuls of the reserved coloured mint cream.

6 Using a dessertspoon handle, gently stir the mixtures together with five or six strokes until it is all marbled together. Freeze the ice cream for 2 hours or until it is firm.

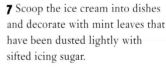

7 Scoop the ice cream into dishes and decorate with mint leaves that have been dusted lightly with sifted icing sugar.

Basil and Orange Sorbet

Basil has a sweet, aromatic flavour that goes very well with citrus fruits. This delicious, fragrant sorbet is refreshing and not too cloying, so it would be perfect after a rich main course or to relax with on a hot summer's afternoon.

SERVES SIX

INGREDIENTS

175g | 6oz | scant 1 cup CASTER (SUPERFINE) SUGAR

105ml | 7 tbsp WATER

30ml | 2 tbsp LEMON or LIME JUICE

500ml | 17fl oz | generous 2 cups FRESHLY SQUEEZED ORANGE JUICE

15g | ½oz FRESH BASIL LEAVES

TINY BASIL LEAVES, to decorate

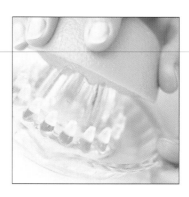

1 Put the sugar and water in a pan and bring slowly to the boil, stirring until all of the sugar has dissolved. Leave the liquid to cool and then stir in the lemon or lime juice.

2 Put half the orange juice in a food processor or blender with the basil leaves and process the mixture in short bursts until the basil has been chopped into small pieces.

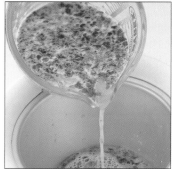

3 Pour the syrup, basil specked orange juice and remaining orange juice into the ice cream maker and churn until thick.

4 Scoop into bowls and decorate with basil leaves or turn into a freezer container and freeze until it is required.

COOK'S TIP *Buy good quality freshly squeezed orange juice, or alternatively you could squeeze your own. You'll need 10-12 small juicing oranges.*

Star Anise and Grapefruit Water Ice

This mildly spiced, refreshing water ice is softer and slushier than a sorbet.

Once the syrup is made, the whole star anise can be set aside for decoration. If the ones you buy

are broken up, use the equivalent of six whole ones for the syrup infusion.

SERVES FOUR

INGREDIENTS

200g | 7oz | 1 cup CASTER
(SUPERFINE) SUGAR

300ml | ½ pint | 1¼ cups WATER

6 whole STAR ANISE

4 GRAPEFRUITS

1 Put the sugar and water in a
pan and heat gently, stirring
occasionally, until the sugar has
dissolved. Stir in the star anise
and heat the syrup gently for
2 minutes. Leave to cool.

VARIATION *This water ice could also
be made using blood oranges in place of
the grapefruit for a dramatic and
refreshing alternative.*

2 Take a slice off the top and
base of each grapefruit, then peel
off the skin and pith. If you want
to use the skin as a bowl, slice the
fruit in half and carefully cut out
the flesh, leaving the pith behind.

3 Chop the flesh of the grapefruit
roughly and put it in a food
processor with any juice.

4 Process the grapefruit flesh until
it is almost smooth, then press the
pulp through a sieve into a bowl.
Discard any pith that is left behind
in the sieve.

5 Strain the star anise and sugar
syrup through the sieve into the
bowl containing the strained
grapefruit juice.

6 Pour into the ice cream maker
and churn until the mixture is
thick and slushy.

7 Spoon the water ice into serving
bowls or hollowed-out grapefruit
shells. If you do not want to eat it
immediately, transfer to a freezer
container and freeze until
ready to serve.

Lemon and Cardamom Ice Cream

The classic partnership of lemon and cardamom gives this rich ice cream a lovely "clean" tang. It is the perfect choice after a spicy main course.

SERVES SIX

INGREDIENTS

15ml | 1 tbsp CARDAMOM PODS

4 EGG YOLKS

115g | 4oz CASTER
(SUPERFINE) SUGAR

10ml | 2 tsp CORNFLOUR (CORNSTARCH)

grated rind and juice of 3 LEMONS

300ml | ½ pint | 1¼ cups MILK

300ml | ½ pint | 1¼ cups
WHIPPING CREAM

FRESH LEMON BALM SPRIGS and
ICING (CONFECTIONERS') SUGAR,
to decorate

1 Put the cardamom pods in a mortar and crush them with a pestle to release the seeds. Pick out and discard the shells, then grind the seeds to break them up slightly.

2 Put the egg yolks, sugar, cornflour, lemon rind and juice in a bowl. Add the cardamom seeds and whisk well.

3 Bring the milk to the boil in a heavy pan, then pour it over the egg yolk mixture, stirring well. Return the mixture to the pan and cook gently, stirring until the custard thickens.

4 Pour the custard into a bowl, cover the surface closely with a circle of baking parchment and leave to cool. Chill until very cold.

5 Whisk the cream lightly into the custard and churn the mixture in an ice cream maker until it holds its shape. Transfer to a container and freeze until needed.

6 Soften the ice cream in the refrigerator for 30 minutes before serving. Scoop into glasses and decorate with the lemon balm and sugar.

COOK'S TIP *Lemon balm is an easy herb to grow. The leaves are best picked before the flowering period, when they are at their most fragrant.*

Saffron, Apricot and Almond Cream

SERVES SIX TO EIGHT

This vibrant, chunky ice cream has a slightly Middle Eastern flavour. Although saffron is expensive, its intense colour and distinctive flavour are well worth it, and you only need a small amount.

INGREDIENTS

150g | 5oz | ⅔ cup DRIED APRICOTS

60ml | 4 tbsp COINTREAU

2.5ml | ½ tsp SAFFRON STRANDS, lightly crushed

15ml | 1 tbsp BOILING WATER

3 EGG YOLKS

75g | 3oz | 6 tbsp CASTER (SUPERFINE) SUGAR

10ml | 2 tsp CORNFLOUR (CORNSTARCH)

300ml | ½ pint | 1¼ cups MILK

300ml | ½ pint | 1¼ cups SINGLE (LIGHT) CREAM

75g | 3oz | ¾ cup UNBLANCHED ALMONDS, lightly toasted

AMARETTI, to serve (optional)

1 Chop the apricots into small pieces and put them in a bowl. Add the liqueur and leave for about 1 hour or until absorbed. Put the saffron in a cup with the boiling water and leave to stand while you make the custard.

2 Whisk the egg yolks, sugar and cornflour with a little of the milk in a bowl. Pour the remaining milk into a pan, bring it almost to the boil, then pour it over the yolk mixture, stirring.

3 Return the mixture to the pan and cook it over a very gentle heat, stirring until the custard thickens. Do not let it boil or it may curdle.

4 Stir in the saffron, with its liquid, then cover the surface of the custard with baking parchment and leave it to cool. Chill until it is very cold.

5 Stir in the cream and churn in an ice cream maker until thick. Add the apricots and nuts and churn for 5 minutes more until well mixed. Spoon into a plastic tub or similar freezerproof container and freeze overnight.

6 Soften the ice cream in the refrigerator 30 minutes before serving. Scoop into glasses and serve with amaretti.

COOK'S TIP *This ice cream looks most attractive served in small glasses or little glass cups with handles.*

Ginger and Kiwi Sorbet

This refreshing sorbet combines freshly grated aromatic root ginger with sweet kiwi fruit

SERVES SIX

INGREDIENTS

150g | 2oz FRESH ROOT GINGER

115g | 4oz | ½ cup CASTER (SUPERFINE) SUGAR

300ml | ½ pint | 1¼ cups WATER

5 KIWI FRUIT

FRESH MINT SPRIGS or CHOPPED KIWI FRUIT, to decorate

1 Peel the ginger and grate it finely. Heat the sugar and water in a pan until the sugar has dissolved. Add the ginger and cook for 1 minute, then leave to cool. Strain into a bowl and chill until very cold.

2 Peel the kiwi fruit and blend until smooth. Add the purée to the chilled syrup and mix well.

3 Churn the mixture in an ice cream maker until it thickens. Transfer to a plastic tub or a similar freezerproof container and freeze until ready to serve.

4 Spoon into glasses, decorate with mint sprigs or chopped kiwi fruit, and serve.

Served during or after dinner this unusual but refreshing sorbet is sure to become a talking point.

SERVES SIX

INGREDIENTS

1 FRESH RED CHILLI

finely grated rind and juice of 2 LEMONS

finely grated rind and juice of 2 LIMES

225g | 8oz | 1 cup CASTER (SUPERFINE) SUGAR

750ml | 1¼ pints | 3 cups WATER

PARED LEMON or LIME RIND, to decorate

1 Cut the chilli in half, removing all the seeds and any pith with a small sharp knife, and then chop the flesh very finely.

2 Put the chilli, lemon and lime rind, sugar and water in a heavy pan. Heat gently and stir while the sugar dissolves. Bring to the boil, then simmer for 2 minutes without stirring. Let cool.

3 Add lemon and lime juice to the chilli syrup and chill until very cold.

4 Churn the mixture in an ice cream maker until it holds its shape. Scrape into a container and freeze until ready to serve. Spoon into glasses and decorate with the thinly pared lemon or lime rind.

COOK'S TIP *Use a medium-hot chilli rather than any of the fiery varieties. For an added kick, drizzle with tequila or vodka before serving. To avoid burning your skin, wash your hands after handling the chilli.*

Turkish Delight Sorbet

Anyone who likes Turkish delight will adore the taste and aroma of this intriguing dessert. Because of its sweetness, it is best served in small portions and is delicious with after-dinner coffee. Decorate with drizzled white chocolate and sugared almonds or slices of Turkish delight.

SERVES EIGHT

INGREDIENTS

250g|9oz ROSE WATER-
FLAVOURED TURKISH DELIGHT

25g|1oz|2 tbsp CASTER
(SUPERFINE) SUGAR

750ml|1¼ pints|3 cups WATER

30ml|2 tbsp LEMON JUICE

50g|2oz WHITE CHOCOLATE,
broken into pieces

roughly chopped
SUGARED ALMONDS,
to decorate

1 Cut the cubes of Turkish delight into small pieces. Put half of the pieces in a heavy pan with the sugar. Pour in half of the water. Heat gently until the Turkish delight has dissolved.

2 Cool, then stir in the lemon juice with the remaining water and Turkish delight. Chill well.

3 Churn the mixture in an ice cream maker until it is firm enough to hold its shape.

COOK'S TIP *You will probably find it easiest to use scissors to cut the cubes of Turkish delight into smaller pieces, rather than a knife.*
If you want to serve the ice cream with Turkish delight instead of sugared almonds, thinly slice 50g|2oz and sprinkle over the top of the ice cream.

4 While the sorbet is freezing, dampen eight very small plastic cups or glasses. Line them with clear film (plastic wrap).

5 Spoon the sorbet into the cups and tap them lightly on the surface to compact the mixture. Cover with the overlapping film and freeze for at least 3 hours or overnight.

6 Make a paper piping (pastry) bag. Put the chocolate in a heatproof bowl and melt it over a pan of gently simmering water.

7 Meanwhile, remove the sorbets from the freezer, let them stand at room temperature for 5 minutes, then pull them out of the cups. Transfer to serving plates and peel away the film. Spoon the melted chocolate into the piping bag, snip off the tip and scribble a design on the sorbet and the plate. Scatter the sugared almonds over and serve.

Mulled Wine Sorbet

This dramatic-looking sorbet provides a brief and welcome respite from the general overindulgence that takes place during the festive season, or any other celebration. It is spicy and flavoursome, with quite a powerful kick to revive you from any seasonal sluggishness!

SERVES SIX

INGREDIENTS

1 bottle MEDIUM RED WINE

2 CLEMENTINES or
1 LARGE ORANGE

16 WHOLE CLOVES

2 CINNAMON STICKS, HALVED

1 APPLE, roughly chopped

5ml | 1 tsp MIXED
(APPLE PIE) SPICE

75g | 3oz | scant ½ cup LIGHT
MUSCOVADO (BROWN) SUGAR

150ml | ¼ pint | ⅔ cup WATER

200ml | 7fl oz | scant 1 cup
FRESHLY SQUEEZED
ORANGE JUICE

45ml | 3 tbsp BRANDY

strips of pared ORANGE RIND,
to decorate

1 Pour the bottle of wine into a pan. Stud the clementines or orange with the cloves, then cut them in half.

2 Add to the wine, with the cinnamon sticks, apple, mixed spice, sugar and water. Heat gently, stirring occasionally, until the sugar has dissolved.

3 Cover the pan and cook the mixture gently for 15 minutes. Remove from the heat and leave it to cool.

4 Pour the mixture through a sieve into a large bowl, then stir in the orange juice and brandy. Chill until it is very cold.

5 Churn the mixture in an ice cream maker until it thickens. Transfer to a plastic tub or a similar freezerproof container and freeze until ready to serve.

6 To serve, spoon or scoop into small glasses and decorate with the strips of pared orange rind.

COOK'S TIP *The better the quality of the red wine you use, the better this sorbet will taste, so try to use one of a reasonable standard.*

Elderflower and Lime Yogurt Ice Cream

These fragrant flowerheads have a wonderful flavour, but they are only in season for a very short time. Fortunately, good quality bought or home-made elderflower cordial is readily available and combines beautifully with limes to make a very refreshing iced dessert.

SERVES SIX

INGREDIENTS

4 EGG YOLKS

50g | 2oz | ¼ cup CASTER (SUPERFINE) SUGAR

10ml | 2 tsp CORNFLOUR (CORNSTARCH)

300ml | ½ pint | 1¼ cups MILK

finely grated rind and juice of 2 LIMES

150ml | ¼ pint | ⅔ cup ELDERFLOWER CORDIAL

200ml | 7fl oz | scant 1 cup GREEK (US STRAINED PLAIN) YOGURT

150ml | ¼ pint | ⅔ cup DOUBLE (HEAVY) CREAM

GRATED LIME, to decorate

3 Pour the custard into a bowl and add the lime rind and juice. Pour in the elderflower cordial and mix lightly. Cover the surface of the mixture closely with baking parchment. Leave to cool, then chill until very cold.

4 Stir the yogurt and cream into the chilled mixture and churn in an ice cream maker until it thickens. Transfer the yogurt ice into individual dishes or a plastic container, cover closely and freeze until required.

5 Soften the yogurt ice in the refrigerator 30 minutes before serving. Decorate with the grated lime rind.

COOK'S TIP *Yogurt gives this ice cream a slightly tangier flavour than cream, but you can use cream if you prefer.*

1 Whisk the egg yolks in a bowl with the sugar, cornflour and a little of the milk until it is pale and frothy. Pour the remaining milk into a heavy pan, bring it just to the boil, then pour it over the yolk mixture, whisking constantly until it is smooth.

2 Return the mixture to the pan and cook over a very gentle heat, stirring constantly until the custard thickens. Do not let it boil or the mixture may curdle.

Pomegranate and Orange Flower Water Creams

Take advantage of the availability of fresh pomegranates when in season to make this wonderfully coloured dessert. The colour will range from pastel pink to vibrant cerise, depending on the type of pomegranates used, but whatever shade you achieve the result will be very impressive.

SERVES SIX

INGREDIENTS

10ml | 2 tsp CORNFLOUR (CORNSTARCH)

300ml | ½ pint | 1¼ cups MILK

25g | 1oz | 2 tbsp CASTER (SUPERFINE) SUGAR

2 LARGE POMEGRANATES

30ml | 2 tbsp ORANGE FLOWER WATER

75ml | 5 tbsp GRENADINE

300ml | ½ pint | 1¼ cups WHIPPING CREAM

extra POMEGRANATE SEEDS and ORANGE FLOWER WATER, to serve

1 Put the cornflour in a pan and blend to a paste with a little of the milk. Stir in the remaining milk and the sugar and cook, stirring constantly, until the mixture thickens. Pour it into a bowl, cover the surface closely with baking parchment and leave it to cool.

2 Cut the pomegranates in half and squeeze out the juice, using a lemon squeezer. Add the juice to the cornflour mixture, with the orange flower water, grenadine and cream. Stir lightly to mix.

3 Churn the mixture in an ice cream maker until it is thoroughly combined and thick enough to hold its shape.

4 Spoon the ice cream into one large, or six individual freezerproof serving dishes and freeze for at least 2 hours, or overnight.

5 Soften the frozen creams in the refrigerator for 30 minutes before serving, to allow them to soften. Top each of them with pomegranate seeds tossed in the extra orange flower water.

VARIATION *To accentuate the Middle Eastern flavour of this dessert, the seeds from 12 cardamom pods can be added with the orange flower water.*

cream-free, low-fat & low-sugar ices

Whether for dietary reasons or simply through choice, many people prefer to use low-fat, low sugar and dairy-free ingredients. On the following pages are some intensely flavoured desserts to suit everyone, ranging from a smooth creamy coconut ice to a refreshing orange and yogurt ice.

Kulfi

This famous Indian ice cream is low in sugar and is lightly flavoured with crushed cardamom and finely chopped pistachios. It is traditionally made by slowly boiling milk until it has reduced to almost one third of its original quantity.

SERVES FOUR

INGREDIENTS

1.5 litres | 2½ pints | 6¼ cups
FULL-FAT (WHOLE) MILK

3 CARDAMOM PODS

50g | 2 oz | ¼ cup CASTER
(SUPERFINE) SUGAR

50g | 2oz | ½ cup PISTACHIO NUTS,
SKINNED, FINELY CHOPPED

To decorate

PINK ROSE PETALS, washed
and dried

thinly sliced PISTACHIO NUTS

1 Pour the milk into a large, heavy pan. Bring to the boil, lower the heat and simmer gently for 1 hour, stirring occasionally. Keep a close eye on the pan to prevent the milk from boiling over.

2 Put the cardamom pods in a mortar and crush them with a pestle. Add the pods and the seeds to the milk and continue simmering for 1-1½ hours until the milk has reduced to 600ml | 1 pint | 2½ cups.

3 Pour the milk through a sieve into a jug (pitcher), then stir in the sugar and leave the mixture to cool.

4 Pour into an ice cream maker and churn until thick. Mix in the pistachios and churn briefly to combine thoroughly.

5 Scoop the soft ice cream into kulfi moulds. Freeze until firm, or overnight. Alternatively, you could leave the mixture churning in the ice cream machine until it is firm and then simply scoop into shallow bowls straight from the machine.

6 To unmould the kulfi, half fill a plastic container or bowl with very hot water, stand the moulds in the water and count to ten. Lift out the moulds and invert them on a baking sheet.

7 Transfer the ice creams to a platter or individual plates. Scatter with rose petals and the thinly sliced pistachios.

Dondurma Kaymalki

This sweet, pure white ice cream comes from the Middle East, where it is traditionally thickened with sahlab and flavoured with orange flower water and mastic, a resin used in chewing gum. As sahlab and mastic are both difficult to obtain in the West, cornflour and light condensed milk have been used in their place.

SERVES FOUR TO SIX

INGREDIENTS

45ml | 3 tbsp CORNFLOUR (CORNSTARCH)

600ml | 1 pint | 2½ cups SEMI-SKIMMED (LOW-FAT) MILK

213g | 7½oz can LIGHT CONDENSED MILK

15ml | 1 tbsp CLEAR HONEY

10ml | 2 tsp ORANGE FLOWER WATER

a few SUGARED ALMONDS, to serve

1 Put the cornflour in a pan and mix to a smooth paste with a little of the milk.

2 Stir in the remaining milk and the condensed milk and bring the mixture to the boil, stirring until it has thickened and is smooth. Pour the mixture into a bowl.

3 Stir in the honey and orange flower water. Cover with a plate to prevent the formation of a skin, leave to cool, then chill in the refrigerator until the mixture is completely cold.

4 Churn in an ice cream maker until firm enough to scoop.

5 To serve, scoop into dishes and serve with a few sugared almonds, if liked.

VARIATION *Light condensed milk is surprisingly low in fat, but if you want to make a richer, creamier version, use ordinary sweetened condensed milk and full-fat (whole) milk.*
You could also substitute rose water for the orange flower water.

Coconut Ice

Despite its creamy taste, this ice cream contains neither cream nor egg and is very refreshing.

SERVES FOUR TO SIX

INGREDIENTS

150ml | ¼ pint | ⅔ cup WATER

115g | 4oz | ½ cup CASTER (SUPERFINE) SUGAR

2 LIMES

400ml | 14fl oz can COCONUT MILK

TOASTED COCONUT SHAVINGS, to decorate (see Cook's Tip)

1 Put the water in a small pan. Tip in the caster sugar and bring to the boil, stirring constantly until the sugar has all dissolved. Remove the pan from the heat and leave the syrup to cool, then chill well.

2 Grate the limes finely, taking care to avoid the bitter pith. Squeeze them and pour the juice and rind into the pan of syrup. Add the coconut milk.

3 Churn the mixture in an ice cream maker until firm enough to scoop. Serve in dishes, decorated with the toasted coconut shavings.

COOK'S TIP *Use the flesh from a coconut to make a pretty decoration. Having rinsed the flesh with cold water, cut off thin slices using a swivel-blade vegetable peeler. Toast the slices under a moderate grill (broiler) until the coconut has curled and the edges are golden. Cool slightly, then sprinkle the shavings over the coconut ice.*

Date and Tofu Ice

Generously spiced with cinnamon, this unusal ice cream is packed with soya protein, contains no added sugar, is low in fat and free from all dairy products.

INGREDIENTS

250g | 9oz | 1½ cups STONED (PITTED) DATES

600ml | 1 pint | 2½ cups APPLE JUICE

5ml | 1 tsp GROUND CINNAMON

285g | 10½oz pack CHILLED TOFU, drained and cubed

150ml | ¼ pint | ⅔ cup UNSWEETENED SOYA MILK

1 Put the dates in a pan. Pour in 300ml | ½ pint | 1¼ cups of the apple juice and leave to soak for 2 hours. Simmer for 10 minutes, then leave to cool. Using a slotted spoon, lift out one-quarter of the dates, chop roughly and set aside.

2 Purée the remaining dates in a food processor or blender. Add the cinnamon and process with enough of the remaining apple juice to make a smooth paste.

3 Add the cubes of tofu, a few at a time, processing after each addition. Finally, add the remaining apple juice and the soya milk and mix well to combine.

4 Churn the mixture in an ice cream maker until very thick, but not thick enough to scoop. Scrape into a plastic tub.

VARIATION *You oould make this tasty ice cream with any soft dried fruits; dried figs, apricots or peaches would be especially good. Alternatively you could use a combination for a vitamin- and fibre-packed feast.*

5 Stir in most of the chopped dates and freeze for 2–3 hours until firm.

6 Scoop into dessert glasses and decorate with the remaining chopped dates.

COOK'S TIP *As tofu is a non-dairy product it will not blend completely, so don't be concerned if the mixture contains tiny flecks of tofu.*

Banana Gelato

This mild, creamy banana ice cream is made with soya milk, making it good for children who are lactose intolerant or allergic to dairy products.

SERVES FOUR TO SIX

INGREDIENTS

115g | 4oz | ½ cup CASTER (SUPERFINE) SUGAR

150ml | ¼ pint | ⅔ cup WATER

1 LEMON

3 RIPE BANANAS

300ml | ½ pint | 1¼ cups UHT VANILLA-FLAVOURED SOYA DESSERT

1 Put the sugar and water in a pan. Bring to the boil, stirring until the sugar has dissolved. Cool.

2 Squeeze the lemon. Put the bananas in a bowl and mash with a fork. Slowly add the lemon juice. Stir in the cooled sugar syrup and the soya dessert.

3 Churn in an ice cream maker until thick, then scrape it into a freezerproof container and freeze for 3–4 hours until firm. Scoop into dishes and serve.

COOK'S TIP *This recipe makes 1 litre | 1¾ pints | 4 cups of frozen gelato, so you may need to churn in two batches if your ice cream maker has a small capacity.*

Honeyed Goat's Milk Gelato

Goat's milk is more widely available than it used to be and is more easily tolerated by some individuals than cow's milk. It makes a surprisingly rich iced dessert.

SERVES FOUR

INGREDIENTS

6 EGG YOLKS

50g | 2oz | ¼ cup CASTER (SUPERFINE) SUGAR

10ml | 2 tsp CORNFLOUR (CORNSTARCH)

600ml | 1 pint | 2½ cups GOAT'S MILK

60ml | 4 tbsp CLEAR HONEY

POMEGRANATE SEEDS, to decorate

1 Whisk the egg yolks, sugar and cornflour in a bowl until pale and thick. Pour the goat's milk into a heavy pan, bring it to the boil, and then gradually whisk it into the yolk mixture.

2 Return the custard mixture to the pan and cook over a gentle heat, stirring constantly until the custard thickens and is smooth. Pour it back into the clean bowl.

3 Stir the honey into the milk mixture. Leave to cool, then chill.

4 Churn the chilled mixture in an ice cream maker until thick enough to scoop.

5 To serve, scoop into dessert glasses and decorate with a few pomegranate seeds.

COOK'S TIP *Make sure the spoon measures are level or the honey flavour will be too dominant.*

VARIATION *This ice cream is also delicious with a little ginger; stir in 40g | 1½oz | ¼ cup finely chopped preserved stem ginger when the ice cream is partially frozen.*

Raspberry Sherbet

Traditional sherbets are made in much the same way as sorbets but with added milk. This modern low-fat version is made from raspberry purée blended with sugar syrup and virtually fat-free fromage frais, then flecked with crushed raspberries.

SERVES SIX

INGREDIENTS

175g | 6oz | ¾ cup CASTER (SUPERFINE) SUGAR

150ml | ¼ pint | ⅔ cup WATER

500g | 1¼lb | 3½ cups RASPBERRIES, plus extra, to serve

500ml | 17fl oz | generous 2 cups VIRTUALLY FAT-FREE FROMAGE FRAIS or CREAM CHEESE

1 Put the sugar and water in a small pan and bring to the boil, stirring until the sugar has dissolved. Pour into a bowl; cool.

2 Put 350g | 12oz | 2½ cups of the raspberries in a food processor or blender. Process to a purée, then press through a sieve placed over a large bowl to remove the seeds. Stir the sugar syrup into the raspberry purée and chill the mixture until it is very cold.

3 Add the fromage frais to the purée and whisk until smooth.

4 Churn the mixture in an ice cream maker until it is thick but too soft to scoop. Scrape into a freezerproof container.

5 Crush the remaining raspberries between your fingers and add them to the partially frozen ice cream. Mix lightly, then freeze for 2–3 hours until firm.

6 Scoop the ice cream into dishes and serve with extra raspberries.

COOK'S TIP *This recipes makes 900ml | 1½ pints | 3¾ cups of mixture. If this is too large a quantity for your machine, you may need to make it in two batches.*

Orange and Yogurt Ice

Serve this refreshing low-fat yogurt ice simply, in cones, or scoop it into bought or home-made meringue baskets and decorate it with blueberries and mint for a more sophisticated treat. If you want a more decadent dessert, use whipping cream or double/heavy cream in place of the yogurt.

SERVES SIX

INGREDIENTS

90ml | 6 tbsp WATER

10ml | 2 tsp POWDERED GELATINE

115g | 4oz | ½ cup CASTER (SUPERFINE) SUGAR

250ml | 8fl oz | 1 cup "FRESHLY SQUEEZED" ORANGE JUICE from a carton or bottle

500ml | 17fl oz | generous 2 cups NATURAL (PLAIN) YOGURT

CONES or MERINGUE NESTS, BLUEBERRIES and FRESH MINT SPRIGS, to serve

1 Put 30ml | 2 tbsp of the water in a small bowl and sprinkle the powdered gelatine over the top. Set aside until spongy.

2 Meanwhile, put the sugar in a small pan, add the remaining water and heat through gently until the sugar has dissolved completely.

3 Take off the heat, add the gelatine and stir until dissolved. Cool, stir in the orange juice and chill for 15–30 minutes.

4 Churn the orange mixture in an ice cream maker until thick, but not thick enough to scoop.

5 Switch off the machine. Remove the paddle, if necessary, add the yogurt to the orange mixture and mix well. Replace the paddle and continue to churn the ice cream for 15–20 minutes until it is thick.

6 Scrape it into a plastic tub or a similar freezerproof container and freeze until firm.

7 Scoop the yogurt ice into cones or meringue nests and decorate with blueberries and mint.

COOK'S TIP *Meringue nests are not difficult to make, but if you do not have the time, bought ones are a perfectly acceptable alternative.*

Mango and Lime Ice Cream

This pale golden iced dessert is flavoured with lime syrup and reduced-fat coconut milk for a light fruity finalé, perfect to follow an Indian main course.

SERVES SIX

INGREDIENTS

2 LIMES, grated rind and juice

75g | 3oz | scant ½ cup CASTER (SUPERFINE) SUGAR

2 MANGOES, each about 350g | 12oz, stoned (pitted) and peeled

400ml | 14fl oz | 1⅔ cups REDUCED-FAT COCONUT MILK

To decorate

FRESH MANGO slices

LIME RIND curls

1 Put the lime rind and juice into a pan with 45ml | 3 tbsp water and the sugar. Heat gently until the sugar has dissolved then bring to the boil.

2 Roughly chop the mango flesh then purée in a liquidizer or food processor until smooth. Mix the purée with the sugar syrup and coconut milk then chill well.

3 Pour the mixture into an ice cream maker and churn until it is firm enough to scoop. Spoon into a freezer container and freeze until required.

4 Scoop into glass dishes and decorate with thin slices of mango and curls of lime rind made with a cannelle knife (zester).

VARIATION *A 400g/14oz can of mango pulp could be used instead of fresh mango purée if preferred.*

Blueberry and Honey Ripple Ice Cream

Packed with vitamin C, blueberries add a vitamin boost to this light honey-flavoured dessert. Frozen blueberries have been used here as they are a handy standby.

SERVES SIX

INGREDIENTS

4 EGG YOLKS

40g | 1½oz | 3 tbsp CASTER (SUPERFINE) SUGAR

5ml | 1 tsp CORNFLOUR (CORNSTARCH)

300ml | ½ pint | 1¼ cups SEMI-SKIMMED (LOW-FAT) MILK

60ml | 4 tbsp CLEAR HONEY

150g | 5oz | 1¼ cups FROZEN BLUEBERRIES, defrosted

200g | 7oz | scant 1 cup FROMAGE FRAIS OR MASCARPONE

To decorate

BLUEBERRIES

FRESH MINT LEAVES

1 Whisk the yolks, sugar and cornflour together in a bowl until thick and pale. Heat the milk in a pan then gradually whisk into the yolk mixture. Return the mixture to the pan and cook over a gentle heat, stirring all the time.

2 When the custard thickens and is smooth, pour it back into the bowl and stir in the honey. Cover and cool, then chill.

3 Meanwhile, place the blueberries in a liquidizer or food processor until purée until smooth, then press through a sieve.

4 Mix the fromage frais or mascarpone into the cooled honey custard then pour into an ice cream maker and churn until thick.

5 Take out one third of the ice cream and mix with the blueberry purée. Add alternate spoonfuls of honey ice cream and blueberry ice cream to a freezer container.

6 Using a dessertspoon handle, stir the mixtures together with five or six strokes to give a swirled effect. Cover and freeze until firm enough to scoop.

7 Scoop into glasses and decorate with a few extra blueberries and some mint leaves.

Bloody Mary Sorbet

Invigorating, refreshing and with a mild alcoholic kick, this delicious blend is great at any time,

particularly on a hot summer's day before lunch or supper.

SERVES FOUR

INGREDIENTS

750g | 1lb 10oz PASSATA
(BOTTLED STRAINED
TOMATOES)

2 CELERY STICKS,
roughly chopped

30ml | 2 tbsp WORCESTERSHIRE
SAUCE or 15ml | 1 tbsp
TABASCO SAUCE

10ml | 2 tsp LEMON JUICE

75ml | 5 tbsp VODKA

CELERY STICKS, to decorate

1 Put half of the passata in a food processor or blender with the celery, and process until smooth. Press the mixture through a sieve into a bowl and stir in the remaining passata.

2 Stir in the Worcestershire or Tabasco sauce, lemon juice and vodka.

3 Pour the mixture into the ice cream maker and churn until thick. Spoon into small glasses and decorate with celery sticks, or transfer to a freezer container and freeze until ready to serve.

COOK'S TIP *Don't be tempted to increase the amount of vodka in the sorbet or it won't freeze. You can always drizzle a little more into the glasses for an extra kick.*

Quantities of this sorbet can easily be increased for a large party, in which case it will need to be churned in batches.

Cinnamon Ricotta Ice with Toasted Granola

Mixed with light, creamy smooth low-fat ricotta this healthy iced dessert is speckled with chunky pieces of cinnamon-flavoured honey-glazed oats and seeds.

SERVES FOUR TO SIX

INGREDIENTS

For the granola topping

30ml | 2 tbsp SUNFLOWER OIL

30ml | 2 tbsp CLEAR HONEY

30ml | 2 tbsp SUNFLOWER SEEDS

30ml | 2 tbsp SESAME SEEDS

30ml | 2 tbsp FLAKED (SLICED) ALMONDS

30ml | 2 tbsp HAZELNUTS, chopped

45ml | 3 tbsp ROLLED OATS

2.5ml | ½ tsp GROUND CINNAMON

For the ice cream

4 EGG YOLKS

75g | 3oz | 6 tbsp CASTER (SUPERFINE) SUGAR

5ml | 1 tsp CORNFLOUR (CORNSTARCH)

2.5ml | ½ tsp GROUND CINNAMON

300ml | ½ pint | 1¼ cups SEMI-SKIMMED (LOW-FAT) MILK

250g | 9oz | generous 1 cup RICOTTA CHEESE

1 Preheat the oven to 180°C | 350°F | Gas 4. Oil a baking sheet. To make the granola, warm the oil and honey together in a pan. Mix in the remaining ingredients then spread into a thin layer on baking sheet. Bake for 7–10 minutes, stirring once until evenly browned. Leave to cool and harden.

2 To make the ice cream, whisk the egg yolks, sugar, cornflour and cinnamon in a bowl until thick and pale. Pour the milk into a heavy pan, bring it just to the boil, then gradually pour it on to the egg mixture, whisking constantly.

3 Return the mixture to the pan and cook over a gentle heat, stirring constantly until the custard thickens and is smooth. Pour it back into the bowl, cover, leave to cool, then chill.

4 Add the ricotta cheese to the cooled custard and whisk together until smooth.

5 Pour the mixture into an ice cream maker and churn until it is thick. Crumble the granola into pieces and mix half into the ice cream. Churn until the ice cream is firm enough to scoop. Transfer the ice cream to a freezer container and freeze until required.

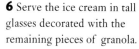

6 Serve the ice cream in tall glasses decorated with the remaining pieces of granola.

COOK'S TIP *The granola topping also tastes delicious sprinkled over other ice creams, or over bananas and yogurt for breakfast.*

Beetroot and Allspice Sorbet

Beetroot is surprisingly sweet, and makes a full-flavoured sorbet that's enhanced with mild spices. Definitely an acquired taste, this idea should appeal to anyone who enjoys the earthy flavour of beetroot juice.

SERVES SIX

INGREDIENTS

1kg | 2¼lb RAW BEETROOT
(BEETS)

150g | 5oz | ¾ cup CASTER
(SUPERFINE) SUGAR

2.5ml | ½ tsp GROUND ALLSPICE

150ml | ¼ pint | ⅔ cup WATER

1 Cut the beetroot into small pieces and push through a juicer to make 600ml | 1 pint | 2½ cups juice. If necessary, make up the quantity with water. Chill.

2 Put the sugar, allspice and water in a small pan and bring slowly to the boil, stirring until the sugar has dissolved. Remove the pan from the heat and cool.

3 Mix the beetroot juice with the syrup and pour into the ice cream maker. Churn until thick. Spoon into glasses or transfer to a freezer container and freeze until ready to serve.

COOK'S TIP *When preparing the beetroot (beets) for juicing, there is no need to trim or peel them first.*

Carrot, Apple and Ginger Water Ice

This sorbet not only tastes good, it's full of vital nutrients. Scrub the carrots but don't bother to peel the apples and ginger. Simply chop them all and push them through a juicer to make a smooth, tangy juice.

SERVES SIX

INGREDIENTS

175g | 6oz | scant 1 cup CASTER (SUPERFINE) SUGAR

150ml | ¼ pint | ⅔ cup WATER

500g | 1¼lb CARROTS, scrubbed

500g | 1¼ lb COOKING APPLES

50g | 2oz FRESH ROOT GINGER

1 Heat the sugar in a pan with the water until the sugar has dissolved. Bring to the boil and remove from the heat.

2 Roughly chop the carrots and apples. Finely chop the ginger. Push half the carrots and apples, then the ginger through the juicer, finishing with the remaining apples and carrots.

3 Pour the juice and syrup into the ice cream maker and churn to a thick slush. Spoon into glasses or transfer to a freezer container and freeze until ready to serve.

VARIATION *Instead of making a water ice, you could make a carrot, apple and ginger spritzer by omitting the sugar syrup and simply pushing the ingredients through a juicer and then adding soda water.*

COOK'S TIP *Fresh root ginger is one of the best natural remedies for indigestion and will help to settle an upset stomach, whether caused by food poisoning, motion sickness or morning sickness.*

shaped & moulded iced desserts

Layered, marbled or speckled with fruit and nuts, bombes and terrines make stunning iced desserts that reveal a feast of colour and texture when cut into. Uncomplicated to assemble, but requiring plenty of freezing time, they're best made several days in advance, ready and waiting for that special occasion.

Cassata

Cassata is an irresistible Italian ice cream, usually comprising three layers and frozen in a bombe mould.

This version, layered in a terrine, combines the complementary flavours of pistachio,

vanilla and tutti frutti.

SERVES EIGHT

INGREDIENTS

6 EGG YOLKS

225g | 8oz | generous 1 cup CASTER (SUPERFINE) SUGAR

15ml | 1 tbsp CORNFLOUR (CORNSTARCH)

600ml | 1 pint | 2½ cups MILK

600ml | 1 pint | 2½ cups DOUBLE (HEAVY) CREAM

75g | 3oz | ¼ cup PISTACHIOS

2.5ml | ½ tsp ALMOND ESSENCE (EXTRACT)

FOOD COLOURING, see method

40g | 1½oz | ¼ cup CANDIED PEEL, finely chopped

50g | 2oz | ¼ cup GLACÉ (CANDIED) CHERRIES, washed, dried and finely chopped

5ml | 1 tsp NATURAL VANILLA ESSENCE (EXTRACT)

1 Whisk the egg yolks, sugar, cornflour and a little milk in a bowl until pale and creamy. Bring the remaining milk and the cream to the boil in a large, heavy pan.

2 Immediately pour into the egg yolk mixture in a steady stream, whisking well. Pour back into the pan and cook over a very gentle heat, stirring until thickened. Remove from the heat and divide into three equal quantities. Cover and cool.

3 Put the pistachios in a bowl. Cover with boiling water and leave for 1 minute. Drain the nuts and spread between several thicknesses of kitchen paper. Rub between the paper to loosen the skins.

4 Pick out the nuts, rubbing off any remaining skins. Roughly chop and add to one bowl with the almond essence and a drop of green food colouring.

5 Stir the candied peel, glacé cherries and a drop of red food colouring into the second bowl. Stir the vanilla essence into the third bowl. Line a dampened 900g | 2lb terrine or loaf tin (pan) with baking parchment.

6 Churn the pistachio ice cream in an ice cream maker and spread into the prepared tin. Level the surface. Place in the freezer.

7 Prepare the remaining ice creams. Follow the same procedure with the vanilla and then the tutti frutti ice cream. Freeze overnight until firm.

8 To serve, dip the terrine or tin in very hot water for 2–3 seconds, then place a long serving plate upside down on top of it. Holding together, turn them over. Lift off the container. Peel away the lining paper. Serve the cassata in slices.

Marzipan and Kumquat Terrine

Tangy poached kumquats make a perfect contrast to the sweet almond paste in this frozen terrine. Any leftover kumquats will keep in the refrigerator for a week, making a lovely topping for vanilla ice cream.

SERVES SIX

INGREDIENTS

350g | 12oz | 3 cups KUMQUATS

115g | 4oz | generous ½ cup CASTER (SUPERFINE) SUGAR

150ml | ¼ pint | ⅔ cup WATER

2 EGG YOLKS

10ml | 2 tsp CORNFLOUR (CORNSTARCH)

300ml | ½ pint | 1¼ cups FULL-CREAM (WHOLE) MILK

200g | 7oz GOLDEN MARZIPAN, grated

2.5ml | ½ tsp ALMOND ESSENCE (EXTRACT)

300ml | ½ pint | 1¼ cups WHIPPING CREAM

1 Cut the kumquats in half and scoop out the seeds with the tip of a knife. Heat the sugar and water gently in a heavy pan until the sugar dissolves. Add the kumquats and cook gently for about 10 minutes until tender. Cool.

2 Whisk the egg yolks in a bowl with the cornflour and 60ml | 4 tbsp of the syrup until smooth. In a heavy pan, bring the milk just to the boil, then gradually pour it over the egg yolk mixture, whisking constantly.

3 Return the custard mixture to the pan and cook over a gentle heat for 2 minutes, stirring constantly, until the custard has thickened. Do not let it boil or the custard may curdle.

4 Transfer the custard to a bowl and stir in the marzipan and almond essence. Cover the surface closely with baking parchment to prevent the formation of a skin on the surface and leave until cold.

5 Line a small terrine or loaf tin (pan) with clear film (plastic wrap).

6 Put a third of the kumquats into a food processor. Pour in a further 60ml | 4 tbsp of the kumquat syrup and blend until smooth and pulpy

7 Stir the cream and pulp into the custard and churn in an ice cream maker until thick. Pour into the tin and freeze for 4 hours.

8 Put the tin in the refrigerator about 1 hour before serving to allow it to soften slightly. Invert on to a plate and remove the tin. Peel away the film.

9 Serve the ice cream topped with the remaining kumquats.

Cranachan Bombes with Raspberry Sauce

This recipe stems from a traditional Scottish dessert comprising a whisky, honey and oatmeal flavoured cream.

This iced version is lovely served with a hot raspberry sauce.

5 To make the sauce, blend the raspberries in a blender or food processor until smooth. Press the pureé through a sieve into a bowl and stir in the remaining icing sugar.

6 Pour the mixture into a saucepan and heat through gently until hot but not boiling.

7 To serve, loosen the edges of the metal moulds with a knife. Dip the bases in very hot water for a few seconds and invert on to serving plates.

8 Pour over the sauce, decorate with extra raspberries and serve.

COOK'S TIP *If you are giving this dessert to small children, you could serve the bombe with cooled raspberry sauce intead of hot.*

SERVES SIX

INGREDIENTS

50g | 2oz | ½ cup medium OATMEAL

600ml | 1 pint | 2½ cups DOUBLE (HEAVY) CREAM

90ml | 6 tbsp CLEAR HONEY

60ml | 4 tbsp WHISKY

50g | 2oz | ½ cup ICING (CONFECTIONER'S) SUGAR

350g | 12oz | generous 2 cups FRESH or FROZEN RASPBERRIES

RASPBERRIES, to decorate

1 Put the oatmeal in a heavy-based frying pan and cook over a gentle heat until it is lightly toasted, stirring frequently. Remove from the heat and leave to cool.

2 Mix 60ml | 4 tbsp of the cream in a bowl with the honey, whisky and half the icing sugar. Stir in the remaining cream and pour into the ice cream maker.

3 Churn until beginning to thicken then add the oatmeal and churn until it is thick.

4 Pack the ice cream into six small dariole moulds and freeze for at least 2 hours or overnight until it is firm.

Tropical Fruit and Bacardi Terrine

Creamy smooth and specked with Bacardi-steeped fruits, this quick and easy iced dessert looks impressive cut into slices and decorated with fresh tropical fruits.

SERVES SIX

INGREDIENTS

75g | 3oz | 6 tbsp each of SWEETENED DRIED MANGO, DRIED PAPAYA, and DRIED PINEAPPLE, finely chopped

30ml | 2 tbsp PRESERVED STEM GINGER, chopped

75ml | 5 tbsp BACARDI

250g | 9oz | generous 1 cup RICOTTA CHEESE

450ml | ¾ pint | scant 2 cups DOUBLE (HEAVY) CREAM

75g | 3oz | ¾ cup ICING (CONFECTIONER'S) SUGAR

a selection of sliced FRESH TROPICAL FRUITS, to decorate

1 Mix together the dried fruits and ginger in a bowl. Add the Bacardi, stir well and leave to stand for 1–2 hours until the Bacardi is all, or mostly absorbed.

2 Beat the ricotta in a bowl to soften it. Gradually whisk in the double cream and icing sugar until thick and smooth.

3 Pour into the ice cream maker and churn until thick. Add the fruits and any Bacardi left in the bowl and churn until thick.

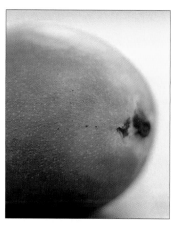

4 Meanwhile dampen a 450g | 1lb loaf tin (pan) and line with clear film (plastic wrap). Spoon the ice cream into the tin and level the surface with a spatula.

5 Freeze for several hours or overnight until firm.

6 To serve, invert the tin on to a flat surface and peel away the clear film. Serve cut into slices topped with sliced fruits.

Layered Chocolate and Chestnut Bombes

Using an ice cream maker takes all the effort out of making these triple flavoured ice creams, which taste delicious and look stunning served on elegant plates drizzled with chocolate. Allow a little extra time for churning each mixture separately and layering them up in the moulds.

SERVES SIX

INGREDIENTS

3 EGG YOLKS

75g | 3oz | 6 tbsp CASTER (SUPERFINE) SUGAR

5ml | 1 tsp CORNFLOUR (CORNSTARCH)

300ml | ½ pint | 1¼ cups MILK

115g | 4oz PLAIN (SEMISWEET) CHOCOLATE, chopped

150g | 5oz | generous 1 cup SWEETENED CHESTNUT PURÉE

30ml | 2 tbsp BRANDY or COINTREAU

130g | 4½oz | generous 1 cup MASCARPONE CHEESE

5ml | 1 tsp VANILLA ESSENCE (EXTRACT)

450ml | ¾ pint | scant 2 cups DOUBLE (HEAVY) CREAM

50g | 2oz PLAIN (SEMISWEET) CHOCOLATE, to decorate

1 Whisk the egg yolks in a bowl with the sugar and cornflour. Bring the milk to the boil in a heavy pan. gradually pour the milk over the egg mixture, whisking well.

2 Return to the pan and cook over a very gentle heat, stirring until thickened. Divide the custard equally among three bowls.

3 While still hot, add the plain chocolate to one bowl, stirring until melted. Leave the mixture to cool, then chill.

4 Beat the chestnut purée until it is soft, then beat it into the second bowl with the brandy or Cointreau until completely combined.

5 Beat the mascarpone and vanilla essence into the third bowl. Leave to cool, then chill.

6 Add one third of the cream to each mixture. Turn the chestnut mixture into the ice cream maker and churn until it has a softly set consistency.

7 Divide the mixture among six 150ml | ¼ pint | ⅔ cup metal moulds, level the surface and freeze.

8 Add the chocolate mixture to the ice cream maker (there's no need to wash the machine) and churn to the same consistency.

9 Spoon into the moulds, level the surface and freeze.

10 Clean out the ice cream machine and churn the remaining mixture to the same consistency. Spoon into the moulds, level the surface and freeze for several hours or overnight.

11 To serve, melt the chocolate for the decoration in a heatproof bowl set oven a pan of gently simmering water.

12 Transfer to a paper piping (pastry) bag and snip off the tip. Scribble lines of chocolate over serving plates.

13 Loosen the edges of the ice cream moulds with a knife. Dip very briefly in hot water, then invert on to a flat surface.

14 Using a palette knife or spatula, transfer the moulds to the decorated plates. Leave to stand for 10 minutes before serving.

VARIATION *If you can't get sweetened chestnut purée use the same quantity of unsweetened purée and add an extra 30ml | 2 tbsp sugar.*

Caramel and Pecan Terrine

Golden caramel and toasted pecans make a fabulous addition to a simple ice cream. When making the caramel, watch it closely and make sure it doesn't start to burn or the ice cream will taste bitter.

SERVES SIX

INGREDIENTS

150g | 5oz | ¾ cup SUGAR

75ml | 5 tbsp WATER

450ml | ¾ pint | scant 2 cups DOUBLE (HEAVY) CREAM

3 EGG YOLKS

2.5ml | ½ tsp CORNFLOUR (CORNSTARCH)

150ml | ¼ pint | ⅔ cup MILK

75g | 3oz | ¾ cup PECAN NUTS, toasted

COOK'S TIP *Watch the caramel syrup closely after removing the pan from the heat. If the caramel syrup starts to turn too dark, dip the base of the pan in cold water to arrest the cooking. If the syrup remains very pale, return the pan to the heat and cook the syrup for a little longer until it starts to darken a bit.*

1 Heat 90g | 3½oz | ½ cup of the sugar and the water in a small, heavy pan until the sugar dissolves. Bring to the boil and boil rapidly until the sugar has turned pale golden. Watching closely, cook the syrup until it turns a deep, dark golden colour.

2 Immediately immerse the base of the pan in cold water to prevent further cooking. Pour 60ml | 4 tbsp of the cream into the caramel and heat gently to make a smooth sauce. Leave to cool.

3 Mix together the remaining sugar, egg yolks and cornflour in a small bowl. Bring the milk and 150ml | ¼ pint | ⅔ cup of the cream just to the boil in a heavy pan.

4 Pour the hot milk over the yolk mixture, whisking well to combine, then tip the custard back into the pan and cook over a very gentle heat, stirring until slightly thickened. Pour the custard mixture into a bowl and leave to cool completely.

5 Dampen a 450g | 1lb loaf tin (pan) and line the base and sides with clear film (plastic wrap). Stir the remaining cream into the custard and pour into the ice cream maker. Churn until thick. Transfer half the ice cream to a freezer container and freeze while making the caramel ice cream.

6 With the paddle working, pour the caramel and nuts into the ice cream and churn until it has the same consistency as the plain ice cream.

7 Spoon a third of the caramel ice cream into the tin and spread with half of the plain ice cream. Repeat layering the ice creams, finishing with a caramel layer. Freeze for at least 3 hours or overnight until firm.

8 To serve the terrine, dip the base of the loaf tin in very hot water for 2 seconds, invert it on to a serving plate and then peel away the clear film. Serve in generous slices.

Chocolate, Rum and Raisin Roulade

This richly flavoured dessert can be assembled and frozen a week or two in advance. Use vanilla, chocolate or coffee ice cream if you prefer, though all versions will be just as enjoyably indulgent.

SERVES SIX

INGREDIENTS

For the roulade

115g | 4oz PLAIN (SEMISWEET) CHOCOLATE, broken into pieces

4 EGGS, separated

115g | 4oz | generous ½ cup CASTER (SUPERFINE) SUGAR

CASTER SUGAR, for dusting

For the filling

75g | 3oz | generous ½ cup RAISINS

60ml | 4 tbsp DARK RUM

425g | 15oz can CUSTARD

50g | 2oz | ¼ cup LIGHT MUSCOVADO (BROWN) SUGAR

200ml | 7fl oz | scant 1 cup WHIPPING CREAM

To decorate

COCOA POWDER (UNSWEETENED)

ICING (CONFECTIONERS') SUGAR

1 To make the roulade, preheat the oven to 180°C | 350°F | Gas 4. Line a 33 x 23cm | 13 x 9in Swiss roll tin (jelly roll pan) with baking parchment. Melt the chocolate in a heatproof bowl set over a pan of simmering water.

2 In a separate bowl whisk the egg yolks and sugar together until thick and pale. Fold in the melted chocolate. Whisk the egg whites in a grease-free bowl until stiff.

3 Fold one quarter of the egg whites into the chocolate mixture to loosen it then gently fold in the remainder.

4 Pour the mixture into the prepared tin and gently ease into the corners. Bake for about 20 minutes until the cake has risen and is just firm. Leave to cool in the tin covered with a piece of baking parchment and a clean dish towel.

5 Meanwhile, warm the raisins in the rum in a small pan for a few minutes, then leave them to cool and plump up for at least 2 hours ready for the ice cream.

6 To make the ice cream, mix the custard, muscovado sugar and cream together and pour into an ice cream maker. Churn the mixture until it is thick then add the raisins and churn until it is stiff enough to spread.

7 Turn the roulade out on to a large sheet of baking parchment dusted with caster sugar and set over a dampened and wrung out dish towel. Spread with the ice cream then roll up from one of the shortest sides, using the paper and dish towel to help.

8 Put on to a serving plate, cover with foil and freeze until ready to serve. Dust with cocoa powder and icing sugar just before slicing.

Spicy Pumpkin and Orange Bombe

Pumpkin has a subtle flavour that is truly transformed with the addition of

citrus fruits and spices. Here, the delicious mixture is encased in syrupy sponge

and served with an orange and whole spice syrup.

SERVES EIGHT

INGREDIENTS

For the sponge

115g | 4oz | ½ cup UNSALTED
(SWEET) BUTTER, softened

115g | 4oz | ½ cup CASTER
(SUPERFINE) SUGAR

115g | 4oz | 1 cup SELF-RAISING
(SELF-RISING) FLOUR

2.5ml | ½ tsp BAKING POWDER

2 EGGS

For the ice cream

1 ORANGE

300g | 11oz | scant 1½ cups
GOLDEN GRANULATED SUGAR

300ml | ½ pint | 1¼ cups WATER

2 CINNAMON STICKS, halved

10ml | 2 tsp WHOLE CLOVES

30ml | 2 tbsp ORANGE
FLOWER WATER

400g | 14oz can UNSWEETENED
PUMPKIN PURÉE

300ml | ½ pint | 1¼ cups
EXTRA THICK DOUBLE
(HEAVY) CREAM

2 pieces PRESERVED STEM
GINGER, grated

ICING (CONFECTIONERS')
SUGAR, for dusting

COOK'S TIP *If you prefer a smooth syrup, strain to remove the cinnamon sticks and cloves before spooning it over the bombe.*

1 Preheat the oven to 180°C | 350°F | Gas 4. Grease and line a 450g | 1lb loaf tin (pan). Beat the softened butter, caster sugar, flour, baking powder and eggs in a bowl until creamy.

2 Scrape the mixture into the prepared tin, level the surface and bake for 30–35 minutes until firm in the centre. Leave to cool.

3 Make the ice cream. Pare thin strips of rind from the orange, scrape off any white pith, then cut the strips into very fine shreds.

4 Squeeze the orange and set the juice aside. Heat the sugar and water in a small, heavy pan until the sugar dissolves. Bring to the boil and boil rapidly without stirring for 3 minutes.

5 Stir in the orange shreds, juice, cinnamon and cloves and heat gently for 5 minutes. Strain the syrup, reserving the orange shreds and spices. Measure 300ml | ½ pint | 1¼ cups of the syrup and reserve. Return the spices to the remaining syrup and stir in the orange flower water. Pour into a jug (pitcher) and set aside to cool.

6 Beat the pumpkin purée with 175ml | 6fl oz | ¾ cup of the measured strained syrup until evenly combined. Stir in the cream and ginger. Cut the cake into 1cm | ½in slices.

7 Dampen a 1.5 litre | 2½ pint | 6¼ cup bowl and line it with clear film (plastic wrap). Pour the remaining strained syrup into a shallow dish.

8 Dip the cake slices briefly in the syrup and use to line the prepared bowl, placing the syrupy coated sides against the bowl. Trim the pieces to fit where necessary, so that the lining is even and any gaps are filled. Chill.

9 Churn the pumpkin mixture in an ice cream maker until very thick, then scrape it into the sponge-lined bowl. Level the surface and freeze until firm, preferably overnight.

10 To serve, invert the ice cream on to a serving plate. Lift off the bowl and peel away the clear film. Dust with the icing sugar and serve in wedges with the spiced syrup spooned over.

Mocha Prune and Armagnac Terrine

This is a really simple yet stylish iced dessert that is perfect for entertaining. Just remember to allow time

for the prunes to soak in the Armagnac.

SERVES SIX

INGREDIENTS

115g | 4oz | ½ cup ready-to-eat stoned (pitted) PRUNES, chopped

90ml | 6 tbsp ARMAGNAC

90g | 3½oz | ½ cup CASTER (SUPERFINE) SUGAR

200ml | 7fl oz | scant 1 cup WATER

45ml | 3 tbsp COFFEE BEANS

150g | 5oz PLAIN (SEMISWEET) CHOCOLATE, broken into pieces

300ml | ½ pint | 1¼ cups DOUBLE (HEAVY) CREAM

COCOA POWDER (UNSWEETENED), to dust

1 Put the prunes in a small bowl. Pour over 75ml | 5 tbsp of the Armagnac and leave to soak for at least 3 hours at room temperature, or overnight in the refrigerator. Line the bases of six 100ml | 2fl oz ramekins with circles cut from baking parchment.

2 Put the sugar and water in a heavy pan and heat gently until the sugar dissolves, stirring occasionally. Add the soaked prunes and any of the Armagnac that remains in the bowl; simmer the prunes gently in the syrup for 5 minutes.

3 Using a slotted spoon, lift the prunes out of the pan and set them aside. Add the coffee beans to the syrup and simmer gently for 5 minutes.

4 Lift out the coffee beans and put about a third of them in a bowl. Spoon over 120ml | 4fl oz | ½ cup of the syrup and stir in the remaining Armagnac.

5 Add the chocolate to the pan containing the remaining syrup and heat gently until melted. Stir in the cream and leave to cool.

6 Pour the mixture into an ice cream maker and churn until thick. Add the prunes and mix together briefly. Spoon into the lined ramekin dishes, level the tops and transfer to the freezer to harden.

7 To serve, loosen the edges of the ramekins with a hot knife, then dip in very hot water for 2 seconds and invert on to serving plates. Remove the lining paper and decorate the plates with a drizzle of the coffee bean syrup and a little cocoa powder.

Rippled Nectarine and Muscovado Terrine

A delicious combination of nectarine ice cream, cream cheese and muscovado sugar, swirled together attractively

and set in the corner of a tilted square cake tin to give an interesting triangular shape.

SERVES SIX

INGREDIENTS

50g | 2oz | ¼ cup LIGHT MUSCOVADO (BROWN) SUGAR

10ml | 2 tsp boiling WATER

3 ripe NECTARINES, halved and stoned (pitted)

10ml | 2 tsp LEMON JUICE

115g | 4oz | 1 cup ICING (CONFECTIONERS') SUGAR

105ml | 7 tbsp WHIPPING CREAM

200g | 7oz | scant 1 cup CREAM CHEESE

90ml | 6 tbsp MILK

1 Line one half of a 20cm | 8in square cake tin (pan) with clear film (plastic wrap) and prop it up at a slight angle on the work surface. Dissolve the muscovado sugar in the boiling water in a small bowl, stirring until it forms a syrup, then leave to cool.

2 Slice the nectarines then put into in a liquidizer or food processor with the lemon juice and three-quarters of the icing sugar and purée until smooth.

COOK'S TIP *Before making this dessert check that you have room in the freezer for the tin at an angle, if not use a 900g/2lb loaf tin instead.*

3 Stir in the cream then pour the mixture into an ice cream maker and churn until thick.

4 Meanwhile mix the cream cheese with the remaining icing sugar and milk until smooth.

5 Add alternate spoonfuls of nectarine ice cream, muscovado syrup and cream cheese along the length of the lined tin, building up layers until the mixtures have been used up.

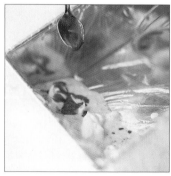

6 Using a dessertspoon handle, gently stir the mixtures together to give a rippled effect. Freeze the tin for a minimum of 4 hours, or overnight, propped up at the same angle until the ice cream is firm.

7 Remove the ice cream from the tin and peel away the clear film. Cut into slices to serve.

Coconut and Lemon Grass Ice Cream

Lemon grass adds an exotic fragrance to this creamy coconut ice cream. If you can't get the fresh ingredient, use the dried stalks or preserved stalks in jars.

SERVES FIVE TO SIX

INGREDIENTS

4 LEMON GRASS STALKS

400ml | 14fl oz | 1⅔ cups COCONUT MILK

3 EGG YOLKS

90g | 3½oz | ½ cup CASTER (SUPERFINE) SUGAR

10ml | 2 tsp CORNFLOUR (CORNSTARCH)

150ml | ¼ pint | ⅔ cup WHIPPING CREAM

finely grated rind of 1 LIME

For the lime syrup

75g | 3oz | 6 tbsp CASTER (SUPERFINE) SUGAR

75ml | 5 tbsp WATER

1 LIME, very thinly sliced, plus 30ml | 2 tbsp LIME JUICE

1 Cut the lemon grass stalks in half lengthways and bruise the stalks with a rolling pin. Put them in a heavy pan, add the coconut milk and bring to just below boiling point.

2 Remove from the heat and leave to infuse for 30 minutes, then remove the lemon grass.

3 Whisk the egg yolks in a bowl with the sugar and cornflour until smooth. Gradually add the coconut milk, whisking constantly.

4 Return to the pan and heat gently, stirring until the custard thickens. Remove from the heat and strain into a clean bowl. Cover with baking parchment and chill.

5 Stir the cream and lime rind into the custard. Churn in an ice cream maker until thick, then spoon into 5–6 dariole moulds. Freeze for at least 3 hours.

6 Heat the sugar and water in a heavy pan until the sugar dissolves. Boil for 5 minutes without stirring. Reduce the heat, add the lime slices and juice and simmer for 5 minutes more. Cool.

7 To turn out, loosen with a knife and briefly dip in very hot water. Serve with syrup and lime slices.

Walnut Castles

This recipe is loosely based on a classic Indian kulfi, using finely chopped walnuts instead of the more familiar pistachios. If you prefer, you could also use finely chopped almonds.

SERVES SIX

INGREDIENTS

2 litres | 3½ pints | 9 cups FULL-CREAM (WHOLE) MILK

15 whole CARDAMOM PODS

75g | 3oz | 6 tbsp CASTER (SUPERFINE) SUGAR

115g | 4oz | 1 cup WALNUTS, finely chopped

30ml | 2 tbsp ROSEWATER

15ml | 1 tbsp LEMON JUICE

CHOPPED WALNUTS, to decorate

1 Put the milk and cardamom pods in a large, heavy pan. Bring to the boil, then simmer vigorously without boiling over. Continue until reduced to about 750ml | 1¼ pints | 3 cups.

2 Pour the milk through a sieve into a bowl, discarding the cardamom pods. Add the caster sugar, chopped walnuts and rosewater and leave to cool then stir in the lemon juice.

3 Chill the mixture, then churn in an ice cream maker until thick.

4 Spoon the ice cream into six 120ml | 4fl oz | ½ cup dariole moulds or plastic cups and freeze overnight or until firm.

5 To serve, briefly dip the moulds in very hot water, then turn out on to individual dessert plates. Serve scattered with chopped walnuts.

Iced Strawberry and Lemon Curd Gâteau

Layer two favourite flavours in this fresh fruit gâteau, which is perfect for summer entertaining and takes only minutes to assemble.

SERVES EIGHT

INGREDIENTS

115g | 4oz | ½ cup UNSALTED (SWEET) BUTTER, softened

115g | 4oz | generous ½ cup CASTER (SUPERFINE) SUGAR

2 EGGS

115g | 4oz | 1 cup SELF-RAISING (SELF-RISING) FLOUR

2.5ml | ½ tsp BAKING POWDER

COOK'S TIP *This dessert is best eaten on the day on which it is made, or the sponge will become soggy. You can, however, make the sponge, ice cream and strawberry sauce ahead and freeze them until required. Then simply allow the sauce to defrost before pouring over the finished gâteau.*

To finish

500ml | 17fl oz | 2¼ cups STRAWBERRY ICE CREAM

300ml | ½ pint | 1¼ cups DOUBLE (HEAVY) CREAM

200g | 7oz | scant 1 cup GOOD QUALITY LEMON CURD

30ml | 2 tbsp LEMON JUICE

500g | 1¼lb | 5 cups STRAWBERRIES, hulled

25g | 1oz | 2 tbsp CASTER (SUPERFINE) SUGAR

45ml | 3 tbsp COINTREAU or other ORANGE-FLAVOURED LIQUEUR

1 Preheat the oven to 180°C | 350°F | Gas 4. Grease and line a 23cm | 9in round springform tin (pan). In a mixing bowl, beat the butter with the sugar, eggs, flour and baking powder until creamy.

2 Spoon into the tin and bake for 20 minutes or until just firm. Leave to cool for 5 minutes, then invert the cake on a wire rack. Cool completely. Wash and dry the cake tin, ready to use again.

3 Line the sides of the clean cake tin with a strip of baking parchment. Using a sharp knife, carefully slice off the top of the cake where it has formed a crust.

4 Fit the cake in the tin, cut-side down. Freeze the cake for 10 minutes, then spread the strawberry ice cream evenly over the cake and freeze until firm.

5 Pour the cream into a bowl, whip it until it forms soft peaks, then fold in the lemon curd and lemon juice. Spoon the mixture over the strawberry ice cream. Cover and freeze overnight.

6 About 45 minutes before you intend to serve the dessert, make the sauce. Cut half the strawberries into thin slices.

7 Put the rest of the strawberries in a food processor or blender and add the sugar and liqueur. Purée the mixture to make a sauce.

8 Arrange the sliced strawberries over the frozen gâteau. Serve with the sauce spooned over.

Soft Fruit and Crushed Meringue Gâteau

This recipe takes five minutes to make but looks and tastes as though a lot of preparation went into it.

Use really good vanilla home-made ice cream.

SERVES SIX

INGREDIENTS

400g | 14oz | 3½ cups MIXED SMALL
STRAWBERRIES or RASPBERRIES

30ml | 2 tbsp ICING
(CONFECTIONERS') SUGAR

750ml | 1¼ pints | 3 cups
CLASSIC VANILLA ICE CREAM

6 MERINGUE NESTS
(or 115g | 4oz meringue)

1 Dampen a 900g | 2lb loaf tin (pan) and line it with clear film (plastic wrap). If using strawberries, chop them into small pieces. Put them in a bowl and add the raspberries and icing sugar. Toss until the fruit is beginning to break up but do not let it become mushy.

2 Put the ice cream in a bowl and break it up with a fork. Crumble the meringues into small chunks and add to the bowl. The meringue nests can be either home-made or bought, depending on how much time you have available. Add the soft fruit mixture.

3 Fold all the ingredients together until they are evenly combined and lightly marbled. Pack into the prepared tin and press down gently to level. Cover and freeze overnight. To serve, invert on to a plate and peel away the film. Serve in slices.

Iced Lime Cheesecake

This cheesecake has a deliciously tangy, sweet flavour, and the sharp lime contrasts wonderfully with the soft cheeses and rich cream. It is not difficult to prepare as it needs no gelatine to set the filling, unlike most unbaked cheesecakes, and it looks pleasantly summery with its citrus decoration.

4 Finely grate the rind and squeeze the juice from five of the limes. Heat the sugar and water over a gentle heat in a small pan, stirring until the sugar dissolves.

5 Bring to the boil and boil for 2 minutes without stirring, then remove the syrup from the heat, stir in the lime juice and rind and leave to cool.

6 Press the cottage cheese through a sieve into a bowl. Beat in the mascarpone, then the lime syrup.

7 Add the cream and churn in an ice cream maker until thick.

8 Meanwhile, cut a slice off either end of each of the remaining limes, stand them on a board and slice off the skins. Cut them into very thin slices.

9 Arrange the lime slices around the sides of the tin, pressing them against the paper.

10 Pour the cheese mixture over the biscuit (cookie) base in the tin and level the surface. Cover and freeze the cheesecake overnight.

11 About 1 hour before you are going to serve the cheesecake, carefully transfer it to a serving plate and put it in the refrigerator to soften slightly.

COOK'S TIP *You could make a lemon and lime cheesecake by using lime for the filling and lemon slices round the side in place of the lime slices.*

SERVES TEN

INGREDIENTS

175g | 6oz AMARETTI

65g | 2½oz | 5 tbsp UNSALTED (SWEET) BUTTER

8 LIMES

115g | 4oz | ½ cup CASTER (SUPERFINE) SUGAR

90ml | 6 tbsp WATER

200g | 7oz | scant 1 cup COTTAGE CHEESE

250g | 9oz | generous 1 cup MASCARPONE CHEESE

300ml | ½ pint | 1¼ cups DOUBLE (HEAVY) CREAM

1 Lightly grease the sides of a 20cm | 8in springform tin (pan) and line it with a strip of baking parchment. Break up the amaretti slightly, put them in a strong plastic bag and crush them finely with a rolling pin.

2 Melt the butter over a gentle heat in a small pan and stir in the amaretti crumbs until they are evenly coated.

3 Spoon the mixture into the tin and pack it down and level the surface with the back of a spoon. Freeze the cheesecake base while you make the filling.

Rhubarb and Ginger Wine Torte

Poached shoots of young forced rhubarb combined with fiery stem ginger and blended with cream and ginger wine make a truly delicious combination. The result is a refreshingly tart flavour, making it the perfect choice for those who prefer less sweet desserts.

SERVES EIGHT

INGREDIENTS

500g | 1¼lb RHUBARB, trimmed

115g | 4oz | ½ cup CASTER (SUPERFINE) SUGAR

30ml | 2 tbsp WATER

200g | 7oz | scant 1 cup CREAM CHEESE

150ml | ¼ pint | ⅔ cups DOUBLE (HEAVY) CREAM

40g | 1½oz | ¼ cup PRESERVED STEM GINGER, finely chopped

a few drops of PINK FOOD COLOURING (optional)

250ml | 8fl oz | 1 cup GINGER WINE

175g | 6oz SPONGE FINGERS (LADYFINGERS)

FRESH MINT or LEMON BALM SPRIGS, dusted with icing (confectioners') sugar, to decorate

1 Chop the rhubarb roughly and put it in a pan with the sugar and water. Cover and cook very gently for 5–8 minutes until the rhubarb is just tender. Process in a food processor or blender until smooth, then leave to cool.

COOK'S TIP *Taste the rhubarb mixture just before churning it and add a little icing (confectioners') sugar if you find the flavour too tart.*

2 Beat the cream cheese in a bowl until softened. Stir in the cream, rhubarb purée and ginger, then a little food colouring, if you like. Line a 900g | 2lb | 6–8 cup loaf tin (pan) with clear film (plastic wrap).

3 Chill the mixture if time permits, then churn in an ice cream maker until firm.

4 Pour the ginger wine into a shallow dish. Spoon a thin layer of ice cream over the bottom of the tin.

5 Working quickly, dip the sponge fingers in the ginger wine, then lay them lengthways over the ice cream in a single layer. Trim the sponge fingers to fit.

6 Spread another layer of ice cream over the sponge fingers. Repeat, adding two to three more layers and finishing with ice cream. Cover and freeze overnight.

7 Put in the refrigerator 30 minutes before serving. Briefly dip in hot water then invert it on to a flat dish. Peel off the clear film and decorate.

elegant iced
desserts

Presentation plays just as important a role with ice creams as it does with any other dessert. Whether scooped into glasses and bathed in a sweet glossy sauce, or cleverly contained in a chocolate case, there is a decorative dessert here to suit the mood of any special occasion.

Ice Cream with Sweet Pine Nut Sauce

The delicious combination of lightly toasted pine nuts, tangy lemon and butter makes an easy sauce, perfect for enlivening vanilla ice cream and lemon sorbet.

SERVES FOUR

INGREDIENTS

75g | 2½oz | 5 tbsp PINE NUTS

25g | 1oz | 2tbsp UNSALTED (SWEET) BUTTER

30ml | 2 tbsp CLEAR HONEY

30ml | 2 tbsp LIGHT MUSCOVADO (BROWN) SUGAR

pared rind and juice of 1 LEMON

250ml | 8 fl oz | 1 cup LEMON SORBET

250ml | 8 fl oz | 1 cup VANILLA ICE CREAM

1 Toast the pine nuts lightly, then chop them roughly. Melt the butter in a small, heavy pan with the honey and sugar. Remove from the heat and stir in the lemon rind and juice.

2 Stir in the chopped pine nuts. Pour into a small jug (pitcher). Leave to cool until ready to serve.

3 To serve, alternate small scoops of the lemon sorbet and the vanilla ice cream in four tall serving glasses.

4 Generously spoon the pine nut sauce over the ices and serve immediately.

COOK'S TIP *The sauce becomes thicker as it cools and is best served before it is quite cold.*

Sorbet in an Ice Bowl

Nothing sets off sorbet quite so effectively as an ice bowl inlaid with fresh flowers and leaves. Ice bowls are easy to make, inexpensive and will grace any special celebration, from a lunch party to a country wedding.

SERVES EIGHT TO TEN

INGREDIENTS

ICE CUBES

COLD WATER

selection of FRESH EDIBLE
FLOWERS AND LEAVES

18–20 scoops of SORBET,
to serve

1 Place some ice cubes in the base of a 3.5 litre | 6 pint | 15 cup clear plastic or glass freezerproof bowl. Tuck some flowers and leaves around the ice.

2 Position a smaller bowl so that it rests on the ice cubes, leaving an even space between the two bowls.

3 Pour cold water into the space between the bowls until the water level starts to come up the sides. Freeze for 2–3 hours until frozen.

4 Tuck more flowers and leaves between the two bowls, mixing the flowers and leaves so that they look attractive through the sides of the larger bowl.

5 Place some kitchen weights or food cans in the central bowl to stop it from rising, then fill the space between the bowls to the rim with more water. Freeze overnight until firm.

COOK'S TIP *If the inner bowl does not sit perfectly, pack crumpled foil between the top edges of the bowls while freezing the base. When unmoulding the bowl, the ice may crack, but it won't fall apart.*

6 Release the inner bowl by pouring boiling water into it almost to the top.

7 Quickly tip out the water and lift away the inner bowl. Repeat the process if the bowl won't come free instantly.

8 To remove the outer bowl, dip it quickly in a large bowl of very hot water until the ice bowl loosens. Return the ice bowl to the freezer.

9 Shortly before serving, scoop the sorbet into the bowl. Return to the freezer until ready to serve.

COOK'S TIP *Use any edible flowers to decorate the bowl, matching the colours to those of the sorbet. Rose petals or small rose buds look lovely, as do any herb flowers, primulas, primroses, pot marigolds, violets, nasturtiums and pansies. Don't place them too closely or the light won't show through and you won't get the full effect.*

White Chocolate Brûlées with Blackberry Coulis

This impressive dessert does not require a blowtorch to finish it off. Here the ice cream is scooped on to plates,

then drizzled with smooth dark blackberry sauce and topped with shards of caramel.

SERVES SIX

INGREDIENTS

4 EGG YOLKS

50g | 2oz | ¼ cup CASTER (SUPERFINE) SUGAR

5ml | 1 tsp CORNFLOUR (CORNSTARCH)

300ml | ½ pint | 1¼ cups SEMI-SKIMMED (LOW-FAT) MILK

150g | 5oz WHITE CHOCOLATE, broken into pieces

5ml | 1 tsp VANILLA ESSENCE (EXTRACT)

200g | 7oz | scant 2 cups BLACKBERRIES

115g | 4oz | generous 1 cup SUGAR

300 ml | ½ pint | 1¼ cups DOUBLE (HEAVY) CREAM

BLACKBERRIES, for decoration

COOK'S TIP *This dessert will taste best if you have picked the blackberries yourself. If you can't find them, however, other summer fruits such as blackcurrants or raspberries will work just as well, or you could use frozen blackberries.*

1 Whisk the egg yolks, sugar and cornflour together until thick and pale. Pour the milk into a heavy pan, bring it just to the boil, then pour it on to the egg yolk mixture, whisking constantly.

2 Return the mixture to the pan and cook over a gentle heat, stirring constantly until the custard thickens and is smooth.

3 Take the pan off the heat and add the chocolate pieces and vanilla essence and stir until the chocolate has completely melted. Cover, leave to cool then chill.

4 Put the blackberries into a pan with 60ml | 4 tbsp water, then cover and cook for 5 minutes until the fruit has softened.

5 Purée the berries in a liquidizer or food processor until smooth. Press through a sieve and discard the seeds.

6 Stir in 30–45ml | 2–3 tbsp extra water to make a spooning sauce.

7 Put the granulated sugar water in a small pan with 45ml | 3 tbsp water and heat gently, without stirring, until the sugar has completely dissolved. Increase the heat and boil for 4–5 minutes until golden.

8 Quickly pour the caramel on to an oiled baking sheet. Leave to cool and harden, then break into pieces.

9 Pour the cooled white chocolate custard and cream into an ice cream maker and churn until firm enough to scoop. Transfer to a freezer container and store in the freezer until required.

10 Scoop the ice cream on to plates and top with the pieces of caramel. Spoon a little sauce on the plate around the ice cream, and add whole blackberries if you like.

Gooseberry and Elderflower Sorbet

A classic combination that makes a really refreshing sorbet. Make it in summer, as a stunning finale for an alfresco meal, or save it for serving after a hearty winter's stew.

SERVES SIX

INGREDIENTS

150g | 5oz | ⅔ cup CASTER (SUPERFINE) SUGAR

175ml | 6fl oz | ¾ cup WATER

10 ELDERFLOWER HEADS

500g | 1¼lb | 4 cups GOOSEBERRIES

200ml | 7fl oz | scant 1 cup APPLE JUICE

dash of GREEN FOOD COLOURING (optional)

a little beaten EGG WHITE

1 Put 30ml | 2 tbsp of the sugar in a pan with 30ml | 2 tbsp of the water. Set aside. Mix the remaining sugar and water in a separate, heavy pan.

2 Heat gently, stirring occasionally, until the sugar has dissolved. Bring to the boil and boil for 1 minute, without stirring, to make a syrup.

3 Remove from the heat and add the elderflower heads, pressing them into the syrup with a wooden spoon. Leave to infuse for about 1 hour.

4 Strain the elderflower syrup through a sieve placed over a bowl. Set the syrup aside. Add the gooseberries to the pan containing the reserved sugar and water. Cover and cook very gently for about 5 minutes until the gooseberries have softened.

5 Transfer to a food processor and add the apple juice. Process until smooth, then press through a sieve into a bowl. Leave to cool. Stir in the elderflower syrup and green food colouring. Chill until very cold.

6 Churn the mixture in an ice cream maker until it holds its shape. Transfer to a freezerproof container and freeze for several hours or overnight.

7 To decorate the glasses, put some egg white in a shallow bowl and a layer of caster sugar on a plate. Dip the rim of each glass in the egg white, then the sugar to coat evenly. Leave to dry. Scoop the sorbet carefully into the glasses, decorate with elderflowers and serve.

Cranberry Sorbet in Lace Pancakes

Pretty lace pancakes make a really stunning decoration for sorbets and ice creams. The sweet yet tangy cranberry sorbet makes an impressive dinner party dessert at any time of the year.

SERVES SIX

INGREDIENTS

500g | 1¼lb | 5 cups CRANBERRIES

225g | 8oz | 1 cup CASTER (SUPERFINE) SUGAR

300ml | ½ pint | 1¼ cups ORANGE JUICE

60ml | 4 tbsp COINTREAU or other ORANGE-FLAVOURED LIQUEUR

ICING (CONFECTIONERS') SUGAR, for dusting

extra CRANBERRIES and LIGHTLY WHIPPED CREAM, to serve

For the pancakes

50g | 2oz | ½ cup PLAIN (ALL-PURPOSE) FLOUR

2.5ml | ½ tsp GROUND GINGER

1 EGG

15ml | 1 tbsp CASTER (SUPERFINE) SUGAR

120ml | 4fl oz | ½ cup MILK

a little OIL, for frying

1 Put the cranberries, sugar and orange juice in a pan and heat gently until the sugar has dissolved. Cover and cook gently for 5–8 minutes more, until the cranberries are very tender. Leave to cool.

2 Tip the mixture into a food processor and process until smooth. Press the purée through a sieve placed over a bowl to extract as much juice as possible. Stir the liqueur into the juice, then chill until very cold.

3 Churn the mixture in an ice cream maker until the sorbet holds its shape. Scrape into a container and freeze overnight.

4 Make the pancakes. Sift the flour and ginger into a bowl. Add the egg, sugar and a little of the milk. Gradually whisk in the remaining milk to make a smooth batter. Heat a little oil in a small frying pan or crêpe pan. Pour off the excess oil and remove the pan from the heat.

5 Using a dessertspoon, drizzle a little of the batter over the bottom of the hot pan, using a scribbling action to give a lacy effect. (The pancake should be about 14cm | 5½in in diameter.) Return the pan to the heat and cook the mixture gently until the lacy pancake is golden on the underside.

6 Carefully turn it over, and cook for 1 minute more. Slide on to a plate and leave to cool. Make five more pancakes in the same way, lightly oiling the pan each time.

7 To serve, lay a pancake on a serving plate, underside upwards. Arrange several small scoops of the sorbet on one side of the pancake. Fold over and dust generously with icing sugar. Scatter with extra cranberries. Serve with whipped cream.

COOK'S TIP *When drizzling the batter into the frying pan, make sure all the lacy edges are connected, otherwise the pancakes will fall apart when you try to turn them.*

Chocolate Millefeuille Slice

Although this stunning dessert takes a little time to prepare, the good news is that it can be assembled

days in advance, ready to impress dinner guests. Simply transfer it to the refrigerator

about 30 minutes before serving so that it becomes easier to slice.

SERVES EIGHT

INGREDIENTS

4 EGG YOLKS

10ml | 2 tsp CORNFLOUR (CORNSTARCH)

300ml | ½ pint | 1¼ cups MILK

175ml | 6fl oz | ¾ cup MAPLE SYRUP

250ml | 8fl oz | 1 cup CRÈME FRAÎCHE

115g | 4oz | 1 cup PECAN NUTS, chopped

To finish

200g | 7oz PLAIN (SEMI-SWEET) CHOCOLATE

300ml | ½ pint | 1¼ cups DOUBLE (HEAVY) CREAM

45ml | 3 tbsp ICING (CONFECTIONERS') SUGAR

30ml | 2 tbsp BRANDY

lightly toasted PECAN NUTS

1 Whisk the egg yolks in a bowl with the cornflour and a little of the milk until smooth. Pour the remaining milk into a pan, bring to the boil, then pour over the yolk mixture, stirring.

2 Return the mixture to the pan and stir in the maple syrup. Cook gently, stirring until thickened and smooth. Do not boil. Pour into a bowl and cover closely with baking parchment to prevent a skin forming. Leave to cool.

3 Churn in an ice cream maker until thick and creamy, then add the chopped pecan nuts. Scrape into a freezerproof container and freeze overnight.

4 Break 150g | 5oz of the chocolate into pieces and melt in a bowl over a pan of simmering water. On greaseproof paper draw four rectangles, each measuring 19 x 12cm | 7½ x 4½in.

5 Spoon a quarter of the melted chocolate on to each rectangle and spread in a thin layer to the edges. Leave to set.

COOK'S TIP *It is a good idea to assemble the millefeuille on the upside-down lid of a rectangular freezer tub. The cover can then be fitted and the dessert frozen. Carefully slide the dessert on to a rectangular plate to serve.*

6 Pare thin curls from the remaining chocolate using a potato peeler. Then whip the cream with the icing sugar and brandy until it forms soft peaks.

7 Carefully peel away the paper from a set chocolate rectangle and place it on a flat freezerproof serving plate. Try not to touch the top too much or you will leave fingerprints. Spread a third of the whipped cream on the chocolate, taking it almost to the edges.

8 Using a dessertspoon, shape small scoops of the ice cream and lay these over the cream. Cover with a second chocolate rectangle. Repeat the layering, finishing with chocolate.

9 Scatter with the toasted pecan nuts and chocolate curls. Freeze overnight until firm. If freezing the slice for longer, cover it loosely with foil once it has frozen solid.

10 Transfer the frozen slice to the refrigerator 30 minutes before serving to soften. Serve in slices.

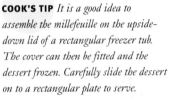

Coconut Ice Cream with Mango Sauce

Halved coconut shells make impressive serving containers for this rich and delicious

ice cream. You'll need to crack open three coconuts to get six serving cups,

plus enough trimmings to use in the ice cream.

SERVES SIX

INGREDIENTS

4 EGG YOLKS

115g | 4oz | ½ cup CASTER (SUPERFINE) SUGAR

15ml | 1 tbsp CORNFLOUR (CORNSTARCH)

5ml | 1 tsp ALMOND ESSENCE (EXTRACT)

600ml | 1 pint | 2½ cups MILK

150g | 5oz | 1½ cups FRESHLY GRATED COCONUT

300ml | ½ pint | 1¼ cups WHIPPING CREAM

For the sauce

1 LARGE RIPE MANGO

30ml | 2 tbsp CASTER (SUPERFINE) SUGAR

15ml | 1 tbsp LEMON JUICE

60ml | 4 tbsp FRESH ORANGE JUICE

1 Beat the egg yolks, sugar, cornflour, almond essence and a little of the milk until combined. If using freshly grated coconut, tip it into a food processor and process with 300ml | ½ pint | 1¼ cups of the remaining milk until fairly smooth.

2 Pour the fresh coconut milk into a heavy pan and stir in the rest of the milk. Bring the milk almost to the boil.

3 Pour the milk over the egg yolks whisking constantly. Return to the pan and cook very gently, stirring until thickened. Pour into a bowl, cover it with a circle of baking parchment and leave to cool.

4 Stir in the cream and churn it in an ice cream maker until it holds its shape. Spoon into a freezer container and freeze overnight.

5 To make the sauce, slice the mango flesh off the stone and put it into a food processor. Add the sugar, lemon juice and orange juice and process until smooth. Pour into a jug (pitcher) and chill.

6 To serve, scoop into the halved coconut shells, or into tall serving glasses. Add the mango sauce and serve immediately.

VARIATION *This ice cream would also be delicious served with passion fruit sauce instead of mango sauce. Simply substitute the flesh of 3 passion fruit for the mango and mix with the sugar, lemon juice and orange juice by hand rather than in the food processor.*

White Chocolate Castles

These impressive chocolate cases serve a wide variety of uses and can be made up to three days in advance and stored in a cool place until they are needed. They can be frozen with iced mousses or other desserts set in them, or, as in this recipe, filled with scoops of ice cream and succulent fresh blueberries.

SERVES SIX

INGREDIENTS

225g | 8oz WHITE CHOCOLATE, broken into pieces

250ml | 8fl oz | 1 cup DOUBLE WHITE CHOCOLATE ICE CREAM

250ml | 8fl oz | 1 cup CLASSIC DARK CHOCOLATE ICE CREAM

115g | 4oz | 1 cup BLUEBERRIES

(UNSWEETENED) COCOA POWDER or ICING (CONFECTIONERS') SUGAR for dusting

1 Put the white chocolate pieces in a heatproof bowl, set it over a pan of gently simmering water and leave until the chocolate has melted. Line a baking sheet with greaseproof paper. Cut out six 30 x 13cm | 12 x 5in strips of baking parchment, then fold each in half lengthways.

2 Stand a 7.5cm | 3in pastry cutter on the baking sheet. Roll one strip of paper into a circle and fit inside the cutter with the folded edge on the base paper. Stick the edges together with tape.

3 Remove the cutter from the paper collar and shape more collars in the same way. Leave the pastry cutter in place around the final collar.

4 Spoon a little of the melted chocolate into the base of the collar supported by the cutter.

5 Using a teaspoon, spread the chocolate over the base and up the sides of the collar, making the top edge uneven. Carefully lift away the cutter.

6 Make five more chocolate cases in the same way, using the cutter for extra support each time. Leave the cases in a cool place or in the refrigerator to set.

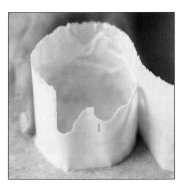

7 Carefully peel away the paper from the sides of the chocolate cases then lift the cases off the base. Transfer to serving plates.

8 Using a large melon baller or teaspoon, scoop the white and dark chocolate ice creams into the cases and decorate with the fruit.

9 Dust with cocoa powder or icing sugar and serve at once.

Miniature Choc-ices

For summer entertaining, these little chocolate-coated ice creams make a fun alternative to the more familiar after-dinner chocolates. You can be creative with toppings and adapt them to suit the occasion, from chopped nuts for adults to multicoloured sprinkles for children.

MAKES ABOUT 25

INGREDIENTS

750ml | 1¼ pints | 3 cups
CLASSIC VANILLA,
CLASSIC DARK CHOCOLATE or
CLASSIC COFFEE ICE CREAM

200g | 7oz PLAIN (SEMI-SWEET)
CHOCOLATE, broken into pieces

25g | 1oz MILK CHOCOLATE,
broken into pieces

25g | 1oz | ¼ cup chopped
HAZELNUTS, lightly toasted

1 Put a large baking sheet in the freezer for 15 minutes. Using a melon baller, scoop balls of the each of the different flavours of ice cream and place these on the baking sheet. Freeze for at least 1 hour until firm.

2 Line a second baking sheet with baking parchment and place it in the freezer for 15 minutes. Melt the plain chocolate in a heatproof bowl set over a pan of gently simmering water. Melt the milk chocolate in the same way in a separate bowl.

COOK'S TIP *If the melted milk chocolate is very runny, leave it for a few minutes to thicken up slightly before spooning it over the ice cream scoops. The milk chocolate can be piped on the choc-ices, using a bag fitted with a writing nozzle.*

3 Using a slim spatula, transfer the ice cream scoops to the paper-lined sheet. Spoon a little plain chocolate over one scoop so that most of it is coated.

4 Scatter the melted chocolate immediately with chopped nuts, before the chocolate sets.

5 Coat the remaining scoops with the dark chocolate. Scatter chopped nuts over half of the chocolate-covered scoops, working quickly so that the chocolate does not set.

6 Once the chocolate has set on the half that are not topped with nuts, drizzle each with milk chocolate, using a teaspoon. Freeze until ready to serve.

Hazelnut Cones with Vanilla Ice Cream and Hazelnut Caramel Sauce

Unlike bought ice cream cones, these hazelnut biscuit cones not only fulfil a function but taste delicious too!

They keep well in an airtight container for several days, but should they start to soften, pop

them into a moderate oven for a minute or two.

SERVES EIGHT

INGREDIENTS

90g | 3½oz | scant 1 cup GROUND HAZELNUTS

50g | 2oz | ½ cup PLAIN (ALL-PURPOSE) FLOUR

50g | 2oz | ¼ cup CASTER (SUPERFINE) SUGAR

2 EGGS, lightly beaten

5ml | 1 tsp NATURAL VANILLA ESSENCE (EXTRACT)

15ml | 1 tbsp MILK

For the sauce

75g | 3oz | 6 tbsp CASTER (SUPERFINE) SUGAR

60ml | 4 tbsp WATER

50g | 2oz | ½ cup HAZELNUTS, lightly toasted and roughly chopped

15ml | 1 tbsp LEMON JUICE

25g | 1oz | 2 tbsp UNSALTED (SWEET) BUTTER

about 500ml | 17fl oz | 2¼ cups VANILLA ICE CREAM

COOK'S TIP *The thickness of the biscuits (cookies) is crucial, so treat the first batch as a trial run. If the mixture is spread too thickly the biscuits will be rather soft; if too thin, they will crack when shaped around the moulds.*

1 Preheat the oven to 180°C | 350°F | Gas 4. Line a baking sheet with baking parchment. Mix the ground hazelnuts, flour and sugar in a bowl. Add the eggs, vanilla essence and milk and mix to a smooth paste.

2 Scoop up a shallow tablespoonful of the mixture and spoon it on to one end of the baking sheet. Add a second spoonful at the opposite end.

3 Using a slim spatula spread each spoonful to a circle about 13cm | 5in in diameter, making sure that the paste is spread to an even thickness. Bake for about 5 minutes until the rounds start to turn pale gold around the edges.

4 Working quickly, lift a round from the paper and turn it over. Wrap it around a cream horn mould to make a cone shape. Repeat with the other rounds.

5 As soon as the rounds become brittle, gently ease the cones away from the moulds. Repeat with the remaining mixture to make eight cones in all.

6 Make the sauce. Heat the sugar and water in a small, heavy pan until the sugar has dissolved. Bring to the boil and boil rapidly, without stirring, until the caramel is a deep golden colour.

7 Immediately immerse the base of the pan in cold water to prevent the caramel from further cooking. Protecting your hand with an oven glove, add 60ml | 4 tbsp water, standing back in case the syrup splutters.

8 Add the hazelnuts, lemon juice and butter to the pan and cook gently until the sauce is glossy. Pour it into a small jug (pitcher).

9 Scoop the vanilla ice cream into the hazelnut cones. Pour over a little sauce and serve immediately.

Chocolate Ice Cream with Lime Sabayon

Sabayon sauce has a light, foamy texture that perfectly complements the rich, smooth flavour of ice cream.

This tangy lime version is delicious with chocolate ice cream but can also be served

with tropical fruit, soft fruit or vanilla ice cream.

SERVES FOUR

INGREDIENTS

2 EGG YOLKS

65g | 2½oz | 5 tbsp CASTER
(SUPERFINE) SUGAR

finely grated rind and juice of
2 LIMES

60ml | 4 tbsp WHITE WINE or
APPLE JUICE

45ml | 3 tbsp SINGLE
(LIGHT) CREAM

500ml | 17fl oz | 2¼ cups
CHOCOLATE CHIP or CLASSIC
DARK CHOCOLATE ICE CREAM

pared strips of LIME RIND,
to decorate

1 Put the egg yolks and sugar in
a heatproof bowl and beat until
combined. Beat in the lime rind
and juice, then the white wine or
apple juice.

2 Whisk over a pan of simmering
water until the sabayon is smooth
and thick, and the mixture leaves a
trail when the whisk is lifted from
the bowl. Lightly whisk in the
cream. Remove the bowl from the
pan and cover with a lid or plate.

3 Working quickly, scoop the ice
cream into four glasses. Spoon the
sabayon sauce over the ice cream,
decorate with the strips of lime
rind and serve immediately.

Chocolate Ice Cream in Florentine Baskets

A similar mixture to that used when making florentines is perfect for shaping fluted baskets for holding scoops of ice cream. For convenience, make the baskets a couple of days in advance, but dip the edges in chocolate on the day you serve them.

SERVES EIGHT

INGREDIENTS

115g | 4oz | ½ cup BUTTER, plus extra for greasing

50g | 2oz | ¼ cup CASTER (SUPERFINE) SUGAR

90ml | 6 tbsp GOLDEN SYRUP or LIGHT CORN SYRUP

90g | 3½oz | scant 1 cup PLAIN (ALL-PURPOSE) FLOUR

50g | 2oz | ½ cup FLAKED (SLICED) ALMONDS

50g | 2oz | ¼ cup GLACÉ (CANDIED) CHERRIES, finely chopped

25g | 1oz | 3 tbsp RAISINS, chopped

15ml | 1 tbsp finely chopped PRESERVED STEM GINGER

90g | 3½oz PLAIN (SEMI-SWEET) CHOCOLATE, broken into pieces

about 750ml | 1¼ pints | 3 cups CLASSIC DARK CHOCOLATE ICE CREAM

1 Preheat the oven to 190°C | 375°F | Gas 5. Line two large baking sheets with lightly greased baking parchment. Melt the butter in a small, heavy pan and add the sugar and syrup. Off the heat, stir in the flour, almonds, cherries, raisins and ginger.

2 Place a shallow tablespoonful of the mixture at either end of one baking sheet, then spread each spoonful to a 13cm | 5in round.

3 Bake for about 5 minutes until each round has spread even more and looks lacy and deep golden. Meanwhile spread more circles on the second baking sheet ready to put in the oven. Have ready several metal dariole moulds for shaping the baskets.

4 Leave the biscuits (cookies) on the baking sheet for about 2 minutes to firm up slightly. Working quickly, lift one biscuit on a spatula and lay it over an upturned dariole mould. Gently shape the biscuit into flutes around the sides of the mould. Shape the other biscuit in the same way.

5 Leave the biscuits in place for about 2 minutes until cool, then carefully lift the baskets away from the dariole moulds. Cook and shape the remaining biscuit mixture in the same way until you have eight baskets in total.

6 Melt the chocolate in a heatproof bowl over a pan of gently simmering water.

7 Carefully dip the edges of the baskets in the melted chocolate and place on individual dessert plates. Scoop the chocolate ice cream into the baskets to serve.

COOK'S TIP *If the biscuits (cookies) feel as though they are going to fall apart when you lift them from the baking sheet, leave them a little longer to firm up slightly. If they become brittle before you've shaped them, pop them back in the oven for a few moments to soften.*

Chocolate Teardrops with Cherry Sauce

These stunning chocolate cases look impressive but are surprisingly easy to make.

Once filled they freeze well, making the perfect choice for a special occasion dessert.

SERVES SIX

INGREDIENTS

90g | 3½oz PLAIN (BITTERSWEET) CHOCOLATE, broken into pieces

115g | 4oz AMARETTI

450ml | ¾ pint | scant 2 cups DOUBLE (HEAVY) CREAM

2.5ml | ½ tsp ALMOND ESSENCE (EXTRACT)

40g | 1½oz | ⅓ cup ICING (CONFECTIONER'S) SUGAR

30ml | 2 tbsp BRANDY or ALMOND LIQUEUR

75ml | 5 tbsp FULL CREAM (WHOLE) MILK

FRESH CHERRIES, to decorate

For the sauce

2.5ml | ½ tsp CORNFLOUR (CORNSTARCH)

75ml | 5 tbsp WATER

225g | 8oz FRESH CHERRIES, pitted and halved

45ml | 3 tbsp CASTER SUGAR

10ml | 2 tsp LEMON JUICE

45ml | 3 tbsp BRANDY or ALMOND LIQUEUR

1 Cut out six Perspex (Plexiglass) strips, each measuring 27 x 3cm | 2 x 1¼in. Put the chocolate in a heatproof bowl over a pan of simmering water. Leave until the chocolate has melted, then remove from the heat and leave for 5 minutes. Line a baking sheet with baking parchment.

2 Coat the underside of a Perspex strip in the chocolate, apart from 1cm | ½in at each end. Try to keep the other side uncoated.

3 Bring the ends of the strip together so the coated side is on the inside. Secure the ends with paper clips, then put on the baking sheet to set. Make five more shapes in the same way. Chill until set.

4 Put the amaretti in a plastic bag, seal and crush with a rolling pin. Put the cream in a bowl and beat in the almond essence, icing sugar and liqueur.

5 Pour into the ice cream maker; churn until thick. Spoon in the milk and scatter with the crushed biscuits (cookies). Churn until mixed.

6 Spoon the mixture carefully into the chocolate cases, making sure they're filled to the rim. If necessary, tap the baking sheet gently to level the mixture. Freeze for at least 2 hours or overnight.

7 Make the sauce. Put the cornflour in a small pan and stir in a little of the water to make a paste. Stir in the remaining water with the cherries, sugar and lemon juice. Bring just to the boil, stirring until thickened. Remove from the heat and leave to cool. Stir in the liqueur.

8 To serve, remove the paper clips from the chocolate shapes and peel away the perspex. Transfer the shapes to dessert plates. Spoon a little sauce beside the cases and serve decorated with fresh cherries.

Iced Cappuccino Cups

Small modern tea cups or coffee cups and saucers make attractive containers for this richly flavoured ice cream. Top with spoonfuls of extra whipped cream and a light dusting of drinking chocolate powder for a refreshing alternative to coffee at the end of a meal.

3 Whisk the egg yolks, sugar and cornflour together in a bowl until the mixture is thick and pale. Return the coffee to the pan, bring it just back to the boil, then gradually pour it on to the yolk mixture, whisking continuously.

4 Return the mixture to the pan and cook over a gentle heat, stirring constantly until the custard thickens and is smooth. Pour it back into the bowl, cover tightly and leave to cool. Chill in the refrigerator until completely cold.

SERVES SIX

INGREDIENTS

150ml | ¼ pint | ⅔ cup WATER

75ml | 5 tbsp GROUND ESPRESSO COFFEE

4 EGG YOLKS

65g | 2½oz | 5 tbsp LIGHT MUSCOVADO (BROWN) SUGAR

5ml | 1 tsp CORNFLOUR (CORNSTARCH)

300ml | ½ pint | 1¼ cups WHIPPING CREAM

30ml | 2 tbsp TIA MARIA or KAHLÚA LIQUEUR

To decorate

lightly whipped CREAM

DRINKING CHOCOLATE POWDER

1 Pour the water into a small pan and stir in the coffee powder. Bring the mixture to the boil, remove the pan from the heat and then leave it to infuse for 15 minutes.

2 Strain the coffee through a muslin- (cheesecloth-) lined sieve into a jug (pitcher).

5 Mix in the cream and liqueur, then pour into an ice cream maker. Churn until the mixture is thick.

6 Spoon the ice cream into cups and level the surface. Transfer to the freezer until hardened and ready to serve.

7 Serve topped with spoonfuls of whipped cream and a light dusting of chocolate powder.

Pear and Gingerbread Sundaes

The best sundaes do not consist solely of ice cream, but are a feast of flavours that melt into each other, as in a trifle. Poach the pears and chill them well in advance, so that the dessert can be assembled in minutes.

SERVES FOUR

INGREDIENTS

65g | 2½oz | ⅓ cup LIGHT BROWN SUGAR

90ml | 6 tbsp WATER

30ml | 2 tbsp LEMON JUICE

40g | 1½oz | ⅓ cup RAISINS

1.5ml | ¼ tsp GROUND MIXED SPICE or APPLE PIE SPICE

4 SMALL PEARS

150g | 5oz MOIST GINGERBREAD

250ml | 8fl oz | 1 cup CLASSIC VANILLA ICE CREAM

1 Heat the sugar and water in a heavy pan until the sugar has dissolved. Add the lemon juice, raisins and spice. Peel, quarter and core the pears and add them to the pan.

2 Cover and simmer very gently for 5–10 minutes until just tender. Cool the pears in the syrup. Lift them out of the syrup and put them in a bowl. Pour the syrup into a jug (pitcher). Chill both.

3 Cut the gingerbread into four pieces and arrange in four serving glasses. Divide the pears among the glasses, then pile ice cream in the centre of each portion. Pour a little of the syrup over each sundae and serve.

VARIATION *This quick and easy dessert can be made just as successfully with tart dessert apples.*

Iced Raspberry and Almond Trifle

This delicious combination of almond sponge, sherried fruit, ice cream and mascarpone topping is sheer indulgence for trifle lovers. The sponge and topping can be made a day in advance, and the assembled trifle will sit happily in the refrigerator for an hour before serving.

SERVES EIGHT TO TEN

INGREDIENTS

For the sponge

115g | 4oz | ½ cup UNSALTED (SWEET) BUTTER, softened

115g | 4oz | ½ cup LIGHT BROWN SUGAR

2 EGGS

75g | 3oz | ⅔ cup SELF-RAISING (SELF-RISING) FLOUR

2.5ml | ½ tsp BAKING POWDER

115g | 4oz | 1 cup finely GROUND ALMONDS

5ml | 1 tsp ALMOND ESSENCE (EXTRACT)

15ml | 1 tbsp MILK

To finish

300g | 11oz | scant 2 cups RASPBERRIES

50g | 2oz | ½ cup FLAKED (SLICED) ALMONDS, toasted

90ml | 6 tbsp FRESH ORANGE JUICE

200ml | 7fl oz | scant 1 cup MEDIUM SHERRY

500g | 1¼lb | 2½ cups MASCARPONE CHEESE

150g | 5oz | ⅔ cup GREEK (US STRAINED PLAIN) YOGURT

30ml | 2 tbsp ICING (CONFECTIONERS') SUGAR

about 250ml | 8fl oz | 1 cup VANILLA ICE CREAM

about 250ml | 8fl oz | 1 cup RASPBERRY ICE CREAM or SORBET

VARIATION *There are many variations on this recipe that work equally well. Try any other soft summer fruits or tropical fruits and complementary ice creams or sorbets.*

COOK'S TIP *The trifle will set better if all the ingredients are thoroughly chilled before assembling. Chill again before serving.*

1 Preheat the oven to 180°C | 350°F | Gas 4. Grease and line a 20cm | 8in round cake tin (pan).

2 Put the butter, sugar, eggs, flour, baking powder, almonds and almond essence in a large bowl and beat with an electric whisk for 2 minutes until creamy and smooth. Stir in the milk.

3 Spoon the mixture into the prepared tin, level the surface and bake for about 30 minutes or until just firm in the centre. Transfer to a wire rack and leave to cool.

6 Spoon over the orange and sherry mixture. Beat the mascarpone in a bowl with the yogurt, icing sugar and remaining sherry.

7 Put the trifle dish and the mascarpone in the refrigerator until you are ready to assemble the raspberry and almond trifle.

8 To serve, scoop the ice cream and sorbet into the trifle dish. Reserve a few of the remaining raspberries and almonds for the decoration, then scatter the rest over the ice cream.

9 Spoon over the mascarpone mixture and scatter the trifle with the reserved raspberries and almonds.

10 Chill the trifle for up to 1 hour before serving.

4 Cut the sponge into chunky pieces and place these in the base of a 1.75 litre | 3 pint | 7½ cup glass serving dish. Scatter with half the raspberries and almonds.

5 Mix the orange juice with 90ml | 6 tbsp of the sherry.

Blackcurrant and Meringue Trifles

These quick desserts, made using meringues, cream and sorbet, are suitable for every day or special occasions.

SERVES SIX

INGREDIENTS

350ml | 12fl oz | 1½ cups
BLACKCURRANT SORBET

3 bought MERINGUES

several sprigs of FRESH MINT, plus
extra MINT SPRIGS, to decorate

30ml | 2 tbsp ICING
(CONFECTIONERS') SUGAR

20ml | 4 tsp LEMON JUICE

300ml | ½ pint | 1¼ cups
WHIPPING CREAM

90ml | 6 tbsp GREEK
(US STRAINED PLAIN) YOGURT

2 Break the meringues into small pieces. Add the icing sugar and lemon juice to the cream. Whip until the mixture just holds its shape. Stir in the Greek yogurt, then fold in the crushed meringues.

3 Spoon a little of the cream mixture into small, deep dishes or glasses. Add layers of sorbet and cream mixture, ending with cream mixture. Decorate with mint sprigs.

COOK'S TIP *The amount this will serve will depend on the size of the dishes used. If you opt for large bowl-shaped glasses, the mixture will probably serve four.*

1 Remove the sorbet from the freezer. Finely chop the mint and put it in a small bowl.

Fig, Port and Clementine Sundaes

SERVES SIX

INGREDIENTS

6 CLEMENTINES

30ml | 2 tbsp CLEAR HONEY

1 CINNAMON STICK, halved

15ml | 1 tbsp LIGHT MUSCOVADO
(BROWN) SUGAR

60ml | 4 tbsp PORT

6 FRESH FIGS

approx 500ml | 17fl oz | 2¼ cups
ORANGE SORBET

1 Finely grate the rind from two clementines and put it in a small, heavy pan. Using a small, sharp knife cut the peel away from all the clementines, then slice the flesh thinly. Add the honey, cinnamon, sugar and port to the clementine rind. Heat gently until the sugar has dissolved, to make a syrup.

The flavours of figs, cinnamon, clementines and port conjure up images of winter and hearty meals.

2 Put the clementine slices in a heatproof bowl and pour over the port and cinnamon syrup. Cool completely, then chill.

3 Slice the figs thinly and add them to the clementines and syrup, tossing the ingredients together gently to combine. Leave for 10 minutes, then discard the cinnamon stick.

4 Arrange half the fig and clementine slices around the sides of six serving glasses. Half fill the glasses with scoops of sorbet. Arrange the remaining fruit slices around the sides of the glasses, then pile more sorbet into the centre. Pour over the port syrup and serve.

hot
ice cream
puddings

Nothing beats the melting texture of cold ice cream as it seeps into a deliciously warm pastry or mingles with the juices of a hot fruit compote, bringing out both the flavour and the temperature contrast. This chapter combines quick-and-easy puddings with make-ahead desserts.

Baby Alaskas with Liqueured Apricots

Just as effective as a traditional baked Alaska, these decadent individual desserts contain a layer of cool, creamy ice cream lavishly covered in hot, soft meringue and contain a heart of sweet, rich apricot filling subtly flavoured with orange liqueur.

SERVES SIX

INGREDIENTS

40g | 1½oz | 3 tbsp SUGAR

60ml | 4 tbsp WATER

150g | 5oz | generous ½ cup READY-TO-EAT APRICOTS, roughly chopped

30ml | 2 tbsp COINTREAU or other ORANGE-FLAVOURED LIQUEUR

500ml | 17fl oz | 2¼ cups VANILLA, HONEY or any NUT-FLAVOURED ICE CREAM

6 LARGE ALMOND BISCUITS (COOKIES) or GINGERSNAPS

3 EGG WHITES

175g | 6oz | scant 1 cup CASTER (SUPERFINE) SUGAR

1 Heat the sugar and water in a small, heavy pan, stirring occasionally, until the sugar has dissolved. Add the apricots and simmer gently for 5 minutes until they have absorbed most of the syrup. Stir in the liqueur and leave to chill.

2 Freeze six small dariole moulds or metal pudding moulds for 15 minutes. At the same time, remove the ice cream from the freezer and leave for 15 minutes to soften slightly.

VARIATION *Feel free to experiment and substitute your favourite liqueur for the orange one recommended here.*

3 Using a dessertspoon, pack most of the ice cream into the moulds, leaving a deep cavity in the centre of each. Return each mould to the freezer once completed.

4 When all the moulds have been lined with ice cream, remove from the freezer and fill with the apricots.

5 Cover the apricots with more ice cream and freeze until firm.

6 Dip each mould in very hot water for 1–2 seconds, then invert. Slide a biscuit (cookie) under each ice cream and transfer to a baking sheet. Place in the freezer.

7 Whisk the egg whites in a grease-free bowl until they are stiff. Gradually whisk in the caster sugar, a tablespoonful at a time, whisking well after each addition until the mixture has become stiff and glossy.

8 Using a slim spatula spread a thick layer of the meringue over each ice cream, making sure that the meringue meets the biscuits and seals in the ice cream.

9 Swirl the surface of the meringue decoratively. Return each of the covered ice creams to the freezer.

10 About 15 minutes before serving, preheat the oven to 230°C | 450°F | Gas 8. Bake the Alaskas for about 2 minutes or until the meringue is pale golden. Serve immediately.

Coconut and Passion Fruit Alaska

A really classic ice cream extravaganza, baked Alaska lends itself to many variations on the basic theme.

This version comprises a passion-fruit-steeped coconut sponge, topped with tropical fruit ice

cream and smothered in a delicious coconut-flavoured meringue.

SERVES EIGHT

INGREDIENTS

For the cake

115g | 4oz | ½ cup UNSALTED (SWEET) BUTTER, softened

115g | 4oz | generous ½ cup CASTER (SUPERFINE) SUGAR

2 EGGS

115g | 4oz | 1 cup SELF-RAISING (SELF-RISING) FLOUR

2.5ml | ½ tsp BAKING POWDER

5ml | 1 tsp ALMOND ESSENCE (EXTRACT)

40g | 1½oz | ½ cup DESICCATED (DRY UNSWEETENED SHREDDED) COCONUT

15ml | 1 tbsp MILK

To finish

1 litre | 1¾ pints | 4 cups MANGO AND PASSION FRUIT GELATO softened

60ml | 4 tbsp KIRSCH

3 PASSION FRUIT

3 EGG WHITES

115g | 4oz | generous ½ cup CASTER (SUPERFINE) SUGAR

50g | 2oz | ½ cup CREAMED COCONUT or FRESH COCONUT, grated

1 Preheat the oven to 180°C | 350°F | Gas 4. Grease and line an 18cm | 7in round cake tin (pan). Whisk all the sponge ingredients in a bowl until smooth. Spoon into the prepared tin, level the surface and bake for 35 minutes until the cake is just firm. Cool on a wire rack.

2 Dampen a 1.2 litre | 2 pint | 5 cup bowl and line it with clear film (plastic wrap).

3 Pack the ice cream into the lined bowl and return it to the freezer for 1 hour. Place the cake on a small baking sheet or ovenproof plate and drizzle the surface with kirsch. Remove the pulp from the fruit and scoop over the cake.

4 Dip the bowl containing the ice cream into very hot water for about 2 seconds to loosen the shaped ice cream. Invert it on to the sponge. Peel away the clear film and put the cake and ice cream in the freezer.

5 To make the meringue, whisk the egg whites in a clean bowl until stiff. Gradually add the sugar, a tablespoon at a time, whisking well after each addition, until the meringue is thick and glossy. Fold in the grated coconut.

6 Using a slim spatula, spread the meringue over the ice cream and sponge to cover both completely. Return to the freezer.

7 About 15 minutes before serving, preheat the oven to 220°C | 425°F | Gas 7. Bake for 4–5 minutes, watching closely, until the peaks are golden. Serve immediately.

Ice Cream Croissants with Chocolate Sauce

A deliciously easy croissant "sandwich" with a filling of vanilla custard, ice cream and chocolate sauce melting inside the warmed bread. Once assembled, serve immediately.

MAKES FOUR

INGREDIENTS

75g | 3oz PLAIN (SEMI-SWEET) CHOCOLATE, broken into pieces

15g | ½oz | 1 tbsp UNSALTED (SWEET) BUTTER

30ml | 2 tbsp GOLDEN SYRUP or LIGHT CORN SYRUP

4 CROISSANTS

90ml | 6 tbsp GOOD QUALITY READY-MADE VANILLA CUSTARD

4 large scoops of CLASSIC VANILLA ICE CREAM

ICING (CONFECTIONERS') SUGAR, for dusting

1 Preheat the oven to 180°C | 350°F | Gas 4. Put the chocolate in a small, heavy pan. Add the butter and syrup and heat gently until smooth, stirring frequently.

2 Split the croissants in half horizontally and place the bases on a baking sheet. Spoon the custard over the bases, cover with the lids and bake for 5 minutes.

3 Remove the lids and place a scoop of ice cream on each croissant. Spoon over half the sauce and press the lids down. Bake for 1 minute more.

4 Dust with icing sugar, and spoon over the remaining chocolate sauce.

Baked Bananas with Ice Cream

Baked bananas make the perfect partners for delicious vanilla ice cream topped with a toasted hazelnut sauce. A quick and easy dessert that looks as good as it tastes.

SERVES FOUR

INGREDIENTS

4 LARGE BANANAS

15ml | 1 tbsp LEMON JUICE

4 large scoops of CLASSIC VANILLA ICE CREAM

For the sauce

50g | 2oz | ½ cup HAZELNUTS

25g | 1oz | 2 tbsp UNSALTED (SWEET) BUTTER

45ml | 3 tbsp GOLDEN SYRUP or LIGHT CORN SYRUP

30ml | 2 tbsp LEMON JUICE

1 Preheat the oven to 180°C | 350°F | Gas 4. Place the unpeeled bananas on a baking sheet and brush them with the lemon juice. Bake for about 20 minutes until the skins are turning black and the flesh gives a little when the bananas are gently squeezed.

2 Toast the hazelnuts for the sauce under a medium grill (broiler). When cool, chop roughly.

COOK'S TIP *Bake the bananas over the dying coals of a barbecue, if you like.*

3 Make the sauce. Melt the butter in a small pan. Add the chopped hazelnuts and cook gently for 1 minute. Add the syrup and lemon juice and heat, stirring, for 1 minute more.

4 To serve, slit each banana open with a knife and open out the skins. Transfer to serving plates and serve with scoops of ice cream. Pour the sauce over.

Hot Ice Cream Fritters

Deep-fried ice cream may seem a contradiction in terms, but once you've made these crisp fritters, you'll be converted! The secret is to encase the ice cream thoroughly in two layers of sweet biscuit crumb. This will turn crisp and golden during frying, and the ice cream inside will melt only slightly.

SERVES FOUR

INGREDIENTS

750ml | 1¼ pints | 3 cups
FIRM VANILLA ICE CREAM

115g | 4oz AMARETTI

115g | 4oz | 2 cups FRESH
BROWN BREADCRUMBS

1 EGG

45g | 1¾oz | 3 tbsp PLAIN
(ALL-PURPOSE) FLOUR

OIL, for deep frying

For the caramel sauce

115g | 4oz | generous ½ cup
CASTER (SUPERFINE) SUGAR

150ml | ¼ pint | ⅔ cup WATER

150ml | ¼ pint | ⅔ cup DOUBLE
(HEAVY) CREAM

1 Line a baking sheet with baking parchment and put it in the freezer for 15 minutes, at the same time removing the ice cream from the freezer to soften slightly.

2 Scoop about 12 balls of ice cream, making them as round as possible and place them on the lined baking sheet. Freeze for at least 1 hour until firm.

3 Meanwhile, put the amaretti in a strong plastic bag and crush them with a rolling pin. Tip the crushed biscuits into a bowl and add the breadcrumbs. Mix well, then transfer half the mixture to a plate.

4 Beat the egg in a shallow dish. Sprinkle the flour in an even layer on to a second plate.

5 Run your hands under the cold tap under they are as cool as possible. Work quickly to roll each ice cream ball in the flour, then dip in the beaten egg until coated.

6 Roll the balls in the mixed crumbs until completely covered. Return the coated ice cream balls to the baking sheet and freeze for at least 1 hour more.

7 Repeat the process, using the remaining flour, egg and breadcrumbs, so that each ball has an additional coating. Return the ice cream balls to the freezer for at least 4 hours, preferably overnight.

8 Make the sauce. Heat the sugar and water in a small, heavy pan, stirring occasionally, until the sugar has dissolved. Bring to the boil and boil the syrup for about 10 minutes without stirring until deep golden.

9 Immediately immerse the base of the pan in a bowl of cold water to prevent the syrup from cooking any more.

10 Pour the cream into the syrup and return the pan to the heat. Stir until the sauce is smooth. Set aside while you fry the ice cream.

11 Pour oil into a heavy pan to a depth of 7.5cm | 3in. Heat to 185°C | 365°F | Gas 4 or until a cube of bread added to the oil browns in 30 seconds.

12 Add several of the ice cream balls and fry for about 1 minute until the coating on each is golden.

13 Drain on kitchen paper and quickly cook the remainder in the same way. Serve the fritters with the caramel sauce.

Toasted Marzipan Parcels with Plums

Melting ice cream, encased in lightly toasted marzipan, makes an irresistible dessert for anyone who likes the flavour of almonds. Lightly poached apricots, cherries, apples or pears can be used instead of the plums.

SERVES FOUR

INGREDIENTS

400g | 14oz GOLDEN MARZIPAN

ICING (CONFECTIONERS') SUGAR, for dusting

250ml | 8fl oz | 1 cup ALMOND ICE CREAM

For the plum compote

3 RED PLUMS, about 250g | 9oz

25g | 1oz | 2 tbsp CASTER (SUPERFINE) SUGAR

75ml | 5 tbsp WATER

1 Roll out the marzipan on a surface lightly dusted with sifted icing sugar to a 45 x 23cm | 18 x 9in rectangle. Stamp out eight 12cm | 4½in rounds.

2 Place a spoonful of the ice cream in the centre of one of the circles. Bring the marzipan up over the ice cream and press the edges together to completely encase.

3 Crimp the edges with your fingers. Transfer to a small baking sheet and freeze. Fill and shape the remaining parcels in the same way and freeze overnight.

4 Make the plum compote. Cut the plums in half, remove the stones, then cut each half into two wedges. Heat the sugar and water in a heavy pan, stirring occasionally, until the sugar has completely dissolved.

5 Add the plums and cook very gently for 5 minutes or until they have softened but retain their shape. Test with the tip of a sharp knife – the flesh of the plums should be just tender.

6 Preheat the grill (broiler) to high. Place the marzipan parcels on the grill rack and cook for 1–2 minutes, watching closely, until the crimped edge of the marzipan is lightly browned. Transfer the parcels to serving plates and serve with the warm plum compote.

COOK'S TIP *Don't let the parcels become too brown under the grill (broiler) or the ice cream will quickly seep out. Use a firm-textured ice cream and make sure the parcels are frozen solid before grilling (broiling) them.*

Filo, Ice Cream and Mincemeat Parcels

Looking rather like crispy fried pancakes, these golden parcels reveal hot chunky mincemeat and melting vanilla ice cream when cut open. They can be assembled days in advance, ready for easy, last-minute frying.

MAKES TWELVE

INGREDIENTS

1 FIRM PEAR

225g | 8oz | 1 cup MINCEMEAT

finely grated rind of 1 LEMON

12 sheets of FILO (PHYLLO) PASTRY, thawed if frozen

a little beaten EGG

250ml | 8 fl oz | 1 cup CLASSIC VANILLA ICE CREAM

OIL, for deep frying

CASTER (SUPERFINE) SUGAR for dusting

1 Peel, core and chop the pear. Put it in a small bowl and then stir in the mincemeat and lemon rind.

2 Cut a filo sheet into two 20cm | 8in squares.

3 Brush one square lightly with beaten egg then cover with the second square.

4 Lay 10ml | 2 tsp mincemeat on the filo, placing it 2.5cm | 1in away from one edge and spreading it slightly to cover a 7.5cm | 3in area.

5 Lay 10ml | 2 tsp of the ice cream over the mincemeat. Brush all around the edges of the filo with beaten egg.

6 Fold over the two opposite sides of the pastry to cover the filling. Roll up the strip, starting from the filled end. Transfer to a baking sheet and freeze. Make 11 more rolls in the same way.

7 When you are ready to serve, pour oil into a heavy pan to a depth of 7.5cm | 3in. Heat it to 185°C | 365°F or until a cube of bread added to the oil browns in 30 seconds.

8 Fry several parcels at a time for 1–2 minutes until pale golden, turning them over during cooking. Drain on kitchen paper while frying the remainder. Dust with caster sugar and serve immediately.

COOK'S TIP *Filo pastry sheets vary considerably in size. Don't worry if you can't get two 20cm | 8in squares from each slice. It won't matter if the squares are slightly smaller or even rectangular as long as they can be rolled to enclose the filling.*

Walnut and Vanilla Ice Palmiers

These walnut pastries can be served freshly baked, but for convenience, make them ahead and reheat them in a moderate oven for 5 minutes. Serve them warm, in pairs, sandwiched with ice cream.

MAKES SIX

INGREDIENTS

75g | 3oz | ¾ cup WALNUT PIECES

350g | 12oz PUFF PASTRY, thawed if frozen

beaten EGG, to glaze

45ml | 3 tbsp CASTER (SUPERFINE) SUGAR

about 200ml | 7fl oz | scant 1 cup CLASSIC VANILLA ICE CREAM

1 Preheat the oven to 200°C | 400°F | Gas 6. Lightly grease a large baking sheet with butter. Chop the walnuts finely. On a lightly floured surface roll the pastry to a thin rectangle 30 x 20cm | 12 x 8in.

2 Trim the edges of the pastry, then brush with the egg. Sprinkle all but 45ml | 3 tbsp of the walnuts and 30ml | 2 tbsp of the sugar. Run the rolling pin over the walnuts to press them into the pastry.

3 Roll up the pastry from one short side to the centre, then roll up the other side until the two rolls meet. Brush the points where the rolls meet with a little beaten egg. Using a sharp knife, cut the pastry into slices 1cm | ½in thick.

4 Lay the slices on the work surface and flatten with a rolling pin. Transfer to the baking sheet. Brush with the rest of the beaten egg and sprinkle with the reserved walnuts and sugar. Bake for about 15 minutes until pale golden.

Peach, Blackberry and Ice Cream Gratin

A wonderfully easy dessert in which the flavours of the hot peaches, blackberries, ice cream and muscovado sugar mingle together. Use large, ripe peaches with enough space for the filling.

3 Using a small teaspoon, take small scoops of the ice cream and pack them into the peach halves, piling up in the centre. Add the blackberries, pushing them gently into the ice cream.

4 Sprinkle the filled peaches with the muscovado sugar and replace under the hot grill for 1–2 minutes until the sugar has dissolved and the ice cream is beginning to melt. Serve immediately.

COOK'S TIP *Don't take the ice cream out of the freezer until just before you are ready to fill the peaches, and then work quickly. The ice cream must still be frozen solid or it will melt too quickly when the dessert is under the hot grill (broiler).*

SERVES FOUR

INGREDIENTS

4 LARGE PEACHES

15ml | 1 tbsp LEMON JUICE

120ml | 4fl oz | ½ cup CLASSIC VANILLA ICE CREAM

115g | 4oz | 1 cup SMALL BLACKBERRIES

40g | 1½oz | 3 tbsp LIGHT MUSCOVADO (BROWN) SUGAR

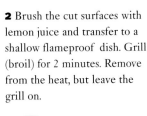

1 Preheat the grill (broiler). Cut the peaches in half and remove the stones (pits). Cut a thin slice off the rounded side of each peach so that they sit flat.

2 Brush the cut surfaces with lemon juice and transfer to a shallow flameproof dish. Grill (broil) for 2 minutes. Remove from the heat, but leave the grill on.

VARIATION *Other soft fruit, such as fresh blueberries, raspberries, recurrants or blackcurrants can be used instead of blackberries, if you prefer.*

Apple Ice Cream with Cinnamon Bread

Rich and creamy but with an apply tang, this ice cream melts irresistibly over the freshly cooked cinnamon bread. Any leftover ice cream is equally good with fruit pies, waffles, pancakes or drop scones.

SERVES SIX

INGREDIENTS

500g | 1¼lb COOKING APPLES

25g | 1oz | 2 tbsp UNSALTED (SWEET) BUTTER

1.5ml | ¼ tsp MIXED (APPLE PIE) SPICE

finely grated rind and juice of 1 LEMON

4 EGG YOLKS

90g | 3½oz | ½ cup CASTER (SUPERFINE) SUGAR

2.5ml | ½ tsp CORNFLOUR (CORNSTARCH)

300ml | ½ pint | 1¼ cups FULL CREAM (WHOLE) MILK

225g | 8oz | 1 cup CLOTTED CREAM

MINT SPRIGS, to decorate

For the cinnamon bread

6 thick slices of WHITE BREAD

1 EGG, beaten

1 EGG YOLK

2.5ml | ½ tsp VANILLA ESSENCE (EXTRACT)

150ml | ¼ pint | ⅔ cup SINGLE (LIGHT) CREAM

65g | 2½ oz | 5 tbsp CASTER (SUPERFINE) SUGAR

2.5ml | ½ tsp GROUND CINNAMON

25g | 1oz UNSALTED (SWEET) BUTTER

45ml | 3tbsp OIL

1 Peel, core and chop the apples into thin slices or small chunks. Melt the butter in a pan, add the apple, mixed spice and lemon rind and juice. Cover and cook very gently for 10 minutes or until the apples are soft. Leave to cool, then tip into a food processor and blend to a smooth purée.

2 Whisk the egg yolks, sugar and cornflour in a bowl. Bring the milk just to the boil in a heavy pan. Pour the milk over the whisked mixture, whisking well to combine. Pour the custard back into the pan and cook over a very gentle heat, stirring until slightly thickened. Tip into a bowl and leave to cool completely.

3 Beat the clotted cream in a bowl to soften it. Gradually beat in the cooled custard. Turn into the ice cream maker and churn until thick.

4 Add the apple purée and churn again until thickened. Transfer to a freezer container and freeze until ready to serve.

5 To make the cinnamon bread, cut the crusts off the bread then slice each diagonally in half. Beat together the egg, egg yolk, vanilla, cream and 15ml | 1tbsp of the sugar. Put the bread triangles in a single layer on a large, shallow plate or tray. Pour the cream mixture over and leave to stand for 10 minutes.

6 Mix the remaining sugar with the cinnamon on a plate. Melt the butter with the oil in a large frying pan. When hot, add half of the bread and fry until it is golden underneath. Turn the slices and fry the other side.

7 Drain the fried bread lightly on kitchen paper then coat on both sides with the sugar. Keep warm while cooking the remainder. Serve immediately, topped with scoops of apple ice cream and decorated with mint sprigs.

Ice Cream with Hot Cherry Sauce

Hot cherry sauce makes a classic yet really simple accompaniment to ice cream for serving on any occasion. Use only good quality chocolate and vanilla.

SERVES FOUR

INGREDIENTS

425g | 15oz can PITTED BLACK CHERRIES

10ml | 2 tsp CORNFLOUR (CORNSTARCH)

finely grated rind of 1 LEMON, plus 10ml | 2 tsp JUICE

15ml | 1 tbsp CASTER (SUPERFINE) SUGAR

2.5ml | ½ tsp GROUND CINNAMON

30ml | 2 tbsp BRANDY or KIRSCH (optional)

400ml | 14fl oz | 1⅔ cups CLASSIC DARK CHOCOLATE ICE CREAM

400ml | 14fl oz | 1⅔ cups CLASSIC VANILLA ICE CREAM

DRINKING CHOCOLATE POWDER, for dusting

1 Drain the cherries, reserving the canning juices. Spoon the cornflour into a small pan and blend to a paste with a little of the reserved juice.

2 Stir in the remaining canning juice with the lemon rind and juice, sugar and cinnamon. Bring to the boil, stirring, until smooth and glossy.

3 Add the cherries, with the brandy or kirsch, if using. Stir gently, then cook for 1 minute. Scoop the ice cream into shallow dishes. Spoon the sauce around, dust with chocolate powder and serve.

Syrupy Brioche Slices with Vanilla Ice Cream

Keep a few individual brioche buns in the freezer to make this fabulous five-minute pudding.

SERVES FOUR

INGREDIENTS

BUTTER, for greasing

finely grated rind and juice of 1 ORANGE

50g | 2oz | ¼ cup CASTER (SUPERFINE) SUGAR

90ml | 6 tbsp WATER

1.5ml | ¼ tsp GROUND CINNAMON

4 BRIOCHE BUNS

15ml | 1 tbsp ICING (CONFECTIONERS') SUGAR

400ml | 14fl oz | 1⅔ cups CLASSIC VANILLA ICE CREAM

1 Lightly grease a gratin dish and set aside. Put the orange rind and juice, sugar, water and cinnamon in a heavy pan.

2 Heat gently, stirring, until the sugar has dissolved, then boil for 2 minutes without stirring.

VARIATION *For a slightly tarter taste, use lemon rind and juice instead of orange.*

3 Remove the syrup from the heat and pour it into a shallow heatproof dish. Preheat the grill (broiler). Cut each brioche vertically into three thick slices.

4 Dip one side of each slice in the hot syrup and arrange in the gratin dish, syrupy sides down. Reserve the remaining syrup. Grill (broil) the brioche until lightly toasted.

5 Turn over and dust with icing sugar. Grill each brioche for 2–3 minutes more until they begin to caramelize around the edges.

6 Transfer to serving plates and top with scoops of ice cream. Spoon over the remaining syrup and serve immediately.

Blueberry and Vanilla Crumble Torte

In this heavenly pudding, vanilla ice cream is packed into a buttery crumble case and baked until

the ice cream starts to melt over the crumble. Remember that you need to start making

this the day before you intend to serve it.

SERVES EIGHT

INGREDIENTS

225g | 8oz | 2 cups PLAIN
(ALL-PURPOSE) FLOUR

5ml | 1 tsp BAKING POWDER

175g | 6oz | ¾ cup UNSALTED
(SWEET) BUTTER, diced

150g | 5oz | ¼ cup CASTER
(SUPERFINE) SUGAR

1 EGG

75g | 3oz | ¼ cup finely
GROUND ALMONDS

10ml | 2 tsp natural VANILLA
ESSENCE (EXTRACT)

5ml | 1 tsp MIXED
(APPLE PIE) SPICE

For the filling

500ml | 17fl oz | 2¼ cups
CLASSIC VANILLA ICE CREAM

175g | 6oz | 1½ cups BLUEBERRIES

ICING (CONFECTIONERS')
SUGAR, for dusting

1 Preheat the oven to 180°C |
350°F | Gas 4. Grease a 20cm | 8in
springform tin (pan). Put the flour
and baking powder in a food
processor. Add the butter and
process briefly to mix.

2 Add the sugar and process
briefly again until the mixture is
crumbly. Remove about 175g |
6oz | 1½ cups of the crumble
mixture and set this aside.

3 Add the egg, ground almonds,
vanilla essence and mixed spice
to the remaining crumble mixture
and blend to a paste.

4 Scrape the paste into the greased
springform tin. Press it firmly on
to the base and halfway up the
sides to make an even case.

5 Line the pastry case with baking
parchment; fill with baking beans.

6 Sprinkle the crumble mixture
on to a baking sheet. Bake the
crumble for 20 minutes and the
case for about 30 minutes until
pale golden.

7 Remove the paper and beans
from the case and bake it for 5
minutes more. Leave both the
crumble and the case to cool.

8 Pack the ice cream into the
almond pastry case and level
the surface. Scatter with the
blueberries and then the baked
crumble mixture. Freeze overnight.

9 About 25 minutes before serving,
preheat the oven to 180°C | 350°F |
Gas 4. Bake the torte for 10–15
minutes, until the ice cream has
started to soften. Dust with icing
sugar and serve in wedges.

COOK'S TIP *You could use other*
flavours of ice cream; Crème Fraîche
and Honey Ice Cream would be
especially delicious.

Orange Crêpes with Mascarpone Cream

Baking these delicate crêpes does not actually make them hot when served. Quite simply, the sorbet and mascarpone start to melt together in their crisp pancake cases to make a delicious dessert that is neither too rich nor too sweet.

SERVES EIGHT

INGREDIENTS

For the crêpes

115g | 4oz | 1 cup PLAIN (ALL-PURPOSE) FLOUR

300ml | ½ pint | 1¼ cups MILK

1 EGG, plus 1 EGG YOLK

finely grated rind of 1 ORANGE

30ml | 2 tbsp CASTER (SUPERFINE) SUGAR

OIL, for frying

To finish

250g | 9oz | generous 1 cup MASCARPONE CHEESE

15ml | 1 tbsp ICING (CONFECTIONERS') SUGAR

90ml | 6 tbsp SINGLE (LIGHT) CREAM

45ml | 3 tbsp COINTREAU or ORANGE JUICE

500ml | 17fl oz | 2¼ cups ORANGE SORBET

ICING (CONFECTIONERS') SUGAR, for dusting

1 Make the crêpes. Put the flour, milk, egg, egg yolk, orange rind and sugar in a food processor and blend until smooth. Pour the batter into a jug (pitcher) and leave to stand for 30 minutes.

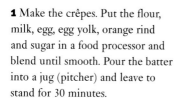

COOK'S TIP *For the crêpe batter, use a jug (pitcher) with a good lip, so that you have good control of the liquid while pouring.*

2 Heat a little of the oil in a medium frying pan or crêpe pan until very hot. Drain off the excess. Pour a little of the batter into the pan, tilting the pan so that the batter coats the base thinly and evenly.

3 Cook the crêpe until the underside is golden, then flip it over with a slim spatula and cook the other side. Slide the crêpe on to a plate and cook seven more crêpes, lightly oiling the pan each time and stacking the cooked ones.

4 Preheat the oven to 200°C | 400°F | Gas 6. In a bowl, beat the mascarpone with the icing sugar, cream and liqueur or orange juice until smooth. Spread the mixture on the crêpes, taking it almost to the edges.

5 Using a dessertspoon, scoop shavings of sorbet and arrange them to one side of each topped crêpe. Fold the crêpes in half and dust with icing sugar. Fold again into quarters and dust with more icing sugar. Lay the crêpes in a large shallow baking dish and bake for 2 minutes until the sorbet starts to melt. Serve immediately.

ice creams
with fruit

Whether served as an accompaniment or churned into ice cream or sorbet, an abundance of tangy fruit gives a light, fresh taste. For an invigorating summer cooler or finale to a rich meal, fruit ices make a vibrant marriage of colour and flavour.

Spiced Sorbet Pears

Pears poached in wine make an elegant dessert at any time of the year and for any special occasion.

In this recipe the poached pears are hollowed out, filled with a wine-and-pear flavoured sorbet

and served with a drizzle of the reduced poaching juices.

5 Cut a deep 2.5cm | 1in slice off the top of each pear and reserve. Use an apple corer to remove the cores.

6 Scoop out the centre of each pear, leaving a thick shell. Put the flesh in a food processor and the hollowed pears and their lids in the freezer. Strain the poaching juices. Set 75ml | 5 tbsp aside for serving and add the rest to the food processor. Blend until smooth.

7 Churn the mixture in an ice cream maker until it holds its shape.

8 Pack the sorbet into the frozen pears. Position the lids and return to the freezer overnight.

9 Remove the pears from the freezer and let them stand at room temperature about 30 minutes before serving. The pears should have softened but the sorbet remains icy. Transfer to serving plates and spoon a little of the reserved syrup around each one.

SERVES SIX

INGREDIENTS

600ml | 1 pint | 2½ cups
RED WINE

2 CINNAMON
STICKS, halved

115g | 4oz | generous ½ cup CASTER
(SUPERFINE) SUGAR

6 PLUMP PEARS

1 Put the wine, cinnamon sticks and sugar in a heavy pan, that is big enough for the pears. Heat gently to dissolve the sugar.

2 Peel the pears, leaving the stalks attached. Stand them upright in the syrup in the pan, taking care not to pack them too tightly.

3 Cover and simmer very gently for 10–20 minutes until just tender, turning so they colour evenly. (The cooking time varies depending on the softness of the pears.)

4 Lift out the pears with a slotted spoon and set them aside to cool. Boil the juices briefly until reduced to 350ml | 12fl oz | 1½ cups. Set aside and leave to cool.

Lemon Sorbet Cups with Summer Fruits

In this stunning dessert, lemon sorbet is moulded into cup shapes to make pretty containers for a selection of summer fruits. Other combinations, such as mango sorbet with tropical fruits, or orange sorbet with blueberries, also work well.

SERVES SIX

INGREDIENTS

500ml | 17fl oz | 2¼ cups
LEMON SORBET

225g | 8oz | 2 cups SMALL
STRAWBERRIES

150g | 5oz | scant 1 cup
RASPBERRIES

75g | 3oz | ¾ cup REDCURRANTS,
BLACKCURRANTS or
WHITECURRANTS

15ml | 1 tbsp CASTER
(SUPERFINE) SUGAR

45ml | 3 tbsp COINTREAU or other
ORANGE-FLAVOURED LIQUEUR

1 Put six 150ml | ¼ pint | ⅔ cup metal moulds in the freezer for 15 minutes to chill. At the same time, remove the sorbet from the freezer to soften slightly.

2 Using a teaspoon, pack the sorbet into the moulds, building up a layer about 1cm | ½in thick around the base and sides, and leaving a deep cavity in the centre. Hold each mould in a dish towel as you work (see Cook's Tip). Return each mould to the freezer when it is lined.

3 Cut the strawberries in half and place in a bowl with the raspberries and red, black or whitecurrants. Add the sugar and liqueur and toss the ingredients together lightly. Cover and chill for at least 2 hours.

4 Once the sorbet in the moulds has frozen completely, loosen the edges with a knife, then dip in a bowl of very hot water for 2 seconds. Invert the sorbet cups on a small tray, using a fork to twist and loosen the cups if necessary.

5 If you need to, dip the moulds very briefly in the hot water again. Turn the cups over so they are ready to fill and return to the freezer until required.

6 To serve, place the cups on serving plates and fill with the fruits, spooning over any juices.

COOK'S TIP *When lining a metal mould with the lemon sorbet it is a good idea to wrap your hand in a dish towel. This not only prevents your fingers from sticking to the metal, but also stops the heat from your hands from warming the mould.*

Cranberry and White Chocolate Ice Cream

A traditional American combination – the creamy sweet white chocolate ice cream complements the slight sharpness of the ruby-red fruits for a richly contrasting marbled ice cream.

SERVES SIX

INGREDIENTS

150g | 5oz | 1¼ cups FROZEN CRANBERRIES

125g | 4½oz | scant ¾ cup CASTER (SUPERFINE) SUGAR

4 EGG YOLKS

5ml | 1 tsp CORNFLOUR (CORNSTARCH)

300ml | ½ pint | 1¼ cups SEMI-SKIMMED (LOW-FAT) MILK

150g | 5oz WHITE CHOCOLATE

5ml | 1 tsp VANILLA ESSENCE (EXTRACT)

200ml | 7fl oz | scant 1 cup DOUBLE (HEAVY) CREAM

extra CRANBERRIES, to decorate

1 Put the cranberries into a pan with 60ml | 4 tbsp water and cook uncovered for 5 minutes until softened. Drain off any fruit juices, mix in 60ml | 4 tbsp of the sugar and leave to cool.

2 Whisk the egg yolks, remaining sugar and cornflour together in a bowl until thick and pale. Pour the milk into a heavy pan, bring it just to the boil, then gradually pour it on to the egg yolk mixture, whisking constantly.

3 Return the mixture to the pan and cook over a gentle heat, stirring constantly until the custard thickens and is smooth. Pour it back into the bowl.

COOK'S TIP *If you find cranberries a bit too tart, add some extra sugar to the cranberries when you cook them, adjusting the amount depending on how sweet you like them.*

4 Finely chop 50g | 2oz of the chocolate and set aside. Break the remainder into pieces and stir into the hot custard until melted. Mix in the vanilla essence then cover, cool and chill.

5 Pour the cooled chocolate custard and cream into an ice cream maker and churn until thick.

6 Gradually mix in the cooled cranberries and diced chocolate and churn for a few more minutes until firm enough to scoop. Transfer to a freezer container and freeze until required.

7 Scoop into tall glasses and decorate with a few extra cranberries.

Iced Summer Pudding

SERVES SIX TO EIGHT

This is a frozen version of the classic and ever-popular soft-fruit dessert. Made using good quality fruit sorbet and strawberry or raspberry ice cream, the result is just as delicious and looks very impressive.

INGREDIENTS

25g | 1 oz | 2 tbsp CASTER (SUPERFINE) SUGAR

60ml | 4 tbsp WATER

75ml | 5 tbsp STRAWBERRY JAM

60ml | 4 tbsp CRÈME DE CASSIS

225g | 8oz | 2 cups SMALL STRAWBERRIES, thinly sliced

250g | 9oz GOOD QUALITY MADEIRA or POUND CAKE

250ml | 8fl oz | 1 cup SOFT FRUIT SORBET

500ml | 17fl oz | 2¼ cups STRAWBERRY or RASPBERRY ICE CREAM

1 Line a 1.5 litre | 2½ pint | 6¼ cup bowl with clear film (plastic wrap). Heat the sugar and water in a heavy pan until the sugar has dissolved.

2 Meanwhile, press 30ml | 2 tbsp of the strawberry jam through a sieve into a small bowl. Stir in 15ml | 1 tbsp of the syrup and brush the mixture up the sides of the lined basin. Press the remaining jam through the sieve into the pan of syrup and stir in the crème de cassis until smooth.

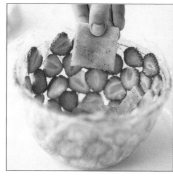

3 Press the strawberry slices in a single layer over the base and sides of the basin, fitting them as tightly together as possible. Chill in the refrigerator whilst you cut the cake into 1cm | ½in slices..

4 Dip the cake slices in the remaining syrup and arrange in a single layer over the strawberries, cutting the sponge to fit and trimming off the excess around the edges. Freeze for 30 minutes.

5 Remove the sorbet from the freezer to soften for about 15 minutes. Using a large metal spoon, pack the sorbet into the basin – it will fill it about three-quarters full – and level the surface.

6 Return the basin to the freezer and leave for 30 minutes. Remove the ice cream from the freezer and leave for 15 minutes to soften.

7 Pack the ice cream over the sorbet, filling the basin. Level the surface and freeze for at least 4 hours or overnight.

8 Shortly before serving, dip the bowl in very hot water for 2 seconds, then invert the iced pudding on to a serving plate. Peel away the clear film. Leave to thaw at room temperature for 10–15 minutes. Serve the pudding in wedges.

COOK'S TIP *Any soft fruit sorbet can be used. Raspberry sorbet has a wonderfully intense colour; blackcurrant or redcurrant sorbet would also be excellent choices.*

Marinated Fruits with Sorbet Sauce

Exotic fruits marinated with lime and sugar, topped with a vodka-spiked mango sorbet sauce, make a refreshing treat on a hot summer's afternoon.

SERVES SIX

INGREDIENTS

12 LYCHEES, peeled

1 MANGO, peeled

1 PAPAYA, peeled

1 KIWI FRUIT, peeled

juice of 1 LIME

15ml | 1 tbsp CASTER (SUPERFINE) SUGAR

30ml | 2 tbsp VODKA

For the sorbet sauce

75g | 3oz | 6 tbsp CASTER (SUPERFINE) SUGAR

200ml | 7fl oz | scant 1 cup WATER

1 LIME, pared rind and squeezed juice

1 large MANGO, peeled

30ml | 2 tbsp VODKA

COOK'S TIP *Any partially frozen sorbet could also be served in this way.*

1 Halve the lychees and remove the stones (pits). Stone (pit) and slice the mango. Halve the papaya, remove the seeds and dice the flesh. Slice the kiwi fruit.

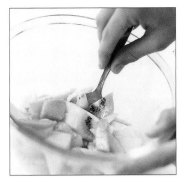

2 Put the fruits into a bowl with the lime juice, sugar and vodka. Cover and chill.

3 To make the sorbet sauce, put the sugar, water and lime rind into a pan. Heat gently until the sugar has dissolved, bring to the boil then leave to cool.

4 Stone and slice the mango and purée in a blender or food processor. Strain the syrup and mix with the lime juice, mango purée and vodka. Pour into an ice cream maker and churn to a thick sauce-like consistency.

5 Stir the marianted fruits and scoop into tall glasses. Pour the sorbet sauce over and serve immediately.

Mascarpone and Raspberry Ripple

Mascarpone makes a perfectly smooth, refreshing base for ice cream, particularly when mixed with a tangy lemon syrup and streaked with raspberry purée.

SERVES EIGHT

INGREDIENTS

250g | 9oz | 1¼ cups CASTER (SUPERFINE) SUGAR

450ml | ¾ pint | scant 2 cups WATER

finely grated rind and juice of 1 LEMON

350g | 12oz | 2 cups RASPBERRIES, plus extra, to decorate

500g | 1¼lb | 2½ cups MASCARPONE CHEESE

1 Put 225g | 8oz | 1 cup of the sugar in a heavy pan. Pour in the water and heat gently until the sugar dissolves. Bring to the boil, add the lemon rind and juice and boil for 3 minutes, without stirring, to make a syrup. Leave to cool.

2 Crush the raspberries lightly with a fork until broken up but not completely puréed, then stir in the remaining sugar.

3 Beat the mascarpone in a large bowl until smooth, gradually adding the lemon syrup.

4 Churn the mixture in an ice cream maker until thick, then transfer to a freezer container.

5 Spoon the crushed raspberries over the ice cream. Using a metal spoon fold into the ice cream until rippled, making sure you reach the corners. Freeze for several hours or overnight until firm.

6 To serve, scoop the ice cream into glasses and decorate with the extra raspberries.

Iced Clementines

The tangy flavours of clementine, lemon and orange are comined here to create a citrus sorbet which is bursting with flavour. The sorbet looks very pretty when served in hollowed-out fruits, and they store well in the freezer so are perfect for an impromptu summer party, a picnic or simply a refreshing treat.

3 Finely grate the rind from the remaining clementines. Squeeze the fruits and add the juice and rind to the syrup.

4 Process the clementine flesh in a food processor or blender, then press it through a sieve placed over a bowl to extract as much juice as possible. Add this to the syrup. You need about 900ml | 1½ pints | 3¾ cups of liquid. Make up with fresh orange juice if necessary.

5 Churn the mixture in an ice cream maker, until it holds its shape, then pack the sorbet into the clementine shells, mounding them up slightly in the centre. Position the lids and return to the freezer for several hours or overnight.

6 Transfer the clementines to the refrigerator about 30 minutes before serving, to soften. Serve on individual plates and decorate.

MAKES 12

INGREDIENTS

16 LARGE CLEMENTINES

175g | 6oz | scant 1 cup CASTER (SUPERFINE) SUGAR

105ml | 7 tbsp WATER

juice of 2 LEMONS

a little FRESH ORANGE JUICE (if necessary)

FRESH MINT or LEMON BALM LEAVES, to decorate

1 Slice the tops off 12 of the clementines to make lids. Set aside on a baking sheet. Loosen the clementine flesh with a sharp knife then carefully scoop it out into a bowl, keeping the shells intact. Scrape out as much of the membrane from the shells as possible. Add the shells to the lids and put them in the freezer.

2 Put the sugar and water in a heavy pan and heat gently, stirring until the sugar dissolves. Boil for 3 minutes without stirring, then leave the syrup to cool. Stir in the lemon juice.

Iced Melon with Pimm's

Freezing sorbet in hollowed out fruit, which is then cut into icy wedges, is an excellent idea. The novel presentation and refreshing flavour make this dessert irresistible on a hot summer's afternoon. The idea works particularly well with melon wedges, laced with chilled Pimm's.

SERVES SIX

INGREDIENTS

50g | 2oz | ¼ cup CASTER (SUPERFINE) SUGAR

30ml | 2 tbsp CLEAR HONEY

15ml | 1 tbsp LEMON JUICE

60ml | 4 tbsp WATER

1 medium CANTALOUPE or CHARENTAIS MELON, about 1 kg | 2¼ lb

CRUSHED ICE, CUCUMBER SLICES and BORAGE LEAVES, to decorate

PIMM'S NO. 1, to serve

1 Put the sugar, honey, lemon juice and water in a small heavy pan and heat gently until the sugar dissolves. Bring to the boil and boil for 1 minute, without stirring, to make a syrup. Leave to cool.

2 Cut the melon in half and discard the seeds. Carefully scoop out the flesh and place in a food processor, taking care to keep the shells intact.

3 Blend the melon flesh until smooth. Then transfer to a bowl, stir in the cooled syrup and chill in the refrigerator until very cold. Invert the melon shells and leave them to drain on kitchen paper, then transfer to the freezer while making the sorbet.

4 Churn the melon mixture in an ice cream maker until the sorbet holds its shape, then pack the sorbet into the melon shells and level the surface with a knife.

5 Use a dessertspoon to scoop out the centre of each filled melon shell to simulate the seed cavity. Freeze overnight until firm.

6 To serve, use a large knife to cut each half into three wedges. Serve on a bed of ice on a large platter or individual serving plates, and decorate with the cucumber slices and borage. Drizzle lightly with Pimm's to serve.

COOK'S TIP *Take care when slicing the frozen melon shell into wedges. A serrated kitchen knife works well.*

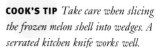

iced drinks

Keep a supply of classic ice creams and sorbets for making a whole range of exciting drinks. Blend with a splash of liqueur for a cooler drink with a kick, scoop into glasses and top up with fizz, or mix with fruit for a wonderful drink and dessert all in one.

Iced Margaritas

This smooth, cooling sorbet drink has all the punch of Mexico's renowned cocktail. Serve it in tall, slim glasses with a capacity of about 200ml/7fl oz/scant 1 cup.

SERVES TWO

INGREDIENTS

35ml | 7 tsp FRESHLY SQUEEZED LIME JUICE

a little CASTER (SUPERFINE) SUGAR, for frosting

4 LIME and 4 LEMON SLICES

60ml | 4 tbsp TEQUILA

30ml | 2 tbsp COINTREAU

6–8 small scoops of ORANGE or LIME SORBET

150ml | ¼ pint | ⅔ cup CHILLED LEMONADE

sprigs of LEMON BALM, to decorate

1 Brush the rims of two tall glasses with 5ml | 1 tsp of the lime juice. Spread out the sugar on a plate. Dip the rims of the glasses in the sugar to give a frosted edge.

2 Carefully add two lime and two lemon slices to each glass, standing them on end, so they will be fully visible through the glass.

3 Mix the tequila, Cointreau and remaining lime juice in a bowl. Scoop the sorbet into the glasses.

4 Spoon an equal quantity of the tequila mixture into each glass. Top up with the lemonade and serve immediately, decorated with lemon balm.

VARIATION *For a "shorter" version of this drink, use cocktail glasses and just one scoop of sorbet. The rims of the glasses can be frosted with salt instead of sugar, as for traditional Margaritas.*

Gin and Lemon Fizz

If gin and tonic is your tipple, try this chilled alternative. The fruit and flower ice cubes make a lively decoration for any iced drink.

SERVES TWO

INGREDIENTS

mixture of small EDIBLE BERRIES or CURRANTS,

pieces of thinly pared LEMON or ORANGE RIND

tiny edible FLOWERS

4 scoops of LEMON SORBET

30ml | 2 tbsp GIN

about 120ml | 4fl oz | ½ cup CHILLED TONIC WATER

1 To make the decorated ice cubes, place each fruit, piece of rind or flower in a section of an ice cube tray. Carefully fill with water and freeze for several hours until the cubes are solid.

2 Divide the sorbet between two cocktail glasses or use small tumblers, with a capacity of about 150ml | ¼ pint | ⅔ cup.

3 Spoon over the gin and add a couple of the ornamental ice cubes to each glass. Top up with tonic water and serve immediately.

COOK'S TIP *When making the decorated ice cubes, choose small herb flowers such as borage or mint, or edible flowers such as rose geraniums, primulas or rose buds.*

Lemonade on Ice

Home-made lemonade may not be fizzy, but it has a fresh, tangy flavour, unmatched by bought drinks.

The basic lemonade will keep well in the refrigerator for up to two weeks and

makes a thirst-quenching drink at any time of day.

SERVES SIX

INGREDIENTS

6 LEMONS

225g | 8oz | 1 cup CASTER (SUPERFINE) SUGAR

1.75 litres | 3 pints | 7½ cups BOILING WATER

For each iced drink

4 scoops of LEMON SORBET

THIN LEMON and LIME SLICES

3 ICE CUBES, crushed

MINT SPRIGS and halved LEMON and LIME SLICES, to decorate

VARIATION *Use freshly squeezed lime juice instead of lemon juice or bruise some mint leaves and add them to the syrup for a subtle mint flavour. For pink lemonade, add a few drops of grenadine to each glass when serving.*

1 Start by making the lemonade. Wash the lemons and dry them thoroughly. Pare or grate all the lemons finely, avoiding the bitter white pith, and put the rind in a large heatproof bowl.

2 Add the sugar. Squeeze the lemons and set the juice aside.

3 Pour the measured boiling water over the lemon rind and sugar. Stir until the sugar dissolves. Leave to cool, then stir in the lemon juice. Strain the lemonade into a large jug (pitcher) and chill.

4 For each glass of iced lemonade, place four scoops of sorbet in a tall glass and tuck some lemon and lime slices down the sides. Add the crushed ice.

5 Top up each glass with about 200ml | 7fl oz | scant 1 cup of the lemonade. Decorate the glass with mint and halved lemon and lime slices, if liked.

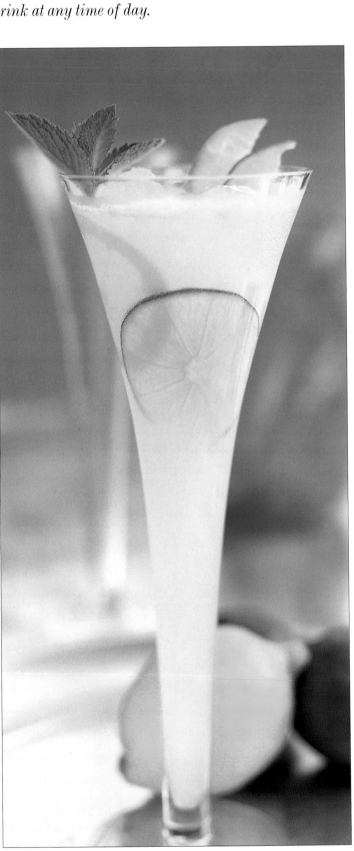

Cranberry, Cinnamon and Ginger Spritzer

Partially freezing fruit juice gives it a refreshingly slushy texture that forms the base of this cooling spritzer. Keep an eye on the machine while it's churning, or the mixture will end up too sorbet-like in consistency.

SERVES FOUR

INGREDIENTS

90g | 3½oz | ½ cup CASTER (SUPERFINE) SUGAR

105ml | 7 tbsp WATER

150ml | ¼ pint | ⅔ cup APPLE JUICE

4 CINNAMON STICKS

600ml | 1 pint | 2½ cups chilled CRANBERRY JUICE

about 400ml | 14fl oz | 1⅔ cups chilled GINGER ALE

fresh or frozen CRANBERRIES, to decorate

1 Put the sugar and water in a small pan and heat gently, stirring until the sugar dissolves. Bring to the boil, remove from the heat and leave to cool.

2 Heat the apple juice in a pan with two cinnamon sticks until almost boiling. Pour into a jug (pitcher) and leave to cool then remove the cinnamon sticks and reserve for decoration. Chill the juice.

3 Stir the syrup into the cranberry juice and churn in the ice cream maker until thickened but still quite slushy. Add the apple juice and churn very lightly until mixed in.

4 Spoon the mixture into glasses. Top up with ginger ale and decorate with cranberries. Push a cinnamon stick into each glass to use as a stirrer.

COOK'S TIP *For convenience the cranberry juice can be churned in advance, then popped in the freezer until ready to serve. Leave it to soften slightly then blend briefly in a food processor with the apple juice to a slushy consistency.*

Soft Fruit and Ginger Cup

A colourful medley of soft fruits steeped in vodka and served with an icy blend of sorbet and ginger ale. You will definitely need spoons for this one.

SERVES FOUR

INGREDIENTS

115g | 4oz | 1 cup STRAWBERRIES, hulled

115g | 4oz | ⅔ cup RASPBERRIES, hulled

50g | 2oz | ½ cup BLUEBERRIES

15ml | 1 tbsp CASTER (SUPERFINE) SUGAR

90ml | 6 tbsp VODKA

600ml | 1 pint | 2½ cups GINGER ALE

4 large scoops of ORANGE SORBET

about 8 ICE CUBES

20ml | 4 tsp GRENADINE

4 PHYSALIS, to decorate

1 Cut the strawberries in half and put them in a bowl with the raspberries, blueberries and sugar.

2 Pour over the vodka and toss lightly. Cover and chill for at least 30 minutes.

3 Put the ginger ale and sorbet in a blender or food processor and process until smooth.

4 Pour the mixture into four bowl-shaped glasses and add a couple of ice cubes to each glass of sorbet mixture.

VARIATION *Any combination of soft fruit can be used for this iced drink. Blackberries, for example, would also work well.*

5 Spoon a teaspoon of grenadine over the ice in each glass, then spoon the vodka-steeped fruits on top of the sorbet mixture and ice.

6 Decorate each glass with a physalis. Serve immediately.

Sparkling Peach Melba

This refreshing fruit fizz is an excellent choice for summer celebrations. As with most soft fruit recipes, its success depends on using the ripest, tastiest peaches and raspberries available.

SERVES FOUR

INGREDIENTS

3 RIPE PEACHES

90ml | 6 tbsp ORANGE JUICE

75g | 3oz | ½ cup RASPBERRIES

10ml | 2 tsp ICING (CONFECTIONERS') SUGAR

500ml | 17fl oz | 2¼ cups RASPBERRY SORBET

about 400ml | 14fl oz | 1⅔ cups MEDIUM SPARKLING CHILLED WHITE WINE

FRESH MINT SPRIGS, to decorate

1 Put the peaches in a heatproof bowl and pour over boiling water to cover. Leave for 60 seconds, then drain the peaches and peel off the skins.

2 Cut the fruit in half and remove the stones (pits). Chop the peach halves roughly and purée them with the orange juice in a food processor or blender until smooth. Scrape the purée into a bowl.

3 Put the raspberries in the food processor or blender. Add the icing sugar and process until smooth. Press the raspberry purée through a sieve into a bowl. Chill both purées for at least 1 hour.

4 Spoon the chilled peach purée into four tall glasses.

5 Add scoops of sorbet to come to the top of the glasses. Spoon the raspberry purée around the sorbet.

6 Top up each glass with sparkling wine. Decorate with the mint sprigs and serve.

VARIATION *When fresh ripe peaches are unavailable, use canned peach halves in juice or light syrup.*

Iced Mango Lassi

Based on a traditional Indian drink, this is excellent with spicy food, or as a welcome cooler at any time of day.

The yogurt ice that forms the basis of this drink is a useful recipe to add to your repertoire –

it is lighter and fresher than cream-based ices.

SERVES THREE TO FOUR

INGREDIENTS

For the yogurt ice

175g | 6oz | ¾ cup CASTER (SUPERFINE) SUGAR

150ml | ¼ pint | ⅔ cup WATER

2 LEMONS

500ml | 17fl oz | generous 2 cups GREEK (US STRAINED PLAIN) YOGURT

For each drink

120ml | 4fl oz | ½ cup MANGO JUICE

2–3 ICE CUBES (optional)

FRESH MINT SPRIGS and WEDGES of MANGO, to serve

1 To make the yogurt ice, put the sugar and water in a pan and heat gently, stirring occasionally, until the sugar has dissolved. Pour the syrup into a jug (pitcher). Cool, then chill until very cold.

2 Finely grate the lemons, avoiding the bitter white pith, and then squeeze them.

3 Add the rind and juice to the chilled syrup and stir well to mix.

4 Churn in an ice cream until it thickens. Stir in the yogurt and churn for 2 minutes more, until well mixed. Transfer the mixture to a plastic tub or a similar freezerproof container and freeze.

5 To make each lassi, briefly blend the mango juice with three small scoops of the yogurt ice in a food processor or blender until it is just smooth.

6 Pour the mixture into a tall glass or tumbler and add the ice cubes, if using.

7 Top each drink with another scoop of the yogurt ice and decorate. Serve at once.

VARIATION *Add one small chopped banana when blending the ingredients together for a more substantial smoothie.*

Tropical Fruit Soda

For many children, scoops of vanilla ice cream, served in a froth of lemonade would make the perfect treat. This more elaborate version will appeal to adults too. Include as much or as little of any combination of tropical fruits as you like, and you can use just vanilla ice cream rather than including any caramel or toffee ice cream.

SERVES FOUR

INGREDIENTS

10ml | 2 tsp SUGAR

1 PAPAYA

1 SMALL RIPE MANGO

2 PASSION FRUIT

4 large scoops of
CLASSIC VANILLA ICE CREAM

4 large scoops of CARAMEL or
TOFFEE ICE CREAM

about 400ml | 14fl oz | 1⅔ cups
CHILLED LEMONADE or
SODA WATER (CLUB SODA)

1 Line a baking sheet with foil. Make four small mounds of sugar on the foil, using about 2.5ml | ½ tsp each time and spacing them well apart. Place under a moderate grill (broiler) for about 2 minutes until the sugar mounds have turned to a pale golden caramel.

2 Immediately swirl each pool of caramel with the tip of a cocktail stick or skewer to give a slightly feathery finish. Leave to cool.

3 Cut the papaya in half. Scoop out and discard the seeds, then remove the skin and chop the flesh. Skin the mango, cut the flesh off the stone (pit) and chop it into bite-size chunks. Mix the papaya and mango in a bowl.

4 Cut each passion fruit in half and scoop the pulp into the bowl of fruit. Mix well, cover and chill until ready to serve.

5 Divide the chilled fruit mixture among four large tumblers, each with a capacity of about 300ml | ½ pint | 1¼ cups.

6 Add one scoop of each type of ice cream to each glass. Peel the caramel decorations carefully away from the foil and press gently into the ice cream. Top up with lemonade or soda and serve.

VARIATIONS *Use a mixture of strawberries and raspberries or other more familiar fruits for children. For adults, a splash of vodka or kirsch can be added to the fruits.*

Snowball

For many of us, a "snowball" is a drink we indulge in once or twice at Christmas time. This iced version,

enhanced with melting vanilla ice cream, lime and nutmeg, may provide the motivation

for drinking advocaat on other occasions too.

SERVES FOUR

INGREDIENTS

8 scoops of
CLASSIC VANILLA ICE CREAM

120ml | 4fl oz | ½ cup ADVOCAAT

60ml | 4 tbsp FRESHLY SQUEEZED
LIME JUICE

FRESHLY GRATED NUTMEG

about 300ml | ½ pint | 1¼ cups
CHILLED LEMONADE

1 Put half the vanilla ice cream in a food processor or blender and add the advocaat and the lime juice, with plenty of freshly grated nutmeg. Process the mixture briefly until well combined.

2 Scoop the remaining ice cream into four medium tumblers. Spoon over the advocaat mixture and top up the glasses with lemonade. Sprinkle with more nutmeg and serve immediately.

COOK'S TIP *Freshly grated nutmeg has a warm, nutty aroma and flavour that works as well in creamy drinks as it does in sweet and savoury dishes. A small nutmeg grater is a worthwhile investment if you don't have one.*

Strawberry Daiquiri

Based on the classic cocktail, this version is a wonderful drink that retains the essential ingredients

of rum and lime and combines them with fresh strawberries and strawberry ice cream

to create a thick iced fruit purée.

SERVES FOUR

INGREDIENTS

225g | 8oz | 2 cups
STRAWBERRIES, hulled

5ml | 1 tsp CASTER
(SUPERFINE) SUGAR

120ml | 4fl oz | ½ cup
BACARDI RUM

30ml | 2 tbsp FRESHLY
SQUEEZED LIME JUICE

8 scoops of STRAWBERRY
ICE CREAM

about 150ml | ¼ pint | ⅔ cup
CHILLED LEMONADE

extra STRAWBERRIES
and LIME SLICES,
to decorate

1 Blend the strawberries with the sugar in a food processor or blender, then press the purée through a sieve into a bowl. Return the strawberry purée to the blender with the rum, lime juice and half the strawberry ice cream. Blend until smooth.

2 Scoop the remaining strawberry ice cream into four cocktail glasses or small tumblers and pour over the blended mixture.

3 Top up with lemonade, decorate with fresh strawberries and lime slices, and serve.

VARIATION *Orange-flavoured liqueur or vodka could be used instead of the rum, if you prefer.*

COOK'S TIP *For the best results use luxury ice cream, or preferably, home-made. This will avoid the risk of a synthetic flavour and garish colour.*

Coffee Frappé

This creamy, smooth creation, strictly for adults, makes a wonderful alternative to a dessert on a hot summer's evening. Use cappuccino cups or small glasses for serving and provide your guests with both straws and long-handled spoons.

SERVES FOUR

INGREDIENTS

8 scoops of
CLASSIC COFFEE ICE CREAM

90ml | 6 tbsp KAHLÚA,
TOUSSAINT or
TIA MARIA LIQUEUR

150ml | ¼ pint | ⅔ cup
SINGLE (LIGHT) CREAM

1.5ml | ¼ tsp GROUND CINNAMON
(optional)

CRUSHED ICE

CINNAMON,
for sprinkling

1 Put half the coffee ice cream in a food processor or blender. Add the liqueur, then pour in the cream, with a little cinnamon, if you like. Whiz briefly to mix.

2 Scoop the remaining ice cream into four cups or glasses. Spoon the coffee cream over the ice cream, then top with the crushed ice. Sprinkle with cinnamon and serve immediately.

VARIATION *For a non-alcoholic version of this iced drink, substitute strong black coffee for the liqueur.*

Warm Chocolate Float

A hot chocolate milkshake and scoops of chocolate and vanilla ice cream are combined here to make a meltingly delicious drink that will prove a big success with children and adults alike.

SERVES TWO

INGREDIENTS

115g | 4oz PLAIN (SEMI-SWEET)
CHOCOLATE, broken into pieces

250ml | 8fl oz | 1 cup MILK

15ml | 1 tbsp CASTER
(SUPERFINE) SUGAR

4 large scoops of
CLASSIC VANILLA ICE CREAM

4 large scoops of
CLASSIC DARK CHOCOLATE
ICE CREAM

a little lightly WHIPPED CREAM

GRATED CHOCOLATE or
CHOCOLATE CURLS,
to decorate

1 Put the chocolate in a pan and add the milk and sugar. Heat gently, stirring with a wooden spoon until the chocolate has melted and the mixture is smooth.

2 Place two scoops of each type of ice cream alternately in two heatproof tumblers.

3 Pour the chocolate milk over and around the ice cream. Top with lightly whipped cream and grated chocolate or chocolate curls.

VARIATION *Try substituting banana, coconut or toffee ice cream for the chocolate and vanilla.*

Picture credits

The publishers would like to thank the following companies for their kind permission to reproduce their photographs: , p13 bottom, p14 top left, AKG Photographic Library; p9 left and right, Charmet; p12 top right and centre, p13 top, p10 right, left and bottom, page 11 top right, bottom right and centre, Hulton Getty; p12 top left, The Advertising Archives; p8 top and bottom, private collection, The Bridgeman Art Library; p 15 top and bottom, The Holmes Group.

All other photographs are by Gus Filgate, William Lingwood and Craig Robertson.

Acknowledgements

The author and publishers would like to thank Magimix, Gaggia, Philips and the Holmes Group for their invaluable help. The research, recipe development and photography for this book would not have been possible without the kind loan of their ice cream machines.

The authors would like to extend their special thanks to Julie Beresford, Annabel Ford and Kate Jay for their enthusiasm and help throughout the busy days of photography and to their families for trying every ice cream that has appeared in this book.

Suppliers

Worldwide, ice cream makers are generally available from electrical suppliers and department stores. Moulds and other equipment are usually available from specialist kitchenware stores and by mail order.

UNITED KINGDOM

ICE CREAM MACHINES

Gaggia UK Ltd
Crown House
Milecross Road
Halifax, West Yorkshire
HX1 4HN
Tel: 01422 330 295 for your nearest stockist of Gaggia ice cream machines
www.gaggia.uk.com

Holmes Products (Europe)
The Piper Building
Peterborough Road
London SW6 3EF
Tel: 0800 052 3615 for your nearest stockist of the Rival soft serve ice cream machine
www.theholmesgroup.com

Magimix (UK) Ltd
19 Bridge Street
Godalming
Surrey GU7 1HY
Tel: 01483 427411 for your nearest stockist of Magimix ice cream machines.

Philips Domestic Appliances and Personal Care
420–430 London Road
Croydon
Surrey CR9 3QR
Tel: 0845 601 0354 for your nearest stockist of the Philips ice cream machine.
www.philips.com

UNITED STATES

WOODEN CONE MOULDS

Randal and Juli Marr
Magdalene House Designs
Magdalene House
Langthorne, Bedale,
North Yorkshire
DL8 1PQ
Tel: 01677 424332

GENERAL EQUIPMENT

Including plastic ice bowl kits,
ice cream machines, ice cream
scoops and containers.

Lakeland Ltd
Alexandra Buildings
Windermere, Cumbria
LA23 1BQ
Tel: 01539 488100 for details of
your nearest shop or to obtain a
mail-order catalogue.

New York Cake & Baking Distributor
56 West 22nd Street
New York, NY 10010
Tel: (800) 94-CAKE-9
Fax:(212) 675-7099

Chef's Catalog
P.O. Box 650589
Dallas, TX 75265-0589
Tel: (800) 884-2433
www.chefscatalog.com

A Cook's Wares
211 37th Street
Beaver Falls, PA 15010
Tel: (800) 915-9788
Fax: (800) 916-2886
www.cookswares.com

Sur La Table
84 Pine St
Seattle, WA 98101-1573
Tel: (206) 448-2244
Fax: (206) 448-2245
www.surlatable.com

Bridge Kitchenware
711 3rd Ave.,
New York, NY 10017
Tel: (212) 688-4220
Fax: (212) 758-5387
www.bridgekitchenware.com

Broadway Panhandler
477 Broome Street
New York, NY 10013
Tel: (212) 966-3434
www.broadwaypanhandler.com

Bowery Kitchen Supply
460 West 16th Street
New York, NY 10011
Tel: (212) 219-1457
www.bowerykitchen.com

Online Site for Ice Cream Makers, Supplies and Info
MakeIceCream.com
89 Long Branch Ave
Long Branch, NJ 07740
Tel: (800) 303-0551
www.makeicecream.com

AUSTRALIA

David Jones and Myer Stores
Stockist of Breville and Philips
ice cream machines.

SYDNEY
Accoutrement
Tel: (02) 9969 1031
Stockist of Gaggia and
Girmi ice cream machines,
anti-freeze ice cream scoops
and Natisco ice cream scoops.

Bay Tree
Tel: (02) 9328 101
Stockist of Gaggia Gelatiera
ice cream machines, French
moulds and ice cream scoops.

Peter's of Kensington
Tel: (02) 9662 1099

MELBOURNE
London & American Supply Stores
Tel: (03) 9329 1052
Stockist of Simo ice cream
machines.

Minimax
Tel: (03) 9826 0022
Stockist of Girmi ice cream
machines.

Scullerymade
The largest range of ice cream
moulds in Australia and distributed
nationally. (Does not supply
ice cream machines.)
Tel: (03) 9509 4003 for your
nearest stockist.

QUEENSLAND
Robins Kitchen
13 stores in Queensland.
Tel: (07) 3375 0200 for details
of your nearest shop.
Stockist of Girmi ice cream
machines, ice cream scoops and
ice cream moulds.

Bibliography

Mrs Mary Eales Receipts (London: Prospect Books, 1733, reproduced from the 1733 edition).

Marshall, A.B. *The Book of Ices* (London: Marshall's, 1885).

Paul, Charlie. *American and Other Iced Drinks* (London: Farrow and Jackson, 1909).

Senn, C. Herman. *Luncheon and Dinner Sweets including the Art of Ice Making* (London: Ward Lock, 1919).

The History of Ice Cream (Washington DC: International Association of Ice Cream Manufacturers, 1978).

Extracts from *Petits Propos Culinaires*, November 1979
Stallings Jr., W. S. *Ice Cream and Water Ices in 17th- and 18th-century England.*
David, Elizabeth. Articles in the same journal.

The Great Ice Cream Book, edited by Edwards, R. and Croft, J. (Absolute Press, 1984).

Beamon, Sylvia P. and Roaf, Susan. *The Ice Houses of Britain* (Routledge, 1990).

Copi, Terri. *The Italian Factor: The Italian Community in Great Britain* (Edinburgh: Mainstream, 1991).

Buxham, Tim. *Icehouses* (Shire Publication, 1992, reprinted 1998).

David, Elizabeth. *Harvest of the Cold Months: The Social History of Ice and Ices* (Michael Joseph, 1994).

Weir, Robin and Liddell, Caroline. *Ices The Definitive Guide* (London: Grub Street, 1995, reprinted 1996, 1998).

Glossary

Bleeding The term used to describe the merging of flavours or syrups when making a layered iced dessert. To prevent this, smooth each additional layer of ice cream or sorbet and freeze until firm before adding the next, so that the layers of the finished ice cream appear well defined.

Cassata This is the name given to an Italian ice cream dessert, that is made with three different ice creams, set in layers in a round, bombe-shaped mould. The mould is sometimes lined with thinly sliced Madeira or Genoese sponge cake, or ready-made trifle sponges.

Dasher A plastic-coated paddle used in ice cream machines.

Float This American-style drink is made with cream soda or fizzy lemonade, fruit syrup and a scoop of vanilla ice cream.

Frappé Similar in texture to a granita, this snow-like iced drink can be made with fruit purée, fruit syrup or liqueur mixed with lots of crushed ice. The best remembered is the vibrant, green crème-de-menthe frappé.

Gelato This is the Italian word for ice cream. The style for a true Italian ice cream is lighter, with less cream and sugar, than American, English or French ice creams.

Granita An Italian water-based iced dessert that is beaten frequently during freezing to form grainy snow-like flakes of ice. Coffee granita is the classic version, but fruit flavours are also popular.

Knickerbocker glory This technicolour American sundae was quickly popularized in Britain and is made with scoops of vanilla ice cream and spoonfuls of different coloured jelly layered in tall sundae glasses, topped with whipped cream, strawberry sauce and sweets, then decorated with a wafer biscuit.

Kulfi This rich Indian ice cream is made by slowly boiling milk over several hours before flavouring with cardamom. It is traditionally frozen in small, conical-shaped moulds.

Neapolitan ice cream First sold in ice cream parlours and tea rooms in the 1850s, this ice cream is made of three contrasting colours of ice cream. It is set in a rectangular mould and served sliced. The most famous combination is chocolate, strawberry and vanilla ice creams.

Parfait This rich, creamy ice cream does not need to be beaten during freezing. It is made by whisking a hot sugar syrup into beaten egg yolks and, because the syrup is heated to the soft-ball stage, the finished ice cream has a wonderful texture even when served straight from the freezer. Parfait is usually set in individual serving dishes or moulds.

Popsicle The American name for an ice lolly, the very first of which was patented in America in 1923 as the Epsicle by Frank Epperson. The original Epsicle was flavoured with lemon.

Saccharometer This glass measuring device is used to check the sugar density of sorbet and ice cream mixtures. If there is too much sugar, the sorbet or ice cream will be too soft; too little and the sorbet or ice cream will have a hard, icy texture. It is used by professionals and enthusiastic

amateurs, but it is not essential unless you intend creating your own recipes or variations.

Semi-freddo This term is used for a semi-frozen Italian ice cream. The ice cream is mixed with crumbled biscuits (cookies), sponge cake or chopped candied fruit and set in containers or moulds. Semi-freddo is never beaten during freezing and is served when only just firm enough to scoop or slice.

Sherbet This is made in the same way as a sorbet, but with the addition of milk or cream. The term is most probably derived from the Arabic "Sharab", an early semi-frozen, sweet, milk-based drink.

Sorbet Classically made with sugar syrup and puréed fruit, this French water ice can also be made using wine or liqueurs. Sorbets are usually mixed with a little egg white to lighten the mixture.

Sorbetti This is the Italian word for sorbet.

Sundae This American iced dessert is served in rounded glass dishes generously filled with scoops of different coloured ice creams, then topped with fruit syrups or sauces, spoonfuls of cream and tiny sweets (candies), grated chocolate or wafers.

Syrup All water ice desserts are based on a simple sugar syrup, which is usually made with caster (superfine) or granulated (white) sugar. If making a large quantity of sorbet, prepare a large batch of syrup. It can be stored in the refrigerator in a covered tub for 2–3 days or until required.

Water ice This is made like a sorbet but usually without the addition of eggs, although egg whites are sometimes added to improve the texture. Water ices were very popular in England during the Georgian and Victorian eras and were often flavoured with flowers, spices, fruits, wine and liqueurs.

Zester This useful, hand-held gadget is used to pare fine curls of rind from citrus fruits. It has four or five tiny metal holes that slice narrow strips of rind. Quick and easy to use, the citrus curls make a pretty finishing touch to even the most simple ice cream desserts and sorbets.

Index